Crisis, Recovery, and the Role of Accounting Firms in the Pacific Basin

Crisis, Recovery, and the Role of Accounting Firms in the Pacific Basin

David L. McKee,
Don E. Garner, and
Yosra AbuAmara McKee

Q

QUORUM BOOKS
Westport, Connecticut • London

Library of Congress Cataloging-in-Publication Data

McKee, David L.
    Crisis, recovery, and the role of accounting firms in the Pacific Basin / David L.
McKee, Don E. Garner, and Yosra AbuAmara McKee.
      p.   cm.
    Includes bibliographical references and index.
    ISBN 1–56720–311–6 (alk. paper)
    1. Accounting firms—Pacific Area.   2. Financial crises—Pacific Area.   I. Garner,
Don E.   II. McKee, Yosra AbuAmara, 1948–   III. Title.
    HF5616.P16M35   2002
    338.7′61657′099—dc21   2001049179

British Library Cataloguing in Publication Data is available.

Library of Congress Catalog Card Number: 2001049179
ISBN: 1–56720–311–6

First published in 2002

Quorum Books, 88 Post Road West, Westport, CT 06881
An imprint of Greenwood Publishing Group, Inc.
www.quorumbooks.com

Printed in the United States of America

The paper used in this book complies with the
Permanent Paper Standard issued by the National
Information Standards Organization (Z39.48–1984).

10 9 8 7 6 5 4 3 2 1

Contents

Preface

Although *Accounting Services, Growth and Change in the Pacific Basin* is still relatively new (McKee and Garner, 1996a), much has occurred in the Pacific Basin since that volume went to press. The 1996 publication highlighted three groups of economies in its analysis. The first group comprised the nations often identified as the Asian Tigers—Hong Kong, Singapore, South Korea and Taiwan. The second group was selected from the emerging nations of the Asia Pacific region. Nations chosen included the Philippines, Indonesia, Thailand and Malaysia. The third grouping included a selection of small Pacific island states.

The authors of the 1996 work are satisfied that they accomplished what they had intended. However, much has transpired in the region that was highlighted. One very obvious change involved Hong Kong's return to China, the consequences of which are still being monitored. Beyond that adjustment has been the dramatic economic and financial crises that have swept the region. Beginning as a financial crisis in Thailand in 1997, the malaise spread to other jurisdictions in the region and became something more than a financial crisis, involving as it did economic and social matters.

At the height of the crises the Asian miracle as it pertained to the Asian Tigers seemed to be very much in doubt. Singapore, South Korea and Taiwan were embroiled in very serious difficulties. The same can be said for the emerging nations that were highlighted in the 1996 study. Although the Pacific island states have not received extensive attention in the media coverage of the crises, this may be more of a symptom of their size and/or global significance than of their avoidance of difficulties.

It seems clear to the present investigators that what has occurred can be assessed more effectively by the publication of a new volume, designed to contribute to an understanding of how fast-moving events have impacted the nations highlighted in the 1996 publication. This volume will not be a revision of the earlier work. Its design should afford it a place in its own right.

The 1996 volume spoke to the role played by producer services, notably those offered by major international accounting firms in facilitating business and economic matters. The general conclusion was that the services in question were helpful contributors to the successes documented involving the jurisdictions that were studied.

A major question to be addressed in the present volume is whether or not the major accounting firms through their service offerings have assisted in the recovery of the economies under consideration. The nations comprising the first two groups to be studied were listed above. The third group, a selection of small island states, includes Papua New Guinea, Fiji and Vanuatu. Thus, the present volume will speak to both the actual and the potential roles of the accounting firms in nations that vary both in size and business and economic strength and potential. More specifically, it will illustrate the facilitative role of the firms in business and economic linkages involving the jurisdictions concerned.

The authors have divided the volume into four sections. Part I provides the parameters for the discussion. Comprised of three chapters, it begins with some general observations concerning the financial roots of the problem. Following that it discusses how the matter expanded to include economic and social issues. The section ends with some general observations concerning the role of the major accounting firms.

In Part II, the legal and institutional constraints governing various aspects of business are reviewed. The emphasis is on the operations of the major accounting firms. Of course, these matters are of some importance if the role of the accounting firms is to be assessed. One of the most significant facilitative functions of the firms in question revolves around the assistance they can offer clients in the face of the rules and regulatory environments of various jurisdictions. Such assistance is of special importance in international business operations and of course doubly significant in the post-crisis environments of the jurisdictions under discussion.

Part III turns the discussion more in the direction of economic considerations. Specifically each jurisdiction mentioned above is reviewed with an eye to understanding its post-crisis economic situation. The facilitative services of the accounting firms in those settings are considered from the point of view of their role in facilitating recovery and/or ongoing economic progress.

In the final section of the book events leading from the prevalence of national accounting standards to a more global approach are reviewed.

Special emphasis is given to how the Asian crisis appears to have accelerated the movement toward more standardized global accounting and auditing practices. Beyond those matters the economic circumstances of the three jurisdictional groupings featured are reviewed and summarized. The intent is to solidify the understanding of the positive role of the major international accounting firms. It is hoped that their contribution to improving the post-crisis business climate can be documented. Clearly their functioning in that environment should add to the understanding of their significance vis-à-vis the facilitation of international business linkages, a service of some significance in the jurisdictions featured.

Acknowledgments

Over the course of this project the authors have benefited from opportunities to present portions of their work as papers at various professional meetings and conferences. Conferences at which presentations were made included those of the American Society for Business and Behavioral Sciences, the American Society for Competitiveness, the International Academy of Business Disciplines and the Western Social Science Association.

The authors are grateful to their respective institutions, California State University, Stanislaus and Kent State University for significant travel support. They are also appreciative of the support of Diane Williams of the Department of Economics at Kent State University for significant assistance with the final preparation of the manuscript.

Parporn Akathaporn, Chief Accountant of the Thai Securities and Exchange Commission and Chair of the Thai Accounting Standards Committee was extremely helpful in providing the authors with materials and information on Thailand accounting. Two of our colleagues at the College of Business Administration, California State University, Stanislaus were very supportive of this project. Dean Amin A. Elmallah provided substantial material and psychological support for our study. Professor David H. Lindsay was most helpful in providing needed assistance.

Part I

The General Frame of Reference

Chapter 1

A Preliminary View of the Crisis

What is sometimes overlooked in analyses of the events which began in Thailand in 1997 and spread through various jurisdictions in the Asia Pacific region, is the fact that those events were fueled by two crises which albeit were interwoven. Thailand was the impact zone for a financial crisis, which as it spread and deepened, spawned an economic crisis. Both crises were international in scope, impacting not just domestic and regional concerns, but global business interests, as well as economic linkages. That being the case, it seems clear with hindsight that lasting solutions, although requiring sometimes extensive domestic adjustments, can hardly be attained without considerable attention to international matters.

Writing in 1999, Jerome Levinson characterized the financial crisis in East Asian jurisdictions, including in addition to Thailand, South Korea, Singapore, Indonesia, Malaysia and Hong Kong, as far more disconcerting than anything that had occurred before (20). He based his opinion on the well-recognized fact that "the economies of East Asia at the center of the recent crisis have been some of the most successful emerging market countries in terms of growth and gains in living standards" (Levinson, 1999, 20 quoting the International Monetary Fund [IMF], May 1998, 3).

The IMF document observed that the countries in question had become models for many others due to their generally prudent fiscal policies and high private savings rates. Certainly Hong Kong, Singapore and South Korea had been widely recognized for their long-standing and successful export-oriented development strategies, and were considered to have joined the ranks of the world's newly industrialized nations. Thailand was not far behind based upon its progress and has frequently been considered as a logical addition to the Asian Tigers. Malaysia, although still considered by some to be among the ranks of emerging nations, had been doing rather well in pursuing its own export strategy.

A World Bank report, that appears dated by today's standards, found East Asia to have had a remarkable record of high and sustained economic growth (1993, 1). During the period 1965–1990 the 23 economies of the region grew more rapidly than all other regions of the world. The World Bank attributed this performance in large part to the success of eight economies—Japan, the Asian Tigers, China, Indonesia, Malaysia and Thailand (1).

Characterizing the eight jurisdictions listed above as high-performing Asian economies (HPAEs), the report found them to have grown at over twice the rate for the remainder of East Asia, roughly three times faster than Latin America and South Asia and 25 times faster than Sub-Saharan Africa (2). The economies in question were also seen to have outperformed the industrial economies and the "oil-rich Middle East–North Africa region" (2).

In answer to its own rhetorical question, "What caused East Asia's success?," the report declared that in large measure the HPAEs attained high growth by getting the basics right (5). It identified private domestic investment and rapidly growing human capital as the principle engines of growth. High-investment levels were sustained by high levels of domestic financed savings. Agriculture enjoyed rapid growth and productivity improvement although it declined in relative importance. Population expansion rates declined more rapidly than was evident in other parts of the developing world. Some of the economies in question had a better-educated labor force and more effective systems of public administration (5).

The report pointed to fundamentally sound development policy as a major ingredient in achieving rapid growth (5). It declared macroeconomic management to have been unusually good and microeconomic performance as unusually stable. This it suggested provided the necessary framework for private investment (5). In addition, policies aimed at increasing the integrity of the banking system, and rendering it more accessible to non-traditional savers, "raised the levels of financial savings" (5). Labor force skills were increased rapidly through educational policies focused on primary and secondary skills. Agricultural policies favored productivity and avoided the excessive taxation of rural economies (5). Beyond all of the above considerations, governments stood ready to intervene for the purpose of fostering development, in some cases the development of specific industries.

The report pointed out that the economies in question are highly diverse in natural resources, culture and political institutions (27). They differ as well vis-à-vis degrees of government intervention in the economy and the manner in which their leaders have shaped and implemented policies (27). Nonetheless, the economies have much in common, most notably their high average rate of economic growth (27). Over the period in question income inequality declined. The report declared rapid growth and reduced inequality as "the defining characteristics of what has come to be known as the East Asian economic miracle" (27).

More specifically the report enumerated six additional characteristics shared by the economies in question, setting them apart (27). To begin with it mentioned more rapid output and productivity growth in agriculture, higher rates of growth of manufacturing exports and earlier and steeper declines in fertility (27). Beyond those the list included higher rates of growth of physical capital, supported by higher rates of domestic savings, higher initial levels of growth rates of human capital and generally higher rates of productivity growth (27). Hindsight being what it is, it may be tempting to ask how such a seemingly euphoric description of circumstances in the region soured so significantly. In fairness, however, it must be acknowledged that what has been documented above was certainly accurate for the period reviewed.

Although the economies reviewed by the report are not coextensive with those that constitute the subject for the present investigation, it seems relevant to review the report since it did encompass an analysis of circumstances holding historical relevance in the case of the various economies that were included in the current study. The report did not consider Taiwan or the Philippines. Nor did it deal with any of the island economies, notably Papua New Guinea, Fiji and Vanuatu. Nonetheless, it did describe the historically strong performance of six economies of interest here, economies that presumably shared a spreading economic strength in the region. Clearly the pre-crisis prognosis for the region was positive. Whether such a prognosis would also apply to the island economies would require further study.

Much has been written concerning the causes of the turnaround in the Asia Pacific region. Space constraints prohibit a general review of that literature in the present context. An attempt will be made to identify the main causes in order to establish a foundation for what is to follow. As already mentioned, the crisis began in Thailand in 1997. Initially it manifested itself in that nation's financial sector. Writing in 1998 Thomas Hoenig suggested that three elements lay at the foundation of the Asian financial crisis (5). First of all some Asian countries relied upon large amounts of short-term debt relative to equity in order to finance growth. Hoenig was of the opinion that carrying a large amount of debt also involves high risk (5). "In times of economic stress, short-term debt is an unstable source of funding" (5). Hoenig appears to have been quite correct in suggesting that investors in the global financial marketplace could quickly move their capital out of an economy (5). As he stated, "This is what happened in these Asian countries" (5).

Second, Hoenig pointed out that each of those countries with a large deficit load maintained a fixed exchange rate (6). That fixed exchange rate tended to generate a false sense of security among businesses and financial institutions vis-à-vis exchange-rate risk (6). Thus those institutions were persuaded to hold a significant part of their short-term debt in dollars (6). Hoenig recognized "the volatile nature of dollar denominated short-term debt as rendering the economies in question especially vulnerable to a crisis in the case of a sudden loss of investor confidence or an unexpected exchange rate depreciation" (6).

He also saw the banking system in each economy as subject to lax lending standards and weak supervision (6). "With short-term foreign capital flowing into a country, a weak banking system allowed loans to be diverted to questionable investment projects and real estate deals" (6). As Hoenig explained when the Asian crisis hit, questionable loans threatened to bankrupt a sizable number of firms and domestic financial institutions (6).

Hoenig used events as they occurred in Thailand to demonstrate his reasoning. That nation suffered an economic slowdown in 1996 and the first half of 1997, causing many questionable investments to become unprofitable (6). "When Thailand floated the baht on July 2, the belief that there was no foreign exchange rate risk quickly disappeared" (6). Investors lost confidence in the currency and tried to convert it into dollars. As the local currency depreciated, the cost to Thai businesses for servicing their dollar-denominated debt increased (6).

Exchange-rate pressures intensified as domestic residents hurried to hedge their external exposure with the result that the crisis spread to other countries in the region (6). Hoenig saw some of the contagion as rational since the depreciation of Thailand's currency reduced the competitiveness of the nation's competitors. Investors saw the same elements in other Asian countries, notably South Korea and Indonesia (6). With hindsight the results appear to have been all too predictable.

Although Hoenig's analysis seems logical and to the point those in the business and economic community appeared unaware of the problems until it was too late. Warren Coats in discussing what he called the Asian meltdown of 1997 saw signs of trouble beneath the surface or what he termed "not so hidden indicators of impending disaster" (1999, 88). He pointed out that the Stock Exchange of Thailand index (SET) "had long exhibited anemic growth, if not downright weakness . . . [and] this was clearly a harbinger of things to come" (88). Beyond that he pointed to the rapid deceleration of export growth, leading to large deficits in the current account, "deceptively masked by large short-term capital inflows" (88).

More specifically he explained that the nation's current account deficit approached 8 percent of GDP, largely financed by massive dollar-denominated short-term borrowing by Thai financial institutions that had been encouraged by financial deregulation introduced in the early 1990s (88). Most notable, according to Coats, were the creation of Bangkok International Banking Facilities which were meant to begin with the building up of the city's image as a regional financial center (88). Coats saw this as turning out to be a regulatory conduit facilitating "excessive Thai bank short-term offshore (Eurodollars) financing for onshore longer-term (domestic) investments" (88).

In more detail than described by Hoenig, with the loss of confidence in the ability of the Bank of Thailand to defend its currency buildup, financial panic caused a sharp reversal in capital flows (88). As suggested by Coats the second half of 1997 saw an exodus of short-term capital generally estimated to have surpassed "the entire capital inflows of the previous eighteen months" (88). With a rapid fall in asset prices, the entire financial system unraveled, pushing the Thai economy into recession (88).

Coats saw the Asian crisis as clearly rooted in the private sector. As he explained, "A surge of private capital inflows in the form of bank loans and portfolio investments led to asset-price inflation that fueled a speculative bubble, as ever larger capital inflows kept pouring into unproductive investments resulting in decreasing returns" (89).

In assessing blame Coats pointed out that the predominant consensus blames crony capitalists, who abused their privileged positions to finance questionable investments, and greedy bankers who channeled the necessary funds (89). Coats saw resource allocation as flawed at two levels—the investment decision level itself and the level of financial intermediation. Either way the public sector was seen to be partially responsible because it supplied false information to firms by following misguided policies (89). Coats included foreign financial institutions in the list of co-conspirators in the financial intermediation saga (91). Despite the custom of blaming Asian business cronyism and corrupt bureaucracies, he felt that foreign financial institutions share half of the blame (91).

In search of causes for the Asian financial crisis Cem Karacadag and Barbara Samuels II asked, "Why were well-known country risk factors overlooked or, if they were not overlooked, why were preemptive decisions not taken by investors and creditors?" (1999, 131). In their opinion inadequate country risk analysis by the private sector and failure to weigh risk and return related to cross-border lending and investment in the region were at the heart of the Asian financial crisis (131). Specifically, "The market was unable to produce and process information adequately in order to perform its allocative role effectively" (131).

They saw three explanations for the failure of risk analysis. To begin with individual market participants and country risk services underinvested in "the human, information and technological resources needed to properly analyse political, economic and financial risks" (131). Second they saw the structure of marketplace analysis production as inefficient, "given the redundancy of individual market participants all performing relatively similar but limited analyses" (131–132). Instead they accused the market place in the aggregate as overinvesting in shortsighted risk analysis (132).

Their third explanation was that analytical processes were fragmented within market institutions, often reflecting institutional biases (132). They accused macro- and micro-level research as being rarely bridged. In addition they suggested that systemic risks were ignored. They saw the processes as lacking the needed sophistication to detect danger signaled by indicators dissimilar from those seen in past crises. "The absence of high quality market analysis allowed dynamics such as cognitive dissonance and herding to take over decisive roles in financial behavior and outcomes" (132).

The authors highlighted two critical market failures that they felt required remedial action. To begin with they saw market participants as underinvesting in the collection and processing of information, which they saw as a problem rooted in the positive externalities associated with those endeavors (140). Second they saw the analytical methodologies themselves as deficient. Those two market failures combined "have allowed hype and herd to become key determinants of market outcomes, undermining faith in the market mechanism as a vehicle for delivering prosperity" (140).

Although much confusion has remained in the aftermath of the Asian crisis, there appears to be little doubt about where it originated. Debate over who or what should be blamed still abounds but it has become clear that both domestic and foreign players share the responsibility for what occurred in Thailand and beyond. There is also debate concerning the roles of public and private elements in the mix. What has become clear, of course, is the international element in the crisis and how what began in one nation (Thailand) quickly spread to other jurisdictions and indeed even threatened the functioning of the global economy.

International concerns were often voiced through international public institutions such as the IMF and the World Bank. The IMF was quick to respond in an effort to restore investor confidence. It agreed to make loans to impacted countries contingent upon the implementation of needed economic reforms (Hoenig, 1998, 60). It required that the nations in question should stabilize exchange rates through temporary upward adjustments in domestic interest rates (6). Simultaneously the nations in question agreed to implement longer term structural adjustments perceived to be essential for reestablishing long-term stability (6).

According to Hoenig, the most important reform was to place the financial systems of impacted nations on sound footings. He saw this as requiring the closure of insolvent financial institutions, the recapitalization of weak yet solvent institutions and the strengthening of financial regulation and supervision. He also endorsed increasing transparency in corporate and government sectors and opening markets to international trade (6).

Prescriptive solutions abound. Those put forward by Hoenig seem generally logical and are supported by others concerned with the problem from both public and private perspectives. What has made these and other prescriptions difficult to implement is the very nature of the problem itself, its international aspect involving a group of countries with a diversity of cultures and traditions, not to mention political systems and business practices. Confronted with such diversity "a one size fits all" approach may not be as simple or obvious as it may seem at first glance.

There is no question that solutions must be based upon stability and workability of the political and economic institutions of the impacted jurisdictions. However, all of the jurisdictions impacted by the crisis had cast their lots with the global economy long before the advent of the crisis. Most were successful in that undertaking. In the post-crisis world those same nations have had little choice but to reestablish their international economic and business linkages.

The global economy is, of course, market driven. Thus individual players make decisions based upon potential for gain. That is where risk and uncertainty become factors to be considered. Implicit in many prescriptive offerings is a recognition of such realities. Prescriptions aimed at eliminating risks and uncertainties through homogenizing the nations concerned may bring with them complications of their own.

The current authors are somewhat skeptical that homogenization on such a scale can work. It seems impractical to suggest that such a degree of intervention can make the region concerned tractable for the operations of international business interests. This position is not an ideological statement but hopefully a more pragmatic approach to the problem.

In preparing the present volume the authors hope among other things to demonstrate a positive role for major multinational accounting firms in the Asia Pacific region. Karacadag and Samuels have pointed to the role of information in the efficient functioning of the region (1999). The present authors are of the opinion that the accounting firms are to some extent facilitating business interests both internationally and within nations, through supplying information on a wide variety of matters impacting their clients. In wearing their consulting hats those firms are assisting clients, many of whom are multinational firms, in functioning within the institutional parameters present in specific nations. To the degree that they are successful, the accounting firms are reducing the risks associated with firms dealing in multiple jurisdictions, with wide ranges of laws, customs and traditions.

No one would suggest that the major international accounting firms hold the key to make the difficulties that caused the Asian crisis go away. However, short of that it does seem that they do have a part to play in facilitating business operations in the region. There is certainly some logic in private firms offering their advisory and perhaps supervisory services to business clients contemplating operations in the Asia Pacific region. In doing that they are certainly contributing to the success of business in the region and beyond. Hopefully the present volume will provide some detail on that subject.

Chapter 2

The Crisis, International Linkages and Recovery

This volume is not intended as an addition to an already substantial library of materials aimed at enumerating the causes or explaining the consequences of the crisis that swept the Southeastern Asian region toward the end of 1997. Instead its task will be to view the nations concerned as they are attempting to regenerate or even initiate roles for themselves in a post-crisis world. More specifically it concerns the real and potential roles that major international accounting firms are playing in the post-crisis linkages of the nations of the region between themselves and the world at large.

Joseph Stiglitz has suggested that "The global financial crisis that began in Thailand on July 2, 1997 has now grown far larger than almost anyone expected at the time (1999, 2). He went on to explain that what many had thought would be no more than a "slight blip in the unrelenting advance of international capital markets has instead become the gravest threat to the stability of the world's market economy since the Great Depression" (2). Those observations dating from 1999 were voiced earlier in his address to the Southern Economic Association in 1998. A partial purpose of the present investigation is to contribute to an understanding of how the Asia Pacific region has faired since the crisis in question and also to provide evidence of the role of major international accounting firms in post-crisis business and economic linkages.

Although much blame for the dual financial and economic crises has been leveled upon residents and institutions of the jurisdictions concerned, Stiglitz was quick to point out that every loan has both a borrower and a lender, each of whom deserves equal shares of the blame (34). He went on to suggest that many foreign lenders were marginal, lending into circumstances where Korean banks, for example, already had huge debt equity ratios (34). In addition he saw those lenders as supposedly well regulated and in possession of sophisticated risk-management systems. Thus he contended that foreign lenders should perhaps have shouldered a larger share of the blame, having been at fault for granting the loans or at least for not requiring higher interest rates, reflecting the true risks (34). He saw these foreign involvements as shedding new light on the view that loans were the result of crony capitalism because the lenders were hardly responding to government pressure (34).

While acknowledging that governments did play a part in bringing about the allocation of capital in some jurisdictions, Stiglitz was skeptical that this could have accounted for the real estate bubble in Thailand, where the crisis began (34). Because of the focus on transparency, Stiglitz saw an immediate implication that blame would fall "not on lenders and investors who should have done due diligence before investing but on crisis countries that were not transparent enough" (34). He saw such shifting of blame as ignoring the fact that transparency problems were well known, and that transparency had been increasing rather than decreasing in recent years (34).

Stiglitz saw a greater awareness of the risks associated with short-term capital investments and a greater skepticism of the gains, and also a greater worry concerning the dangers of inappropriate responses, a heightened awareness of the importance of supplying stronger safety nets and building institutional infrastructures (35). Clearly his analysis would support the view of the crisis as an international phenomenon, capable of impacts that may be very difficult to mitigate from the perspective of individual impacted jurisdictions. Clearly a case can be made for the facilitative inputs of the major international accounting firms and other purveyors of business services on the international scene. Whether or not such practitioners have had roles in the recovery of the economies of the Asia Pacific region remains to be seen.

Writing in 1999, Marcus Noland observed that Asia was emerging from the financial crisis and that indeed its economic performance was more robust than most had anticipated (1). However, he saw the sustainability of the region's recovery as questionable. Among the economies most heavily impacted by the crisis he saw South Korea as having made the most progress and saw it experiencing strong growth in 1999 (3). Unfortunately he seemed skeptical of that nation's ability to sustain its recovery into the year 2000 and beyond (3).

He based his concern on the fact that "Much of the current growth has been due to a rebound in consumption from extremely depressed levels in 1998, inventory restocking, and fiscal stimulus" (3). He went on to explain that employment in the core sectors of the economy, including industry, agriculture and services, has remained weak, with the bulk of recent job increases in self-employment and the public sector (3). He reported considerable restructuring in the smaller Chaebol and the small and medium enterprise sector (3). He saw the significant question as to whether fiscal stimulus in the absence of restructuring and improvements in efficiency is an adequate recovery strategy.

The present crisis in the region seems ironic considering what many of the nations concerned were able to accomplish in previous years. As has been pointed out, "In less than a generation many Asian economies transformed themselves from underdeveloped agricultural economies to efficient industrialized economies" (Putnam Retail Management, Inc., 1998, 1). The Putnam appraisal suggested that such changes were accompanied by the arrival of foreign banks, attracted by inexpensive labor and governments friendly to business. The banks provided much of the capital required for large infrastructure projects, including factories, highways, airports, skyscrapers and multi-media super corridors (1).

The countries involved were seen to be successful, enjoying high rates of economic growth and savings accompanied by low inflation and interest rates (1). Behind all of this, current account deficits arose and became large when Southeast Asia's exports slowed in 1996 and 1997. Such a deficit in a specific nation indicated that that country was taking in more capital, goods and services than it was exporting, which made the repayment of foreign debts more difficult (1).

The Putnam analysis pointed out that deficits in the current account can be handled if the nation concerned has an advanced and well-capitalized banking system to provide for the efficient allocation of capital (1). The Southeast Asian countries were lacking in that regard. "Instead their economies relied on a high degree of cronyism between government, business, and banks." Financial disclosure and regulation were seen as inadequate (1). In the face of rapid growth banks did not question the repayment capabilities of borrowers, and corporations did not release damaging information to investors. Banks did not build adequate reserves, believing that governments would keep them from failing (1). Thus the banking system was seen as ill prepared to respond to the financial panic that resulted from Thailand and Malaysia devaluing their currencies in July 1997 in answer to growing current account deficits (1–2).

The Asian crisis is said to have disclosed the weaknesses of financial systems in the crisis countries, especially their vulnerability to large outflows of foreign capital (Cambodian Centre for Conflict Resolution, 2000, 4). Foreign capital has the potential for generating a wide range of benefits including the augmentation of the shortage of domestic capital, the transfer of new and appropriate technology, the improvement of the quality of human resources and the earning of foreign currency (5). However foreign capital is said to magnify rather than smooth fluctuations in developing economies due to its volatile and pro-cyclical characteristics (5). Beyond that inflows of foreign capital are volatile since they are influenced by economic conditions and fluctuations in the home countries of foreign investors (5).

This view seems to be in accord with one opinion of the cause of the Asian crisis referred to by Martin Khor (2000a, 1). That view blamed the crisis on developments in the global financial system, including the combination of financial deregulation and liberalization across the world, the increasing interconnection of markets and speed of transactions through computer technology, and the development of large institutional financial players such as the speculative hedge funds, the investment banks and the huge mutual and pension funds (1). Khor noted that US $184 billion entered developing Asian countries as net private capital flows in 1994–1996 (2). "In 1996 US $94 billion entered and in the first half of 1997 $70 billion poured in" (2). He stated that with the onset of the crisis $102 billion went out in the second half of 1997, adding that the massive outflow has continued (2). He suggests that the figures show how large flows in and out can be, how volatile and sudden shifts can be and how market leaders in pulling out trigger a herd instinct causing a panic withdrawal by large institutional investors and players (2).

He explains that in some countries the first outflow by foreigners was followed by domestic outflows since local people feared further depreciation or were concerned about the safety of financial institutions (2–3). Among events leading to a worsening of the crisis Khor cited financial liberalization, currency depreciation and debt crisis, liberalization and debt in the Malaysian case, local asset boom and bust and liquidity squeeze, the fall in output and the easing of fiscal and monetary policy (3–5).

With respect to financial liberalization, the nations concerned made foreign exchange convertible with local currency for trade and direct investment purposes as well as for autonomous capital inflows and outflows. In addition large inflows and outflows of funds were largely deregulated and permitted (3). With respect to currency depreciation and debt crises, Khor states that the build-up of short-term debts was becoming alarming. He suggests that what turned this into a crisis in Thailand, Indonesia and South Korea was the sharp sudden depreciation of their currencies, together with the sudden reduction of their foreign reserves in anti-speculation attempts. Depreciated currencies increased debt-service burdens vis-à-vis local currency needed for repaying loans (3).

According to Khor, "the financial crisis has been transformed to a full-blown recession in the real economy of production (4). He cited Indonesia as the worst affected "with a 6.2% fall in GDP in the first quarter of 1998, and a newly projected negative growth rate for 1998 of 15%, inflation of 80% and expected unemployment of 17% or 15 million" (4). He pointed to a drop of 3.8 percent in South Korea's GDP in the first quarter of 1998 and cited an expected drop of 4 to 5.5 percent in the GDP of Thailand for 1998 (4). Hong Kong experienced a 2 percent drop in GDP for the first quarter of 1998 and Malaysia suffered a 1.8 percent decline in GDP over the same period, following a 6.9 percent expansion in the last quarter of 1997 (4). Although Singapore boasted a larger than 5 percent growth in the first quarter, it was expected to experience a decline in the second half of 1998 (4).

Khor was of the opinion that the IMF policy of squeezing domestic economies through high interest rates, tight monetary policies and cuts in government budgets may have made matters more difficult. He suggested that some economists have warned from the start that IMF treatment for Thailand, Indonesia and South Korea would transform a financial problem into a full-blown economic crisis (5). This has occurred with the three nations alluded to above slipping into deep recession. In part due to spillovers, other jurisdictions such as Malaysia and Hong Kong have experienced negative growth during the first quarter of 1998 and Singapore was teetering on the brink (4).

In the three nations seemingly impacted by IMF policies, "there are many thousands of firms (most of them small and medium sized) that have now been affected in each country" (5). In the same vein Putnam Retail Management, Inc., pointed out that "The IMF secured large bailout packages for Thailand, Indonesia and South Korea in exchange for tough fiscal measures and the promise that governments would not aid insolvent businesses" (1998, 3).

This posture was accused by critics of exacerbating the problems of the region by forcing countries to raise interest rates and reduce spending (3). IMF loan programs in Thailand and South Korea have caused layoffs in large industrial conglomerates (4). Nonetheless those two nations have accumulated large foreign reserves and have attracted investment from international companies (4). Putnam Retail Management, Inc. pointed to discussions between General Motors and Daewoo Motor Company aimed at the American firm purchasing roughly half of the Korean firm (4). "Direct corporate investment along these lines would provide the capital needed to restore economic growth and help to open up previously closed business relationships in Asia" (4).

In a continuation of his analysis of the Asian crisis, Martin Khor reviews the need for regulating the global financial system (2000b, 1). He suggests that the crisis has shown the dangers of volatile and large short-term capital flows to the economic stability of emerging nations and calls for greater transparency vis-à-vis the operations of global players and markets, coupled with reforms at both national and international levels aimed at regulating speculative flows (1). Certainly it seems clear that most international accounting firms and other international facilitative service providers may have significant contributions to make to both public and private participants in this scenario.

According to Khor, happenings in the international financial arena have been the most important contributors to the East Asian financial crisis, a crisis that he suggests is spreading (1). He criticizes a lack of transparency in what constitutes the financial markets, who the major players are, what they are doing and how money moves with what effect. Although Khor is hardly a strong supporter of the policies of the IMF in the region, he has an ally in Stanley Fischer, First Deputy Managing Director of the IMF, with respect to transparency. In an address delivered on the Asian crisis and its implications for other economies, Fischer called among other things, for improving the transparency of corporate and government accounts (1998, 6). Khor stresses that financial crises cannot be prevented or resolved unless the lack of transparency is removed (2000b, 1).

Khor details many facets of the transparency issue, including the need to identify the major institutions and players with respect to the ownership of financial assets, the need to understand their operational methods and their markets (2). He asks, "What is the system by which central banks of the major Northern countries regulate, deregulate (or decide not to regulate) the behavior of funds, speculators and investors?" (2). In addition he calls for transparency on the part of the IMF concerning how policies and conditions are set globally and on a country-specific basis (2).

Although Khor has drawn many policy lessons from the Asian crisis, some are more important than others in the present context. He stresses the importance for emerging nations to properly manage the interface between global developments and national policies, in particular in planning a nation's financial system and policy (4). He stresses the need for policy makers to understand what is occurring and the policy instruments to deal with it, including "adequate regulatory policy and legal frameworks and the enforcement capability" (5). In addition private sector players such as banks and other financial institutions and private corporations, must also understand and control processes such as fund inflows from loans and portfolio investment, and their appropriate recycling, not to mention the handling of risks of changes in foreign currency rates (5). Clearly, major international service suppliers have much to offer.

Although the financial element in the region's difficulties is certainly crucial, it must also be remembered that the crisis was economic as well as financial. Oxfam International was of the opinion that recession threatened to reverse human development gains in East Asia and that, barring effective international action, "contagion effects would spread the region's crisis to other parts of the developing world" (October 1998, 1). They likened the crisis to the destructive impact of the Great Depression of 1929, observing that what began as a financial crisis has been permitted to become a full-fledged social and economic crisis with what they termed as devastating consequences for human development (1).

Elaborating on that assessment they noted that incomes that had been rising have reversed direction and unemployment and underemployment have reached alarming levels (1). The social conditions of the poorest have been worsened by rising food prices and falling social spending (1). They indict international response as not only inadequate but having "exacerbated the severity of the situation, and contributed to poverty" (1). They attach much of the responsibility to the IMF since its prescriptions based on high interest rates to restore confidence have not been justified by developments (1).

Oxfam saw the economic prospects for East Asia as bleak. The worst impacts have occurred in Indonesia, where GDP was expected to fall by 20 percent (2). Thailand and South Korea were expected to experience drops in output in the 6–8 percent range (2). Among underlying causes of the crisis Oxfam mentions domestic mismanagement, corruption and the politicization of loans through an unaccountable and nontransparent banking system (4). This assessment supports the view that the macroeconomic collapse began as a crisis of confidence with the most immediate cause being massive capital flights, initially from Thailand and following that from Indonesia, Malaysia and to a lesser extent the Philippines (Sussangkarn, Flatters and Kittiprapas, 1999, 1).

Those last mentioned authors explained that in the most heavily impacted jurisdictions, the loss of confidence resulted from a large and fast-rising dependence on short-term private capital flows and corresponding current account deficits (August, 2000, 1). They pointed out that the financial sectors in all countries were experiencing a variety of regulatory and prudential weaknesses that were hidden or "made to appear irrelevant in the face of rapid growth and the seemingly endless appreciation of real estate and stock market assets (1).

Recession followed in Thailand, signaled by a rapid and unpredicted contraction of domestic demand (1). Malaysia and the Philippines suffered less than Indonesia and Thailand in the early days of the crisis since they did not have the same levels of accumulated short-term debt liabilities (2). As the crisis advanced, the Philippines were thought to have suffered least in aggregate terms, while Indonesia suffered most as measured by the depth of the economic contraction and the estimated time for recovery (2).

Sussangkarn et al. noted that the effects of the crisis in the jurisdictions alluded to above varied in magnitude and composition while displaying some broad similarities (3). They saw labor market impacts as much more severe in urban areas, with declines in employment, hours and wages appearing to have been concentrated much more in formal rather than informal sectors (3). In the formal sector, construction and financial services encountered the heaviest impacts (3).

In the Philippines, upper and middle class, especially urbanites, were seen as potentially the most affected (5). They were seen to be at risk from massive business closures (5). This the authors predicted might make income distribution more equal (5). The authors suggested that middle- to upper-income-class families depend to a large extent on re-mittances from Filipino workers abroad, who in turn were facing falling employment and incomes themselves (5).

Commenting on Indonesia, Hadi Soesastro suggests that the crisis has taken on a dynamic of its own (July 10, 2000a, 1). It began as a currency crisis in the third quarter of 1997, turned into a deep financial crisis with wide ranging economic and social impacts and became a serious political crisis (1). The size of the nation has potential externalities from the crisis putting the whole region at further risk, a problem well understood by Soesastro.

Soesastro suggests that banks have been hardest hit by the crisis in Indonesia (7). Depositors withdrew money while at the same time cor-porate borrowers ceased to pay interest or to pay back their debts. Thus nonperforming loans rose from 15 percent at the outset of the crisis to 50 percent at the height of the crisis (7). Indeed in some states non-performing loans were estimated to have reached 70 percent (7). As part of an agreement with the IMF, a regimen of bank and corporate restruc-turing was introduced, a major component of which called for bank re-capitalization (7).

The same author refers to "a lot of talk about 'industrial policy after the East Asia crisis' " and identifies two trends in that regard (7). One involves shifting from outward orientation to new internal capabilities that would signal the emergence of competition policy to replace the role of activist government (8).

Soesastro sees this as an enormous challenge to governments to gen-erate new public administration skills, designed to deal with the more complex mandate (10). The other trend harkens back to "old style in-dustrial policy of selective targeting, including a shift from an outward orientation to a new rationale for import substitution (10). Soesastro seems rightly disturbed by all of this. At the very least it seems clear that Indonesia, one of the world's largest nations, faces a good deal of uncertainty in the face of the ongoing impacts of the confirmed financial and economic crises that have ravished Southeast Asia. The uncertainties of the situation are impacting government agencies at all levels, as well as elements of all sizes in the private sector. It seems clear that there is great scope for the assistance available through major purveyors of facilitative services for business. The major international accounting firms seem especially well equipped to contribute needed expertise.

No overview of the Asian crisis would be acceptable without some reference to Hong Kong. The Hong Kong Trade Development Council has suggested that jurisdiction's economic recovery from the crisis has been slower than those of other economies in the region (1999, 1). The council reported that the scale of the contraction in Hong Kong during the Asian crisis was significant and the rebound has been slower than those of many other Asian economies (1). In 1998 Hong Kong's real GDP fell by 5.1 percent and continued its decline in the first quarter of 1999 with a loss of 3.4 percent (1). "During the same period, the other three 'dragon' economies have all experienced positive growth" (1).

The Council attributed Hong Kong's significant economic contraction and slower-than-expected rebound as having much to do with weak consumer demand (2). The weakness in consumer demand in turn is attributed to a relatively high level of consumer debt (3). "Many people in Hong Kong pledged their property to banks for a loan in order to get the finance they need to build up their own businesses, either in Hong Kong or overseas (including Mainland China)" (3). As explained, the Asian crisis led to a significant decline in asset values. Residential property prices fell by an average of about 50 percent causing many people to lose a substantial part of their wealth (4).

Beyond such matters Hong Kong is characterized by large numbers of small and medium-sized firms which are described as flexible, mobile and able to get in and out of business quickly (5–6). However the firms in question are subject to a high casualty rate and industries rise and fall as large numbers of these firms enter or leave (6). Most of the firms under discussion must rely on their ability to pledge assets to banks to obtain financing (6). Thus the fall in asset values in Hong Kong, together with a deteriorating business value on the mainland have resulted in liquidity problems for many enterprises (6). In addition the weak, uncertain economic environment has resulted in weak investments (6). Thus it can be seen that the crisis has faced Hong Kong with a unique set of financial and economic difficulties.

To date the discussion in this chapter has moved from jurisdiction to jurisdiction in examining the circumstances that the crisis has generated. Beyond that it must be recognized that the successful reestablishment of strong economies is dependent in many ways on successful business. According to Charles In-Chang Chun and John C. Beck the rules of business in Asia are being rewritten, meaning that individual firms will have to assess how such rules will transform competition and impact their businesses (1999, 4).

Those authors suggest that early in the crisis companies were optimistic about opportunities that it might hold but they have not adjusted their strategies accordingly (1). They labeled company responses as mostly defensive, the immediate priority for them being the improvement of short-term cash flow, which was seen as the lifeblood of survival (1). "Currency devaluation, capital flight from debt and equity markets, and high debt-to-equity ratios weighed heavily on companies whose valuations plummeted as quickly as liquidity drained away" (1).

The authors in question went on to suggest that companies initially tried to better their cash positions by quick fixes, such as cutting costs, postponing investments, rationalizing their businesses and restructuring investment portfolios and debt payments (1). "Banks and finance companies either stopped lending, delayed building reserves or turned to foreign partners for fresh capital" (1). The authors pointed out that consumer-goods makers reduced their range of products, laid off employees, cut excess capacity and renegotiated contracts with existing customers (2). Industrial-products companies entered price wars and sold off businesses to generate cash, while natural resource–related firms streamlined operations or searched for new export markets (2). Other firms froze investments or looked for foreign partners (2). Marketing outlays were reduced by telecommunications firms as were systems maintenance costs, while new investments were halted (2).

The authors caution that each short-term decision will impact the long-term capabilities of the firm (2). "The market will no longer condone debt-financed diversification, loose corporate governance and limited-cost competitiveness (2). The litany of don'ts from the authors continues, as they suggest that delaying payments to suppliers or dissolving business relationships may harm goodwill and interfere with future business contacts (2). They advise against cutting research and development, information technology, operational improvements and product offerings on grounds that such actions may erode market share and the ability to innovate (2).

They see the traditional home-market advantages enjoyed by Asian conglomerates to be rocked by market opening reforms in some countries in the region and suggest that the era of limited competition and preferential treatment will fade as market changes are adopted and as fewer decisions are impacted by political concerns (3–4). Reforms are predicted that will force competition with foreigners to a level playing field with less government intervention (4). Also predicted are restricted access to capital, greater transparency and exposure to world-class standards (4). It seems clear that the private sector bears a heavy responsibility in the realm of efficient operating procedures if the region has hopes of a complete recovery from the crisis, not to mention a resumption of successful international economic linkages and a consequent sustained expansion.

The discussion above was prompted by a piece in *Outlook Magazine*, a trade organ of Andersen Consulting, the firm in which Charles Chun is an associate partner in Bangkok. The article is an example of the expertise that professionals in major consulting firms can bring to bear on concerns precipitated by the Asian crisis. Clearly such firms have much to offer, as do the major international accounting firms and their consulting arms, as facilitators of economic and business goals.

The current authors are hardly new supporters of the hypothesis that various business services and notably those offered by major international accounting firms have assumed major facilitative roles in the global economy. "Once services emerged as facilitators in both the operation and expansion of modern economies, the extension of that role beyond national boundaries was all but inevitable" (McKee and Garner, 1992, 65). McKee and Garner were of the opinion that the world economy would hardly have been feasible without substantial inputs from various categories of sophisticated services.

Certainly this view of the global economy does no violence to the understanding of the Asian Pacific region and the roles of its various constituent jurisdictions in that economy. Beyond that it appears to set the stage for a better understanding of the potential roles of services in the region and hopefully in what such enterprises may have to contribute to moving players in the region beyond the crises of 1997.

Writing in 1991 William J. Coffey and Antoine Bailly saw increasingly complex national and international financial environments as broadening service needs (100). In light of financial mechanations described above, it seems hardly surprising that the Asia Pacific region was fertile soil for growth in service needs in the post-crisis environment. Coffey and Bailly in their pre-crisis discussion mentioned that "Functions relating to raising capital, foreign exchange, and mounting or assisting takeovers and/ or mergers are occurring over wider geographical areas" (100). Beyond that they alluded to additional service needs arising as a result of the international integration of both production and consumption (100). Such observations brought the current authors to the contention that "it would appear that legal, accounting and insurance sub-sectors should experience ongoing increases in client interest" (McKee, Amara and Garner, 1995, 259).

"Services appear to assert a stabilizing influence while at the same time making expansion and integration more feasible both within nations and internationally" (260). This statement appears to have acquired a more acute significance in the regional post-crisis environment, a significance that may become clearer during the present investigation as the role of major accounting firms is examined.

KPMG is one of the major international accounting firms active in the region. "Understanding local business process, culture, customs, and regulations is an essential part of doing business in the region. KPMG can assist your organization to understand and meet those challenges"

(KPMG, March 2000a). The firm is located throughout the region and boasts a staff of international specialists who can assist clients with trans-regional business activities (2000a). The firm's Asia Pacific consulting network is designed to facilitate cross-border investment and trade activities in what they term "a seamless and integrated fashion" (2000a). The firm considers its network to be a point of contact for clients establishing market entry strategies or engaging in cross-border transactions.

The firm's specialties include international tax, investigative accounting, market surveys, business process improvement, global supply-chain management, SAP implementation and international finance (2000a). From earlier discussions in the current Chapter it is easy to endorse the value of such expertise in the region. In another context the firm suggests that Asia Pacific is known to be a very complex region, as well as a region of change (2000b). "To operate successfully throughout the region, an enterprise must first hurdle barriers presented by language, cultural diversity and wide geographic coverage" (2000b). The firm sees itself as the essential link to assist businesses in meeting and managing those challenges (2000b).

Writing in 1999 Corichita Manibat, the managing partner of C.L. Manibat & Co. in the Philippines observed, "As the 20th century comes to a close, the world is confronted with a myriad of concerns putting to the test one's ability to manage change" (Deloitte Touche Tohmatsu, 1999). Manabat went on to explain the fact that traders and businessmen change with time and with the insatiable desire to create wealth which is the driving force that has broadened the playing field. This has made it difficult to talk about any single nation's economy without considering its major trading partners or immediate neighbors (2). Manabat seems correct in observing that the economies of various countries are becoming more and more enmeshed as time goes by. This, of course, speaks to the seriousness of what has transpired in Southeast Asia. That there is a major role for the international accounting firms in the region seems self evident.

Chapter 3

The Role of the Accounting Firms

Writing in 1996, David L. McKee and Don E. Garner documented a significant role for the large international accounting firms in the Pacific Basin. The nations covered in that study were selected on the basis of their orientation toward export activity. Indeed their economic status was seen to be related to their participation in the world economy, as facilitated by the various service offerings of the major accounting firms that they were hosting (McKee and Garner, 1996b).

The nations that were featured represented three distinct groupings which differed substantially from each other in terms of what might be termed material success. The most prosperous group comprised what have been called the Asian Tigers, Hong Kong, Singapore, South Korea and Taiwan. The second group included a selection of emerging nations, notably Indonesia, Malaysia, the Philippines and Thailand. The final group was composed of a selection of small island economies which included Papua New Guinea, Fiji, Vanuatu and Western Samoa.

The prognosis for the Asian Tigers and the emerging nations considered was for the most part positive in terms of expansion potential and material betterment. For the islands in question the expectations were somewhat less robust. With respect to services offered by the major accounting firms it seemed clear that there were significant parts to play. "It seems clear that accounting services are important to economies enjoying various levels of development" (1996, 155). Indeed such services expand in volume and diversity in keeping with needs of their business clients (155).

It may well be that the turmoil that has occurred in various Pacific Basin economies during the closing years of the 1990s may have caused adjustments in the service menus of various international accounting firms, if indeed those firms have responded to the changing needs indicated by their clients. It may also be that the accounting firms through their ongoing operations may have assisted clients both public and private to weather the crises that have occurred. It may also be that the firms have actually facilitated the emergence of various Asian nations from recent crises. If that proves to be the case it will speak eloquently to the importance of the major accounting firms and their services.

In a recent statement concerning its functions and activities in the region, KPMG displays the importance of such a firm vis-à-vis the international efficiency of business in the nations concerned. KPMG suggests that understanding local business process, culture, customs, and regulations is an essential part of doing business in the region (KPMG, April 1998).

The firm sees itself as both able and willing to assist with relevant issues. In support of its credentials for such an undertaking the firm claims to be present throughout the region with a cadre of international specialists designed to assist its clients with their transregional business activities (April 1998). The regional consulting network was designed to facilitate cross-border investment, and its client's trade-related activities "in a seamless and integrated fashion" (April 1998). As it explains, its network presents a point of contact for its clients developing strategies for market entry or for taking part in cross-border activities.

The firm has developed specialized service networks to help its Australian, Canadian, Chinese, Dutch, German, Japanese, Korean and U.S. clients (April 1998). It is clear that the firm recognizes the importance of its services. Those services are designed to assist a wide-ranging clientele and in doing that it can be expected to reinforce or strengthen the economies of the nations where they are available.

KPMG goes on to explain that its specialties include international tax, investigative accounting, market surveys and business process improvement, as well as the management of global supply chains, SAP implementation and international finance. The firm's regional consultants are also willing to provide integrated services on commercial and public-sector projects throughout the region (April 1998).

The fact that such a firm describes its international role in such an explicit fashion for potential clients clearly signals its matter of fact willingness to operate as an international facilitator of business operations and linkages. It may be that the operations of that firm and/or its competitors can do much to maintain, restore or even generate linkages for clients to the global economy. In the case of the Asian Pacific region that seems to suggest that the major accounting firms may be willing and able to assist clients whether public or private in ways that facilitate renewed international economic viability in the post-Asian-crisis environment.

The importance of what international accounting firms or networks are about in the global economy can be seen in a recent Internet release by Independent Accountants International (1998). Speaking of their consulting activity they see themselves "as an organization conceived and structured specifically for cross-border operations" (1998). They go on to state, "We offer the same authority and reliability that business leaders already recognize in IA's extensive international accounting and auditing network, drawing on our well established offices in over 70 countries in all continents" (1998).

They see a unique advantage for themselves and their clients in their supply of reliable data and advice on the country of interest and also in their ability to assign in-house IA business managers with direct experience with local business cultures as well as those of other nations to be dealt with (1998). "Each of IA's Business Services affiliates is equipped to provide complete, swift response to your local business needs, identify potential pitfalls and opportunities during all phases of your venture" (1998).

Such aims were to be accomplished through offering market research, strategic planning and mergers and acquisitions (M&A) assistance and by coordinating legal and tax advisory services. Beyond such matters offerings include administrative services covering accounting services as well as the comprehensive financial management of subsidiaries. The organization can also conduct executive searches and can provide professional staffs for subsidiaries with guarantees relating to unbiased reporting, external hands on management, professional levels otherwise unattainable, and flexibility in scope and cost (1998). If such a network can successfully deliver on this menu of assistance, it speaks to the power they can wield in the global economy.

According to Independent Accountants International cross-border operations were traditionally the preserve of major multinational firms but are now becoming "an unavoidable fact of life for medium-sized companies" (1998). As they explain, "The breaking down of trade barriers, marketing integration and ever shortening distances within the global economy, are combining to bring this multinational challenge to the doorstep of companies that once could rely on a single national market" (1998). They suggest that regardless of years of experience and knowhow in home markets, many large firms are struggling with unfamiliar and costly obstacles in foreign operations (1998).

In such cases they suggest that the firms concerned find themselves involved with an expensive learning curve and a loss of time, effort and money (1998). Managers find themselves moving from regional to international concerns. The most obvious issues to be faced, such as fiscal and auditing arrangements are rarely the sole root of managerial problems (1998). Among additional key elements are "The supply of prompt, accurate and relevant financial and economic data on an on going and permanent basis" (1998). Beyond that is a required understanding of the human, cultural and economic context of the new operating environment (1998). Other issues revolve around developing the appropriate scale and cost of the subsidiaries management, a problem that may not benefit significantly from home-country experience (1998).

The network under discussion is a global consultancy corporation, offering business advice "on issues that involve transnational inquiries or management advisory services in many areas" (1998). Among specialized services that participating IA member firms can provide are market surveys, investigations and analyses, as well as productivity analysis and improvement (1998). They also offer legal, administrative or secretarial services, human resources services, and advice concerning mergers and acquisitions (1998). Other assistance available includes personal computer and software consulting services, healthcare consulting and translation services (1998). Information can be provided on individual or corporate investments and beyond that assistance with respect to asset management can be given, involving representing troubled companies, acting as trustees and handling asset disposal (1998).

The organization also consults on tax matters and government contracts and, beyond such matters, offers business-valuation services and litigation-support services (1998). Judging from their offerings, Independent Accountants International are very much involved on a global basis in facilitating the operation of international business interests. Their services, where available in the Asia Pacific region, can do much to reassert international linkages in ways that should certainly assist with both recovery and advancement.

Kreston International is a world-wide network of independent accounting firms that is active in the Asia Pacific region. It is represented in all of the jurisdictions featured in the current study save for the Pacific Islands. "The Kreston network has been established to facilitate the need of international companies to find reliable accounting services in the countries where their business is conducted" (1999a).

Each firm in the network is solely responsible for its own work, staff and clients (1999a). However, "To ensure local knowledge and understanding of current business laws, customs, conditions and their fiscal implications, international assignments will be coordinated by the Kreston firm in the client's country of origin and completed by accountants who are nationals of the country where the business is being conducted" (1999a).

The organization offers the usual auditing and accounting services (1999a). It does taxation compliance work and offers taxation planning and consulting for both individuals and companies. It advises firms on potential acquisitions and mergers, on acquiring finance and on selecting computers, as well as both software and hardware. It offers other computer services as well. It helps with corporate recovery, insolvency and liquidation and receiverships. It gives investment advice and manages investment portfolios. It consults on internal systems and controls and assists with business and strategic planning. It can perform company secretarial work and help with staff recruitment. It conducts business valuations and can help clients with personal financial planning (1999b). The Kreston organization's service menu appears to be representative of the offerings of major accounting firms and/or networks.

Supply-chain management has been significant among KPMG's regional consulting activities. In that regard the firm has put together a regional initiative, geared to the expanding significance of specific industry and product areas. Kuala Lumpur has been host to its Asia Pacific Global Supply Chain Management Practice (KPMG, February 1998, 1). According to KPMG, supply-chain management is prominent on board room agendas and is seen as a critical business issue in various locations including the United States, Europe and Australia (February 1998, 1). "The recent establishment of the Practice comes at a critical time for local and multinational companies in Asia who are keen to reduce operational costs in light of the ailing economies" (February 1998, 1). The firm has been intent upon developing a self-sustaining team in the region, designed to assist local practices in responding to the needs of both new and existing clients (February 1998, 1–2).

Among the services offered by KPMG Asia Pacific Global Supply-Chain Management are supply-chain diagnostic and future visioning and supply-chain strategy formulation and testing (February 1998, 2). Other service offerings included supply-chain process review and alignment, technology-driven supply-chain optimization and supply-chain improvement and cost-reduction programs (February 1998, 2). The firm notes that "Given the current economic situation in the region, this quantitative and qualitative combination has proven to be extremely appealing to business" (February 1998, 2).

The firm has suggested that there is no single survey that establishes what firms around the world are doing, or how they compare vis-à-vis supply-chain management (February 1998, 2). Because of this the firm undertook a benchmarking study intended to establish how supply chains are managed, "what market concerns and future plans were" (February 1998, 2). The results of their survey suggested that many firms were not in sufficient control of their supply chains to drive them to winning performance levels.

Some firms "still operated it as a series of functional or company silos creating waste and inefficiency at the interface points" (February 1998,

1). KPMG found that others had moved to an integrated process organization, while leaving their control and measurement systems organized by function. The firm was of the opinion that process-based organizations provide chances for improved intra-company material and information flows, with subsequent reductions of time scales and inventory levels. Clearly KPMG was developing in-depth knowledge of business operations that could well facilitate the functioning of their clients.

KPMG is also operating an Asia Pacific Financial Sector Consulting Practice that focuses on servicing the banking and finance industries (November 1998a). That practice is based in Kuala Lumpur and Taipei but functions throughout the region. It has risk solutions as its principle service offering with an eye to assisting clients to control capital leakage and optimize earnings (November 1998a, 3). "Specific areas of expertise include market risk, credit risk, operational risk, risk adjustment performance measures, capital allocation and treasury management" (November 1998a, 3).

Services offered by the KPMG risks-solutions team include such matters as the identification and measurement of business risks and the development of management frameworks and individual risk-response plans. The team can also design risk organization structures, enhancing risk management processes (November 1998a, 3). It can assist with reengineering trading operations and designing and implementing market, credit and operational risk management systems and can implement pragmatic risk-adjusted performance measures to improve capital allocation processes (November 1998a, 4)

It also stands ready to evaluate financial risk strategy and to implement operational improvements in corporate treasuries (November 1998a, 4). The team also "controls reviews to support statutory or regulatory audit work" and conducts feasibility reviews of corporate plans (November 1998a, 4). Once again it is clear in this subset of its service menu that KPMG stands ready to provide very specialized assistance to clients, assistance that should be expected to impact business operations within and beyond the Asia Pacific region.

According to KPMG, "Organizations increasingly face more complex business issues and must rapidly change to keep pace with today's dynamic market" (November 1998a, 5). The firm is willing to help in that regard. KPMG suggests that organizations "now require total service solutions based on global knowledge, experience and best practices" (November 1998a, 5). The firm sees their clients as requiring solutions crafted to meet specific needs and supplied by a highly skilled consulting team if they hope to attain their goals (November 1998a, 5).

According to the firm, its KPMG Consulting's BPI Methodology is "an internationally proven service and technique for achieving rapid business transformation and performance improvement" (November 1998a,

5). They see their approach as enabling the delivery of solutions that range from strategy formulation through business transformation to systems implementation and the monitoring of benefits (November 1998a, 5). Indeed they cite their approach as addressing all key elements of organizational change (November 1998a, 5).

In promoting its assistance potential KPMG asserts that bridging the gap between what it termed "old habits" and "better business" requires an effective improvement in performance, a need that it asserts can be met with the help of its Business Performance Improvement Methodology (November 1998a, 5). "Whatever challenges you have KPMG understands the interdependencies of process, technology and people, and how change impacts an organization" (November 1998a, 5). Driving home its selling points the firm asserts that its methodology fosters the acceptance of change from the starting point, promoting behaviors that will drive success. It claims its methodology to be a single unified framework for designing, constructing and implementing solutions (November 1998a, 5).

Judging from the offerings of the major accounting firms and networks discussed above, it appears as though those organizations have developed a detailed understanding of corporate operating procedures. Those understandings go well beyond the traditional preserves of accounting and auditing. Clearly the firms can supply their services within specific nations or internationally between nations. By assisting their clients they may also be strengthening the economies in which those clients operate and in addition they may be strengthening international linkages, not to mention the global economy and the regional subsets comprising it.

Vis-à-vis the Asia Pacific region an earlier study argued that various business services, including those provided by major accounting firms, impact events in economies of varying sizes and levels of development but that the extent of those influences may differ dramatically from place to place (McKee and Garner, 1996b, 152).

Historical variations have become moot in light of the recent crises that emerged in various economies that will be the focus of the current volume. Certainly the major accounting firms and networks and/or other purveyors of business services were unable to avert the crises in question. Nonetheless they may still hold importance as facilitators of business and economic operations in a recovering region. They may also be very important with respect to world-wide corporate linkages and mechanations.

As suggested in the earlier study "nations that cast their lots with export industries will have definite and increasing needs with respect to services that facilitate international business operations" (1996, 152). Certainly all of the newly industrialized nations to be discussed in this volume fall within that category. The same can be said for Thailand and

Malaysia. At this juncture it seems probable that all of the export-oriented nations to be discussed stand to benefit from the involvements of major international accounting firms or networks.

The manner in which such gains impact domestic economic activities in the nations concerned may vary significantly. In jurisdictions such as Hong Kong and Singapore it seems probable that services offered locally by the firms and of course demonstration effects from the firms' operations will add strength to local economies. Local and domestic impacts may be less visible in the other export-oriented nations.

Prior to the crises of the late 1990s the firms were supplying some assistance with external linkages to clients in Indonesia and the Philippines (152). Unfortunately, it seemed as though the spread effects from the firms' activities may not have been having major impacts beyond Jakarta and Manila where they were concentrated (152). It was suggested that "Even in those two rather large metropolitan complexes, the impact of the firms may have limited visibility because of the sheer size of the cities in question" (152). Although it doesn't appear that matters have changed much in these last mentioned nations more definite statements may be feasible at the conclusion of the current project.

Thailand which has been a center of concern during recent crises in the Asia Pacific region may certainly benefit in its recovery from the international ministrations of major accounting firms. However in the pre-crisis era during which Thailand displayed rather impressive growth statistics it was thought that the concentration of the firms in Bangkok may have been limiting in the nation at large (152). Whether things have changed in that regard at this writing remains to be seen.

Recent crises may not have impacted the island economies of the Pacific in the way that they have the larger jurisdictions. It was thought that islands hosting major accounting firms were enjoying strengthened foreign linkages and that the smallness of the islands in question "May insure more visible domestic impacts from the firms relative to what is occurring in the larger nations" (1996, 152). At this juncture there appears to be little justification for revising that assessment.

Writing in 1993 Susan Segal-Horn saw merger processes generating very large international accounting and consulting firms for the purpose of more efficient capacity use and improved productivity by implementing standardized methodologies (41). Evidence supporting her position has been presented in the current Chapter. She claimed the existence of "de facto evidence that international chains exist in virtually all types of service businesses, even highly local, regulated, and cultural specific services.

It has been suggested that "Within and between national economies services facilitate the passage of materials, personnel and funds within and between business units" (McKee, Amara and Garner, 1995, 255).

That statement illustrates the impact of the service offerings of the major accounting firms in the Asia Pacific region. "Financial, legal and accounting practitioners as well as many other specialized service groups have produced collective impacts to render business more efficient and better integrated" (McKee, Garner and AbuAmara McKee, 1998, 4).

Services have had a part to play in strengthening business linkages and thus strengthening the economies hosting the businesses in question. That being the case they should be expected to contribute to the resurgence of regional economies since the abatement of the crises of the late 1990s. According to Peter Enderwick, "Conventional views of development seriously understate the importance of the service sector in economic growth" (1991, 292). He saw the most widely held view as labeling a growing service sector to be a result of rather than a cause of development. He acknowledged an enabling role for services in development while suggesting that such a function alone "does not do justice to their importance" (294).

He saw services typically as characterized by significant economic linkages and the generation of externalities (294). Enderwick saw a potential role for service multinationals. Multinational service firms provide "both a competitive and a complementary role in stimulating through competition, the quality of service provision and in complementing indigenous service offerings with those targeted at new market segments" (295).

"Service opportunities are emerging on a global basis, aimed at facilitating international business operations, which are crossing long standing national boundaries" (McKee, Garner and AbuAmara McKee, 1998, 7). It seems clear that the operations of major international accounting firms and networks being considered here serve as a good illustration of this phenomenon, "Independent of individual firms and industries and presumably governments, such service groups may enjoy a level of stability or staying power rarely seen among businesses in the past" (McKee, Amara and Garner, 1995, 258). That stability has been exhibited by the accounting organizations that have survived the recent economic and financial crises that have impacted the Pacific region.

As was suggested in a recent publication, "As firms and industries come and go as leading sectors of the world economy, the services facilitating them adjust to the needs of this changing clientele and thus add a certain stability while aiding in the processes of change" (McKee, Garner and AbuAmara McKee, 1998, 7). This of course speaks to one of the central concerns of the present volume. It seems reasonable to ask how the major international accounting organizations have adjusted during and after the recent crises. Some evidence of the strength and perhaps the depth of the mission of the accounting organizations has been reviewed in the present Chapter.

Part II

Institutional Parameters for Accounting Practice

Chapter 4

Accounting and Business Environments Facing the Asian Tigers

With the stronger economies of the four jurisdictions discussed in this chapter, Hong Kong, Korea, Singapore and Taiwan would be expected to have more developed national accounting and reporting systems than the remaining countries covered in this volume. Harmonization of their national standards with international accounting standards might be expected to be at an advanced stage. This Chapter explores the financial and accounting infrastructures of these economies with an eye toward these expectations.

HONG KONG

As Hong Kong reverted to China in 1997, China gave assurances that it will until at least the year 2047 preserve the present legal system, financial autonomy and independent business arrangements, including Hong Kong's market economy, free port status, industrialization practices and access to world markets. China drew up a Constitution for Hong Kong, referred to as the Basic Law, which does provide that the current capitalist system and lifestyle will be upheld for at least 50 years. The Basic Law promises a high degree of autonomy, an independent judiciary system and guarantees of individual property rights.

In Hong Kong, which is largely a service center for banking, finance, research and development, and market research, the business language is English. Cantonese Chinese may become a second official language as it is widely spoken. The Hong Kong dollar is legal tender. There are no exchange control restrictions with regard to movement of funds into or out of Hong Kong for any purpose (Diamond and Diamond, 2000, 13–15).[1]

Each business in Hong Kong, be it a proprietorship, partnership or corporation, must register each year with the Business Registration Office and receive a certificate to operate after payment of annual fees. Proprietorships, which have unlimited liability, are not required to publicly disclose or to have audited financial statements. For partnerships, liability may be limited or unlimited. At least one partner in a limited partnership must have unlimited liability for partnership obligations. The Partnership Ordinance does not specify accounting or auditing rules but does require partnerships to keep true accounts such that full information on the partnership is available (35).

The Inland Revenue Ordinance as amended established two kinds of partnerships. A partnership which has 20 partners or less is referred to as a designated partnership and profits and losses are taxed to the individual members of the partnership in their profit and loss sharing ratios. A partnership with more than 20 members is treated for taxation as though the partnership were a company (36).

Foreign corporations must register with the Hong Kong Companies Registrar and provide required documentation. Should the corporation be a public one, audited financial statements must be filed annually together with a director's report. Private foreign companies may apply for relief from these reporting requirements (35).

The Companies Ordinance as amended regulates corporations in Hong Kong. Companies may be formed as either private or public and may be formed by persons of any nationality whether resident in Hong Kong or not. The corporation may have limited or unlimited liability. Limited liability may be attained by a corporation organizing as limited by shares, by guarantee or by guarantee with a share capital.

Incorporators who seek to form a private company must restrict rights of share transfer, must limit shareholders to 50 or less, and must not offer stock or debentures for sale to the public. The private company must have at least two incorporators of any nationality who need not be residents of Hong Kong. Each must subscribe to at least one share if the company issues capital stock. The private company is not required to file financial statements with the Registrar of Companies. Stockholders, however, must be provided with audited statements unless all shareholders agree not to receive such statements.

A registered office in Hong Kong must be maintained by a private limited company. There must be no fewer than two shareholders, two directors and a corporate secretary. The secretary is required to be a Hong Kong resident or a corporation with a Hong Kong registered office or place of business. The private company is permitted to purchase its own shares even from capital so long as creditors' and minority shareholders' rights are protected. Redeemable ordinary or preferred shares may be issued (31).

Hong Kong companies that do not meet the requirements for a private company are automatically considered public companies. Each public company is required to file its financial statements with the Registrar of Companies. A shareholders' meeting must be held between one month and three months after the company begins operating so that a report on allotment of shares and capital receipts can be made. There must be no less than two incorporators who must subscribe to at least one share if capital stock is issued. There must also be two directors who must be individuals not corporations (32).

The Companies Ordinance governs accounting and auditing provisions. Each Hong Kong company is responsible for maintaining adequate accounting records and proper statutory records, such as stockholder registers. These records may be kept at the registered office of the company or at another location decided upon by the company directors. While there is no mandatory chart of accounts required, records should be sufficient to show a true and fair view of the state of affairs and to explain company transactions. The records should encompass, at a minimum, all company assets, liabilities and equities. Entries must be kept for all money received and expended including particulars of goods purchased and sold. Should these records be kept outside of Hong Kong, sufficient information must be sent at least semi-annually to allow the preparation of reports on financial position and for necessary statutory reports required by the Hong Kong Companies Ordinance (KPMG, 2001).

The annual company statutory report under the Ordinance must include audited financial statements for the current and preceding year. The report should include balance sheet, profit and loss statement, cash flow statement and all required notes thereto. The annual statutory report must be presented to a general stockholders' meeting. The company may set the date of the financial year-end, however all member companies in a group should have the same year-end.

Companies whose shares are held by the public must file the annual reports with the Registrar of Companies where they are available to the public. Private companies are exempt from this requirement. The reports may be in either English or Chinese. The financial records and reports must give a true and fair view including required disclosures. The Hong Kong Inland Revenue Department requires that corporation tax returns must have audited financial statements submitted with them (KPMG, 2001).

The Professional Accountants Ordinance in 1973 designated the Hong Kong Society of Accountants as the only official Hong Kong accounting body and as the authority responsible for formulating Hong Kong accounting and auditing standards. The Society is also the organization responsible for conducting accountancy examinations, prescribing experience requirements for the practice certificate and for issuing practice certificates for accounting practice in Hong Kong (Price Waterhouse, 1992a, 9).

The Hong Kong Society of Accountants issues Statements of Standard Accounting Practice that in effect constitute Hong Kong generally accepted accounting principles (GAAP). In the past, Hong Kong GAAP tended to allow more alternative treatments and more judgments than U.S. GAAP. In fact, there were substantial differences between the two. Since the financial crisis in 1997, the Society has set the goal of developing standards, which will provide a comprehensive framework for Hong Kong companies that will be harmonized with international accounting standards (IAS). The Hong Kong Society has issued a substantial number of revised and new standards.

For the year ending December 31, 1999 there were six standards. Four were seen as being in compliance with applicable IAS. An International Forum for Accountancy Development sponsored study, "GAAP 2000—A Survey of National Accounting Rules in 53 Countries," was conducted to gauge whether written national accounting standards in 53 countries were harmonized with IAS, including interpretations issued by the IAS Standing Interpretations Committee. The rules effective for reporting periods ending on December 31, 2000 were used in the study (Nobes, 2000, 47)

Respondent CPAs were asked to identify nonalignment where national rules would not permit the international treatment because of inconsistent rules or would not require the international treatment because of missing or permissive rules (1). The survey summary for Hong Kong listed 31 instances in which differences were reported between Hong Kong standards and international accounting standards. These covered 15 International Accounting Standards and two interpretations. Reasons for the differences fell into three categories: Hong Kong accounting standards differ from IAS because of the lack of specific Hong Kong rules, five instances cited; there are no specific rules in Hong Kong which require disclosures required by IAS, three instances cited; and inconsistencies between the two sets of standards could lead to differences for many enterprises in certain areas, 13 instances were cited under Hong Kong rules and 10 instances were cited under IAS rules.

Local levels have province governments headed by a governor and city governments headed by a mayor. Within the city or municipality there are barangays; each has a barangay captain as its leader. All of the local levels of government have boards of councilmen (99).

SINGAPORE

Singapore's beginnings were as a British trading colony in 1819. Independence came in 1965, when the nation state separated from Malaysia. For a century and a half, Singapore has been a leading entrepot center of East-West trade, remaining so today with harbors and shipyards among the busiest in the world (Diamond and Diamond, 2000, 24). Singapore is increasingly recognized as an exceptional investment location in the Asian Pacific area, not only because of its strategic location but also because of its positive and productive environment for business. The nation state has infrastructures that are among the best in the world. There are excellent systems of education, telecommunications, information technology, transportation and healthcare. The social and political infrastructures have been stable and constitute a market-oriented growing economy that weathered the effects of the 1997 financial crisis.

The labor force is highly skilled and motivated toward success. The government is geared to innovation and planning and carries through to productive results. Singapore is a regional financial center and since the 1997 financial crisis in the region has been in the process of investing on a wider global basis with the goal of becoming a world financial center. Arthur Andersen believes that "Singapore has evolved into a truly vibrant, cosmopolitan, and international global business center" (Arthur Andersen, 1999, 1).

The population in 2000 was estimated at 4.2 million with a population growth rate of 3.54 percent. The ethnic group make up was Chinese 77 percent, Malay 14 percent, Indian 7.6 percent and other 1.4 percent. The literacy rate is estimated at over 91 percent, with Chinese, English, Tamil and Malay all official languages. The usual language of business is English (CIA, 2000c, 1)

There is a parliamentary style government in which the chief of state is the president of the republic and the prime minister is the head of government. The parliament has 83 seats elected by popular vote for five-year terms of office. Following the 1997 election, the Peoples' Action Party held all Parliament seats save three (1).

The judiciary consists of a Supreme Court and Court of Appeals. The president with the advice of the prime minister appoints the Supreme Court chief justice. Other judges are appointed by the president upon the advice of the chief justice (2).

Services and exports, led by electronics and chemicals, drive the highly developed economy. Services accounted for 72 percent and industry 28 percent of GDP in 1998. Agriculture's share in GDP is negligible. The labor force was occupied 38 percent in financial, business and other services, 21.6 percent in manufacturing, 21.4 percent in commerce, 7 percent in construction and 12 percent in other areas (6).

Government-linked and -owned companies operate as commercial entities and produce 60 percent of GDP. The government spends heavily in education and technology. A government-mandated savings scheme helps promote savings and investment. For 1999, real growth in the economy was estimated at 5.5 percent with a 0.4 percent inflation rate in consumer prices (5,6). The Singapore dollar is the national currency unit, with rates of exchange against the U.S. dollar of S $1.67 in 2000, 1.695 in 1999, 1.6736 in 1998, 1.4848 in 1997, and 1.41 in 1996 (7).

The country supports free trade and does not impose protectionist restrictions, quotas or tariffs on imports. Excise duties in a material amount are collected on a limited set of goods, for example tobacco, alcohol, automobiles and petroleum products (2). Goods from Singapore have preferential duties in other ASEAN countries.

Singapore has become one of the world's three largest offshore financial centers. As regional and global political and business environments have changed over the years, Singapore has become ever more attractive to multinational companies and cross-border investors. The country provides generous tax incentives in a solid business infrastructure. The government is stable. The currency is strong, being viewed as the most attractive Asian currency after the Japanese yen. And, the living conditions in the republic are comfortable (Diamond and Diamond, 2000, 1).

With government encouragement, appropriate legislation and incentive programs, Singapore has grown into a sophisticated financial center with substantial offshore banking, an Asian dollar market, mature futures and stock exchanges. Incentives have been established for financial-center growth in fund management, debt securities market, unit trusts and venture capital (Arthur Andersen, 1999, 2).

Domestic equity shares are traded on the Singapore Exchange (SGX) through its Securities Trading Division. SGX was officially launched in December 1999 as a result of the merger between the Stock Exchange of Singapore and the Singapore International Monetary Exchange. The merger was authorized by the Exchanges (Demutualisation and Merger) Act 1999 and was designed to update Singapore's markets and enhance its position in the world markets. Through its subsidiary Singapore Exchange Securities Trading Limited (SGX-ST), equities are traded via an electronic platform for a wide range of domestic and foreign securities on a script-less basis. Since March 2000 SGX-ST Trading Limited (SGX-ST), equities are traded via an electronic platform for a wide range of domestic and foreign securities on a script-less basis. By March 2000 SGX-ST had 426 list companies with combined market capitalization in excess of S $440 billion. Of the total companies, 342 were listed on the Main Board of SGX-ST. The remaining 84 companies were listed on

SESDAQ of SGX-ST. The listing requirements for SESDAQ are less stringent than those for the Main Board and allow small and medium-sized companies to raise funds through the equity markets. Trading of derivatives products is carried on by the Derivatives Trading Division of SGX.

The government takes active roles in promoting Singapore as a regional operational and business headquarters location for multinational companies. In effect, operational business units of a multinational company in the Asian Pacific region are directed from a company's headquarters in Singapore. The government grants tax and business incentives. Direct help from governmental agencies is also provided in identifying, exploring and establishing business opportunities in Asia. Business parks are now operating in Indonesia, China, Vietnam and India (3).

The Registry of Companies and Businesses controls the registration of unincorporated businesses as well as the incorporation of companies in Singapore. The Registrar keeps the registration documents on file available for public access (David Tong & Company, 1993, 25). Neither foreign investors nor Singapore citizens are restricted in the form of business they may use. An unincorporated business can be registered either as a sole proprietorship or a partnership with the Registry (Arthur Andersen, 1999, 1). In order to carry on a business to import and/or export goods, a business must additionally register with the Trade Development Board. Certain other activities do require licensing from appropriate government agencies, for example banking, production of beer, and operation of a restaurant or bar (Government of Singapore, 2001, 1).

A local manager must be appointed for all businesses except where the sole proprietor, a partner, a company director or a company secretary in said business has a local address and is long-staying. Such managers may be Singapore citizens or non-Singapore citizens who have a Singapore permanent-resident status, or an employment pall from the Ministry of Manpower (5).

Each business firm must display its full registered name in a conspicuous position on the outside of every place where business is carried on, including all branches. In addition, each letterhead, invoice, bill or other document used for business purposes must have the full registered business name and the Certificate of Registration number displayed (2).

The company is a legally incorporated entity that when registered under the Companies Act has a separate legal personality. Such corporate bodies must commonly include in their corporate name the words "Pte Ltd" or "Ltd." Corporations may be of three main types: private limited companies, public companies and branches of foreign companies. The private limited company may not have more than 50 shareholders nor can shares be offered for sale to the general public. A public company may have more than 50 shareholders and may offer shares and debentures to the public. A Prospectus must be registered with the Registrar prior to making a public offer of shares or debentures for sale (Government of Singapore, 2001, 1).

The Registrar must first approve the proposed company name. After the name is approved, the company may proceed to register by filing appropriate incorporation documents, including Memorandum & Articles of Association setting out the objectives and bylaws of the proposed company. Each company must have at least two directors, one of whom must be a resident in Singapore (How to Register a Local Company in Singapore, 1, 2). After approval, the Registrar issues a certificate of incorporation.

Foreign investors are permitted to operate a business in Singapore as a sole proprietorship, by setting up a partnership, by establishing a branch, or incorporating a local subsidiary company. With a few exceptions, 100 percent foreign ownership of corporations is allowed (Arthur Andersen, 1999, 4).

Branches of foreign companies have a country of origin outside Singapore. These branches are registered but not incorporated under the Companies Act, Chapter 50. To register the branch in Singapore appropriate documents must be submitted to the Registrar, including information about the parent company. Two natural persons who are residents in Singapore must be appointed as agents with formal appointment made with the Registrar (7).

Foreign companies may also have representative offices in Singapore. Such offices must register with the Trade Development Board. These representative offices must not carry on business. Their purposes are to perform liaison services and establish business contacts, usually in preparation for full-scale business activities in Singapore. Representative offices are not required to maintain accounting records, or to file tax returns (4).

All companies are required to maintain books of account and other records such that a "true and fair" accounting can be drawn up. Such records must be available in Singapore. There must be adequate internal control over the accumulation of the accounting and related records (David Tong & Company, 1993, 97).

Singapore companies must have their financial statements audited by approved auditors (Arthur Andersen, 1999, 4). Branches of foreign companies are also required to undertake audit of their financial statements by approved auditors. In the case of the branch, auditors who qualify in the foreign firm's country of origin may perform the audit (David Tong & Company, 1993, 97).

An approved auditor in Singapore is a Certified Public Accountant registered as a member with the Institute of Certified Public Accountants. The Institute of Certified Public Accountants of Singapore, established

in 1963 under the Accountants Act as the Singapore Society of Accountants, is the national professional accountants' organization. The Society
was reorganized and renamed in 1989 under the Accountants Act 1987
(Institute of Certified Public Accountants of Singapore, 2001, 1).

The Public Accountants Board was also established by the 1989 Accountants Act as a statutory board under the Ministry of Finance to regulate the practice of public accounting in Singapore. To insure
professional practices and conduct, the ten member board registers public accountants and deals with disciplinary matters (2).

The Public Accountants Board Rules set forth and the Institute administers the requirements to become a registered public accountant. The
applicant must successfully complete the professional accounting examination, have acquired the prerequisite experience, have taken necessary preregistration courses and must demonstrate proficiency in local
laws (David Tong & Company, 1993, 98).

Standards for conduct of the audit, set by the Institute, are with few
exceptions the same as international auditing standards. The Companies
Act does require the auditor to review the internal control structure of
the client company and make a report to the audit committee of the
board of directors. Further, auditors must report on the compliance of
client companies with the Companies Act. The auditor must report any
uncorrected deficiencies to the Registrar. And in the case where material
fraud or dishonesty has occurred in a client company, a report must be
made to the Minister of Finance. The trustees acting for debenture holders must be provided a copy of all reports issued to the client company
and must be informed of any matters relevant to their trustee duties. The
Companies Act gives the auditor right of access to company records at
all times. Penalties are levied for obstruction of an audit (David Tong &
Company, 1993, 9).

The Companies Act contains the legislated requirement to prepare audited financial statements that present a "true and fair view" of the results of operations and financial conditions of the company. However,
there is no legislated legal requirement that financial statements comply
with accounting standards. The burden of insuring compliance with accounting and reporting standards rests with the CPAs who audit the
financials, as they are obligated to follow the Institute's accounting and
auditing standards as well as other Institute pronouncements. The Institute "uses its leverage over its practicing members, who are auditors of
companies, to enforce compliance with accounting standards" (Disclosure and Accounting Standards Committee, 2001, 3).

Currently, the applicable accounting standards in Singapore are the
Statements of Auditing Standards (SAS) promulgated by the Accounting
Standards Committee. The SASs are with a few minor exceptions iden-
tical to the International Accounting Standards (IAS). The Stock

Exchange of Singapore, now the Singapore Exchange, allows listed companies to use SASs, IASs or U.S. GAAP as the basis for listing company financial reports (5).

The Institute has been in the process of aligning the SASs completely with IAS. And, because of the inefficiencies in the process, the Disclosure and Accounting Standards Committee set up jointly by the Ministry of Finance, the Monetary Authority of Singapore and the Attorney-General's Chambers, has recommended that Singapore eliminate SAS and its redundant processes and adopt IAS and U.S. GAAP as acceptable accounting standards (4).

In a study by Nobes referenced earlier in this chapter respondent CPAs were asked to identify nonalignment where national rules would not permit the international treatment because of inconsistent rules or would not require the international treatment because of missing or permissive rules (2000, 1). The survey summary for Singapore listed 20 instances in which differences were reported between Singapore SASs and international accounting standards. These covered 12 International Accounting Standards and one interpretation. Reasons for the differences fell into four categories: Singapore accounting standards differ from IAS because of the lack of specific Singapore rules; there are no specific rules in Singapore which require disclosures required by IAS; and inconsistencies between the two sets of standards (Nobes, 2000, 94).

The Institute has been working to harmonize Singapore standards with IAS with considerable success but the Nobes study is indicative of differences which remain. A number of exposure drafts remained outstanding in April 2001. The Institute indicated that it will in the future issue exposure drafts and standards for SAS simultaneously with the release of exposure drafts for IAS. And, the Institute plans to make the SAS based on each IAS effective in the quarter following adoption of the IAS.

SOUTH KOREA

The vast majority of Korean business organizations are small in size and are family controlled. Large conglomerates called Chaebol dominate the economy, however. And even though government policy is to foster free competition, the government heavily regulates business organizations through its ministries.

The Ministry of Finance and Economy formulates the national budget and directs the entire economy through its fiscal policies. It controls foreign currency transactions and oversees the government-owned banks. The Bank of Korea, the central bank, under the chairmanship of the Minister of Finance and Economy controls monetary and credit policies within the country. The Korean Securities and Exchange Commission supervises the stock market and is said to be similar in its responsibilities to the United States Securities and Exchange Commission. Both the Office of National Tax Administration and the Office of Customs Administration are within the Ministry of Finance and Economy. The Ministry of Health and Welfare has wide authority to control and prevent air and water pollution under the Environmental Protection Act of 1977.

Although there are no formal price controls, the Ministry of Finance and Economy effectively controls foreign and domestic prices through its authority to set price ceilings on most goods and services and through its considerable influence on pricing decisions within the country. It is not technically illegal in Korea for a monopoly to exist but through the Antimonopoly Law, market dominators are in effect prohibited from acting like monopolies. Penalties for monopolistic abuses can be significant punitive tax penalties or government takeover. The Office of Fair Trade monitors actions of companies perceived as market dominators (Price Waterhouse Coopers, 2000, chapter 6).[2]

The Commercial Code is the primary law governing Korean business. In December 1998, in an attempt to alleviate the continuing foreign currency and economic crisis, the National Assembly revised the Commercial Code. Revisions were directed at simplifying business restructuring and promoting mergers and acquisitions; allowing more funds to be taken in by companies by reducing minimum par value requirements, allowing stock splits and interim dividends; and promoting shareholder control through a new cumulative voting system (Ernst & Young, 2001a). Although further revisions to the Commercial Code have been proposed by the Consultants for the Financial and Corporate Restructuring Assistance Project and the International Bank for Reconstruction and Development of the World Bank (Ernst & Young, 2001b), the passage by the National Assembly of further revisions remains to be seen.

Sole proprietorships do not have separate entity legal recognition in Korea but must be registered with tax administrators. Joint ventures, as well, are not recognized in Korea as legally separate entities. To participate in a joint venture, a limited liability company may be formed under the Foreign Capital Inducement Act, which may then carry out a joint venture agreement. Foreign corporations may operate branch offices by registering with the civil court and with the approval of the Bank of Korea. Liaison or representative offices are also permitted to carry out approved, limited business junctions (Price Waterhouse Coopers, 2000 chapter 9).

Businesses are most often formed as limited liability or unlimited liability companies. There are four principal classes of companies. Limited liability companies are Chusik Hoesa under which seven or more promoters may incorporate with liability limited to contributed capital and Yuhan Hoesa under which two to fifty persons may incorporate with liability limited to each member's company contribution. Unlimited companies are Hapmyong Hoesa under which two or more persons incorporate to jointly and severally bear liability for company obligations and Hapja Hoesa under which some members have unlimited liability while other members have limited liability (chapter 9).

Partnerships in Korea operate as a Hapmyong Hoesa or a Hapja Hoesa. The Hapmyong Hoesa may be entered into by two or more partners, all of whom have unlimited liability for partnership obligations. Professional lawyers or accountants are typical users of this form. A Hapja Hoesa may have one or more partners with unlimited liability and one or more partners with liability limited to contributed capital.

Each Korean company must keep proper accounting records at the company's registered office, which must be situated within the Republic of Korea. Statutory records such as shareholder registers, directors' lists, and minute books are required. Books of account must use generally accepted accounting principles. Such records must be retained for 10 years under the Commercial Code (chapter 11).

Semiannual reports must be filed by companies listed on the Korea Stock Exchange—one for the first six months of the fiscal year and the other for the entire year. The annual report must contain a statement of financial position audited by a certified public accountant and be filed with the Securities and Exchange Commission (SEC) as well as the stock exchange (chapter 9).

For a Chusik Hoesa, a statutory auditor must be appointed who examines company accounts, monitors company operations and reports to shareholders. The External Audit Law of Joint-Stock Companies requires all companies with more than W6 billion in assets, those listed on the Korean Stock Exchange or those registered with the SEC to undergo annual examination of financial statements by a licensed Korean CPA (chapter 9). The Securities Law requires that consolidated statements be audited. Foreign companies and branches of foreign entities that remit dividends or are in the process of liquidation also require audit. Year-end balance sheets of corporations must be published in a newspaper. Copies of all required audit reports must be filed with the Securities Supervisory Board. This board is responsible for compliance with audit standards (chapter 11).

The Korean Institute of Certified Public Accountants is the central professional accounting organization with approximately 5,000 members of which about 77 percent are in public accounting practice, 14 percent in industry or commerce, 9 percent in education and less than 1 percent in the public sector. The CPA is registered only after passing the CPA examination, after completing an apprentice program for two to three years and after approval from the Ministry of Finance and Economy (Korean Institute of Certified Public Accountants, 2001).

Auditing standards are set by the Securities Supervisory Board with approval from the Ministry of Finance and Economy. Audit procedures are similar to those in English-speaking countries and are designed to insure uniformity, objectivity and auditor independence (Price Waterhouse Coopers, 2000, chapter 11).

Korean Financial Accounting Standards were set in the past by the Securities and Exchange Commission assisted by the Accounting Standards Advisory Board of the Korean Institute of Certified Public Accountants and the Bank of Korea. Approval of the Ministry of Finance and Economy was necessary (chapter 12).

As a result of consultations between the Korean government and the World Bank in the aftermath of the financial crisis of 1997, Korea has acted on a number of fronts to improve financial reporting. International Accounting Standards were adopted as the benchmark for comparison of Korean accounting standards (Deloitte Touche Tohmatsu, 2001b).

In December 1998, new accounting standards for banks, financial institutions and insurance companies were enacted. The new standards for the financial sector call for receivables to be categorized into three classes: collectable, collection uncertain and uncollectable. Provisions for bad debts are required for each category. Stocks and receivables must now be carried at market value. The interest income, dividend income and gain on disposal of securities components of income must now be described in detail (Ernst & Young, 2001a).

In July 1999, the Korean Accounting Institute was created to oversee the operations of a new, private sector, Korea Accounting Standards Board that in turn came into existence in September 1999 as an independent board. The board's stated aim is to bring Korean accounting standards to the level of international best practices. The board has begun its work with two research reports and four discussion papers. The research reports review prior working rules and interpretations, including comparisons with International Standards and U.S. generally accepted accounting principles. The discussion papers deal with changes in accounting policy and estimates, correction of errors, intangible assets, revenue recognition, and valuation of equity securities and debts securities (Ernst & Young, 2001c).

Differences between Korean accounting standards and U.S. standards remain substantial. Asset values are originally recorded at acquisition costs but may be revalued when cumulative inflation of asset costs is 25 percent or more. Investments in affiliated companies over which the parent has significant influence can be carried at cost even when market value is below cost. Under Korean GAAP, goodwill is capitalized and amortized over estimated useful life of between five and ten years. Negative goodwill is charged to the paid-in capital account. Some costs may be amortized over three to five years: organizational, pre-operating, new stock issuance, debenture issuance and certain defined research and development expenses. The effects of all accounting changes are given retrospective treatment. Tax rules are permitted in financial accounting reports for some expenses such as depreciation and bad debt. Segment reporting is not required. Income tax allocation is not permitted. Most leases under Korean rules are classed as operating leases. Interim reports are semi-annual instead of quarterly and they are not required to be on a consolidated basis. This list is incomplete but clearly there are large differences between Korean and U.S. GAAP (Ernst and Young, 2001c).

The same can be concluded about differences between Korean GAAP and International Accounting Standards (IAS). Korea was included in the GAAP 2000 survey discussed in the Hong Kong section of this book. The Korean responses indicated 15 differences between Korean standards and IAS. These included 11 IAS and two Korean interpretations. Reasons for the differences fell into three categories: Korean accounting standards differ from IAS because of the lack of specific Korean rules, three instances cited; there are no specific rules in Korea which require disclosures required by IAS, two instances cited; and inconsistencies between the two sets of standards could lead to differences for many enterprises in certain areas, seven instances cited under Korean rules and three instances cited under IAS rules (Nobes, 2000, 66).

TAIWAN

Since 1949, when two million Nationalists fled mainland China, Taiwan has prospered. The country has maintained high growth rates benefiting from the entrepreneurial strengths of its people. The country's conservative approach to financial matters has allowed it to weather the Asian financial crises, suffering little as compared to other Asian countries (CIA, 2001d, 1).

Taiwan's population in 2000 was estimated at 22.3 million people, making an average population density in the country of 620 people per square kilometer or over 1,500 per square mile, one of the densest in the world. They are, of course, unevenly distributed with most living on the plains and basins to the west of the Chungyang Range. The three largest cities are Taipei, Kaohsiung, and Taichung. In 1952 the birth rate was 46.6 births per 1,000 people, while in 2000 it stands at 14.5 per 1,000. Over the years, educational levels and economic well being have risen (Encarta, 2001, 1). Public education is compulsory for 12 years that includes six years of elementary and three of middle school and three of secondary or vocational school. A number of colleges and universities are available (Price Waterhouse Coopers, 2000, chapter 1, 2).

The people of Taiwan are overwhelmingly ethnic Han Chinese. Most were born or have ancestors who were born on the mainland. The three primary population groups are based on the native Chinese dialects of

Taiwanese, Hakka and Mandarin. A small population of aborigines, about 2 percent of the Taiwan population, are members of nine aborigine tribes that each speak a different form of Formosan. The official language is Mandarin Chinese (1). English is taught starting in the seventh grade of middle school to all students as their first foreign language. In 1998, literacy was reported as 94 percent (CIA, 2001d, 4).

There are 12 officially recognized religions with approximately one half the populace professing a faith. About 93 percent of these are Buddhist, Confucian or Taoist followers (3).

The government is a multiparty democratic regime. A constitution was enacted in 1947 and amended in 1992, 1994 and 1997. The constitution provides for a National Assembly and a five-branched government consisting of the executive, the legislative, the judicial, the examination and the control. The executive branch is headed by a premier. Under the central government are the Taiwan Provincial Government, the Taipei Municipal Government, and the Kaohsiung Municipal Government. There are various county and municipal local governments with mayors, county magistrates and provincial, county and municipal assemblies, which are elected by the people (Price Waterhouse Coopers, 2000, chapter 1, 2).

The legal system of Taiwan is based in the continental European system and particularly on the Civil Code system. In the past, the National Assembly elected the president. The first direct elections for president and vice-president occurred on March 23, 1996. The elected president appoints the premier who is regarded as Head of Government. In the judicial branch, the president with the consent of the National Assembly appoints justices.

The economy is market based, dynamic and successful. GDP growth has averaged about 8 percent over the past three decades. Exports have grown even more, providing the impetus for industrialization (CIA, 2001d, 6). The outstanding record of growth is based on the success of the manufacturing industry. There is a proliferation of small family-owned companies that are very adaptable in changing products as the foreign market demands change. Currently within this sector there is a trend to higher-quality and value-added products, which includes high technology. Government policy now encourages development in the services areas, as well (Price Waterhouse Coopers, 2000, chapter 2, 2).

Unemployment and inflation have been low. The country's trade surplus is substantial, creating the world's third largest foreign reserves total. The guidance by government authorities is gradually decreasing on matters of investment and foreign trade. Privatization of government-owned banks and industrial firms is underway.

Agriculture in 1952 accounted for 35 percent of GDP but had dropped to 3 percent in 1999. In 1999, services accounted for 64 percent of GDP and industry 33 percent. The labor force was 55 percent in services, 37 percent in industry and 8 percent in agriculture. Labor-intensive industries are steadily moving offshore being replaced with capital and technology. Taiwan is reported to be the largest foreign investor in China, Thailand, Indonesia, the Philippines, Malaysia and Vietnam (CIA, 2001d, 6). The currency is the New Taiwan dollar. Exchange rates for US $1 were 31.4 in 1999, 32.22 in 1998, 32 in 1997, 27 in 1996 and 27.5 in 1995 (chapter 7, 8).

The Ministry of Economic Affairs has the responsibility for business laws and regulations in Taiwan. The Ministry of Finance is responsible for administration of the finance, insurance, and taxation sectors of government. There are price controls only for basic living commodities. The government fosters competition under the Fair Trade Law, which governs acts of monopoly, consolidation and collusion. Monopolies are approved where they benefit the economy as a whole (chapter 6, 2).

The Securities and Futures Commission (SEF) oversees the issuance of public offerings of securities and the securities markets (3). The SEF is also responsible for public reporting requirements for public companies and oversight on standards. Securities are traded on the Taiwan Securities Exchange on a bid basis or on the over-the-counter market on a negotiated basis. To be listed on the Taiwan Securities Exchange or be traded over-the-counter a company must have its annual and semi-annual financial statements certified by a Certified Public Accountant and have the coming year's financial forecast reviewed by CPAs within four months after fiscal year end. CPAs are also required to review the first and third quarter results issued by the company. Company monthly operations statements must be issued publicly within ten days after the end of each month. An event that has the probability of making a material impact on the stock price of the company must be publicly disclosed within two days of occurrence. Should a director, corporate supervisor, officer or shareholder hold more than 10 percent of the total company stock, such individual must disclose transactions in the stock monthly (6). Entry into the banking or insurance sectors is strictly controlled by the Ministry of Finance and the Bank of China (8).

Businesses may be formed in Taiwan as single proprietorships, partnerships or companies. A foreign corporation may enter the business sector by establishing a subsidiary corporation, a branch, a job-site office, a representative office or a liaison office. Only Taiwan citizens are permitted to operate single proprietorships (Soong, 1992, 19). The sole proprietor must register with the tax authority. Filing fees and minimum capital requirements are the same as for a partnership. Only general partnerships are permitted in Taiwan. Every partner is fully liable for all partnership obligations. A corporate entity may not be a partner. Partnerships are governed by the Civil Code and must be registered with appropriate government agencies, usually the municipal, city or county government. Minimum partnership capital requirement is NT $3,000. A joint venture is not a separate legal or taxable entity in Taiwan. Such ventures are generally accomplished by establishing a company that is jointly owned by the principals (Price Waterhouse Coopers, 2000, chapter 9, 3).

A foreign company branch, after registering with the Ministry of Finance and receiving a certificate of recognition, may engage in trading or service activities. The branch must have working capital of at least NT $1 million. Branch capital and earnings can be repatriated up to NT $5 million per year. A registered branch manager must be appointed as well as a branch representative for litigious and non-litigious matters. If the branch manager is a foreigner who will stay in Taiwan, a work permit and an alien resident certificate must be obtained. A job-site office is used for contracting and construction activities and is beneficial for tax and operating purposes. Such an office must be registered with the tax authorities and it must have a business registration certificate. Its head office must remit all job-site office expenses to Taiwan. The representative or liaison office activities are restricted. Such offices have tax-free status and may not conduct business or generate operating income (chapter, 3, 9).

Corporations are authorized in four classes. The unlimited company must be organized by at least two shareholders who undertake joint and several liability for the company's obligations. A limited company needs between 5 and 21 shareholders and each is liable only up to the limit of contributed capital. An unlimited company with limited shareholders must be organized by one or more shareholders who have unlimited liability and one or more shareholders who have limited liability for company obligations. All of the unlimited shareholders have unlimited joint and several liability for company obligations while limited shareholders are liable only for contributed capital. For a company limited by shares, the total capital of the corporation is divided equally in shares. This form must have seven or more shareholders. Shareholders are liable only up to the amount of contributed capital. This type of corporation may be either a public or a private company (2). A foreign investor may be a shareholder in any of these corporate forms and may participate with Taiwan residents in the formation processes (3).

The company limited by shares is the usual form of incorporation in Taiwan. Under the Company Law, a company name must first be reserved with the Ministry of Economic Affairs. Before the incorporation is approved by the appropriate government agency the original capital, which must be at least 25 percent of authorized capital, must be paid in and a CPA's verification obtained. Special licenses are also required in a number of business sectors (5).

Minimum capital of NT $1 million is required for incorporation. A company in the importing or exporting sector must have minimum paid-in capital of NT $5 million. Shares must have a par value, which is the lowest issuance price per share. Preferred stock may be issued if the rights of the preferred stock are clearly set forth in the articles of incorporation. Up to 50 percent of any class of stock may be bearer stock (5).

If paid-in capital exceeds NT $200 million, the company is considered a public company even though not listed on an exchange and must register with the Securities and Futures Commission. A public company must publicly disclose its financial statements. To increase its capital, a public company must have approval from the SEF. These conditions do not attach to a foreign-owned company incorporated in Taiwan that has received the status of Foreign Investment Approved (FIA) enterprise under the Statute for Promotion of Industrial Upgrading (chapter 3, 6).

Foreign nationals may wholly own an FIA company. Directors, corporate supervisors including the chairman may all be foreign nationals residing outside of Taiwan. For a company that does not have FIA status, a majority of shareholders must be local shareholders in the first year of incorporation. The company chairman and at least one company supervisor must be a Taiwan national. If a company has the minimum seven shareholders, at least four, including the chairman and one supervisor, must be nationals. After one year, all seven shareholders may be foreigners so long as at least one of these is a foreign corporation that will appoint two Taiwan representatives as chairman and supervisor (5). The role of company supervisor is similar to a member of the audit committee. A supervisor's term may be three years and is renewable (7).

Incorporators must approve the articles of incorporation that include the scope of the business, total capital, tenure and number of directors and supervisors, and classes of stock to be issued together with the rights and obligations of each class. Shareholders must have one regular meeting per year convened by the board of directors. Voting rights must be established in the articles of incorporation. Those holding voting shares must have one vote per share, except that the articles of incorporation are required to prescribe a restriction on the number of votes of any shareholder holding 3 percent or more of the total number of shares outstanding (7).

The board of directors must have at least three directors elected from and by the shareholders. Directors may have terms of up to three years and are eligible for reelection. A director, who engages in a business similar to company operations, either on his own or on behalf of others, must explain to and have the approval of the shareholders' meeting. There must be a minimum of three managing directors but not more than one-third of the board can be managing directors. The chairman and vice-chairman of the board are to be elected from and by the managing directors. One half of the managing directors, the chairman and the vice-chairman are required to be Taiwan nationals who reside in Taiwan. This requirement does not apply to an FIA company. At least one supervisor must be selected from among the shareholders. The supervisor may not be a director, management officer or staff of the company. Any executive officer position of the company must be defined in the articles of incorporation and appropriate duties specified. Executive officers must be appointed and discharged only by a majority of the board of directors. An executive officer must be resident in Taiwan. Companies must register the names of its directors, supervisors and executive officers with appropriate government authorities within 15 days of appointment or election (7).

After incorporation, the Company Law directs that at least 10 percent of each year's net income after tax be set aside as a legal reserve until the total of the reserve equals the total company capital. The Company Law does not set restrictions on the accumulation of earnings but the Income Tax Law requires a profit-seeking entity to distribute earnings that exceed 50 percent of paid-in capital. Shares may be transferred freely except that shares held by incorporators must be retained for one year after incorporation, registered shares may not be transferred one month before the annual shareholders' meeting, 15 days before a special shareholder meeting or five days before the date of distribution of dividends or other benefits and transfers of stock in FIA companies must be government approved (6).

Each business organization management is charged with the responsibility to keep proper accounting and related records. They must also assure proper financial reports such that both shareholders and tax authorities are provided fair presentations. With the exception of small-scale enterprises, accounting books, including computerized systems, must be approved by the tax authorities before use. Proper documentation of transactions is required. A unified invoice is prescribed and controlled by the tax authorities as proper documentation for the purchase of goods and services. The tax authorities through the printing, pre-numbering, binding, and issuance processes, maintain strict control of the invoices (chapter 11, 1).

Audited financial statements are required for a number of situations, in addition to the listed companies discussed above. Companies that have capital of NT $30 million must be audited. Those whose bank credit reaches NT $30 million are required to have audited financials sent to the Credit Center of the Taipei Bankers' Association. Companies with revenues of NT $100 million need to have their income tax returns CPA certified (Soong, 1992, 10). The audit of financial statements is governed by Regulations Governing the Examination and Certification of Financial

Statements by CPAs, a joint issuance of the Ministry of Economic Affairs and the Ministry of Finance (12).

The Securities and Futures Commission, formerly named the Securities and Exchange Commission, within the Ministry of Finance is charged by the Certified Public Accountants Law with responsibility to regulate CPAs in Taiwan. In accordance with the CPA Law, the Examination Yuan, or branch of government, administers the CPA examination once a year. Recent changes have allowed foreigners, as well as Taiwan citizens, to sit for the examination (Securities and Futures Commission, 1999, VI). The Ministry of Finance registers those who are qualified as Certified Public Accountants in Taiwan (Price Waterhouse Coopers, 2000, chapter 11, 3).

T. N. Soong & Company reported that as of the beginning of 1991 approximately 2,100 CPAs were registered in Taiwan with 43 percent in public practice (Soong, 1992, 5). The Securities and Futures Commission reported that at the end of 2000, a total of 1,123 CPA firms in Taiwan of which 855 were said to be sole practitioners with 268 partnerships. Of these, 125 CPA firms were approved to provide attestation service to publicly held companies (Securities and Futures Commission, 2000, vi).

Taiwan has several professional associations, which include the Taipei Certified Public Accountants Association, the Taiwan Certified Public Accountants Association, the Kaohsiung Certified Public Accountants Association, CPA Association of R.O.C. and the Accounting Research and Development Foundation of R.O.C.

The CPA Association of R.O.C. had issued seven statements in the Code of Professional Ethics by 1992. Topics covered include principles of execution and technique, business promotion restrictions and the conduct of business by CPA firms.

The Accounting Research and Development Foundation, which was established in 1984, was designated by the Securities and Futures Commission to issue accounting and auditing standards for Taiwan. It has done so through the Financial Accounting Standards Board and the Auditing Standards Board of the Foundation. Auditing standards are set forth in Auditing Standards Bulletins and are in general similar to those of the United States (Price Waterhouse Coopers, 2000, chapter 11, 3). By 2000, 34 Statements of Auditing Standards had been issued. The accounting standards are issued as Statements of Financial Accounting Standards, of which 31 had been issued by 2000 (Securities and Futures Commission, 2000, 2).

Statements of Financial Accounting Standards which became effective for years ending on or after December 31, 2000 are: SFAS 17, Statement of Cash Flows (Revised December 9, 1999); SFAS 22, Accounting for Income Taxes (Revised November 11, 1999); SFAS 23, Interim Financial Reporting and Disclosures (Revised July 29, 1999); SFAS 28, Disclosures in the Financial Statements of Banks (issued March 31, 1999); and SFAS 29, Accounting for Government Grants (issued June 24, 1999). The statements that will be effective for years ending on or after December 31, 2001 are: SFAS 30, Accounting for Treasury Stock (issued on July 7, 2000); and SFAS 31, Accounting for Joint Ventures (issued on September 7, 2000). Two statements were under revision in October 2000: SFAS 3, Capitalization of Interest Cost; and SFAS 18, Accounting for Pensions (revision) (Deloitte Touche Tohmatsu, 2000e, 1).

As discussed earlier in this chapter, an International Forum for Accountancy Development–sponsored study gauged differences between written national accounting standards in 53 countries with International Accounting Standards (IAS). Rules that were in force for reporting periods ending on December 31, 2000 were studied (Nobes, 2000, 103). CPAs responding identified nonalignment of the two sets of standards where national rules would not permit the international treatment because of inconsistent rules or would not require the international treatment because of missing or permissive rules. The summary of survey responses for Taiwan listed 22 instances of differences between Taiwan rules and IAS. These involved 16 IAS. The reasons for the differences fell into three categories: Taiwan accounting standards differ from IAS because of the lack of specific Taiwan rules; there are no specific rules in Taiwan which require disclosures required by IAS and inconsistencies between the two sets of standards (1).

NOTES

1. In the editions of their work, *Tax Havens of the World* (1998 and 2000), the Diamonds supply detailed information on 60 jurisdictions. The jurisdictions covered are listed in alphabetical order and pagination is internal to each jurisdiction. In the present volume references to the work in question are to the jurisdiction being discussed and page references are to that jurisdiction.

2. The CD-ROM *Doing Business and Investment Series 2000 Edition*, published by Price Waterhouse Coopers in 2000, contains information guides to 80 countries. Here references will be to the CD-ROM and not to individual information guides. Chapter references are internal to guides for particular jurisdictions being discussed.

Chapter 5

Accounting and Business Environments in Developing Asian Nations

In each of the developing countries included in this Chapter there is a marked movement toward more sophisticated handling of business and accounting matters. The governments in question, Indonesia, Malaysia, the Philippines and Thailand, were each in various degrees affected by the Asian financial crises. And, each has moved closer to a globalized viewpoint on financial reporting. Together, they provide wide information on the changes made in countries at their development stages.

INDONESIA

Indonesia became independent of the Netherlands in 1949 and for most of its history has been ruled by authoritarians. The nation currently is said to be in the process of transition to a popularly elected government. The unicameral House of Representatives has 462 members elected by popular vote and 38 appointed by military representatives. The president who is both chief of state and head of government is selected by vote of the People's Consultative Assembly for a five-year term of office. The People's Consultative Assembly is made up of the entire House of Representatives and 200 indirectly selected members. This body meets every five years to select the president and to authorize national policy in broad outline (CIA, 2001a, 5). The legal system is based in Roman–Dutch law modified by indigenous procedures and concepts. The president appoints Supreme Court members.

For most of the years since its independence the country sustained substantial economic growth and remained stable politically. In the aftermath of the Asian economic crisis in 1997, the Suharto government resigned. The government of B.J. Habibie became what is viewed as a transitional government with the responsibility to completely overhaul the electoral process and restore economic stability.

The CIA *World Factbook* (CIA, 2001a) cited a number of severe national problems with the business situation of the country near the forefront. Changes are thought to be needed in the business environment that now is said to be dominated by the Chinese business class. The IMF-mandated reforms of the banking system are also among major obstacles that must be overcome if the country is to resume economic growth.

In 2000 the population was estimated at just less than 225 million. Eighty-eight percent of the populace is Muslim, 8 percent Christian, 2 percent Hindu and 1 percent Buddhist. The literacy rate is estimated at 84 percent. Bahasa Indonesia, a modified form of Malay, is the official language. English, Dutch and Javanese are also spoken. Large numbers of Indonesians enter the labor market in each year. Unemployment is high with wages low. Technical and managerial skills are in scarce supply and education of the populace is a significant challenge for the country.

In 1999, the agricultural sector accounted for 21 percent of the GDP while industry produced 35 percent and services 44 percent. The labor force in agriculture was 45 percent of the populace. Nineteen percent was in the trade, restaurant and hotel sector, with 11 percent in manufacturing, 5 percent in transportation and communications and 4 percent in construction (7).

The Indonesian rupiah is the country's currency. The exchange rate was 7,279 to the U.S. dollar in January 2000, 7,855 to $1 in 1999, and 10,000 to $1 in 1998 as compared to 2,909 to $1 in 1997 and 2,343 to $1 in 1996.

The real GDP growth rate in 1999 was zero. This followed a sharp contraction of the economy and high inflation of 1998. During 1998 inflation rose to 70 percent but by 1999 inflation had been reduced to 2 percent. Interest rates had spiked to 70 percent in 1998 but rapidly returned to the 10- to 15-percent range. Since the collapse of the banking system, the government has been able to capitalize a few private banks but has yet to complete recapitalizing the state-owned banking sector. The pace of bank and debt restructuring has been slow and dissatisfaction continues to make Indonesia unattractive to private investment (6). The banking sector is in the process of overhaul, administered by the Indonesian Bank Restructuring Agency. The Jakarta Stock Market, growing until 1997, now finds most listed companies technically bankrupt.

Although Price Waterhouse Coopers (2000, chapter 2, 1) indicates that "many Indonesians do not yet see their society as being wholly "capitalist," the country appears to be on a track away from governmental direction and toward a more market-based economic system. Most large businesses remain state-owned or dominated by a small handful of family groups (2). The government declares that it is committed to deregulation and does appear to have accelerated the process since the financial crisis.

In recent years, Indonesia has removed many of the fiscal and other barriers to trade and commerce (6). In 1994 the government opened a number of areas that were previously unavailable to private foreign investors. Joint ventures are now allowed in a wide array of public services. Previously state-owned telephone companies and mining companies have been privatized. Private and publicly owned industrial estates to facilitate factory operations in ready-to-use complexes are growing in number. Free trade and bonded zones for re-export manufacturing are in use (3).

The Indonesia 1945 Constitution declares that all natural resources of the country are under control of the government to use for the greatest citizen welfare. In line with this, Mining Law No. 11 declares that the government has ownership of minerals in the ground and foreigners may enter into contracts of work for developing mineral deposits or recently into production-sharing contracts (13). The Law did not set forth the contract requirements. The Department of Mining and Energy controls the contracting. A related aspect is that exploitation of minerals is allowed through mining authorizations that can only be held by Indonesians, wholly Indonesian-owned companies or partnerships. These are frequently government-owned companies. Contracting must be done with both the government mining department and the holders of mining authorizations. Accounting, reporting and all other aspects of such business arrangements are contained in the contract of work (18).

A major step forward in the modernization of business came in 1995 when the Parliament approved a new Indonesian Company Law (chapter 9, 1). Prior company law was based on outdated Dutch commercial codes that had not been updated as changes were made in the Netherlands. Forms of business permitted under the 1995 Company Law include limited liability company, joint venture company, partnership, foreign company representative office, foreign company branch and sole proprietorship. Indonesian citizens may operate proprietorships, however foreigners may not use the proprietorship form of business (20). And, as a matter of policy, partnerships are not open to foreign participation (10).

Foreign companies are authorized to register branches in Indonesia but such registrations are permitted only in exceptional cases on a case-by-case basis. Should registration of a branch be accepted an appropriate ministry would determine the procedures and reporting for the branch.

A representative office may also be established generally only for auxiliary services (2). When registered under the Ministry of Trade, they may not operate businesses or enter into trading activities (19). When registered under the Ministry of Public Works, a representative office may be established for construction or construction-consulting purposes. Foreign construction and engineering companies, through representative offices and in cooperation with Indonesian companies, are permitted to explore possible construction and consulting markets, participate in tender offers, submit proposals and carry a project to completion (20).

Business entities may take the form of a basic partnership, disclosed partnership or limited partnership. The basic partnership is governed by the Indonesian civil code. Professionals such as lawyers, notaries and accountants often use this form. The existence of the basic partnership may, but need not, be disclosed to third parties (10). The partnership agreement may be written, oral or even implied by the actions of the principals. The partners must agree on each partner's contributions and must have the intention to share profits in order for a partnership contract to be valid. One partner may be appointed as the manager able to act in the name of the partnership and bind the partnership to third party agreements. Should a partner not be designated as the manager, then all partners are considered to have been authorized by the others to act on behalf of the partnership (11). Each partner is liable only for a pro-rata portion of partnership debts. There is no provision for several liabilities. Unless the partnership agreement provides otherwise, an interest in the partnership may be transferred only with the consent of all partners. The partnership is terminated: upon the withdrawal of a partner; at a certain date if set in the partnership agreement; death, bankruptcy or guardianship status of a partner; or the completion or termination of the partnership's purpose.

Commercial partnerships designed to trade or operate in the service sector are generally formed as a Disclosed partnership. They are established with the intention of holding a continuing business name. This class of partnership is governed by the Commercial Code but the provisions which apply to a basic partnership also apply. Any partner may act in the name of and bind the partnership except where the given partner has been expressly denied these rights in the partnership agreement. Partnership liability is jointly and severally liable without limit for the partnership debts (12).

The limited partnership consists of partners at least one of whom must be an active partner liable personally for all partnership debt. The remaining partners may be silent partners whose liability is limited to their contributions to the partnership. The silent partner has no rights to and must not manage the partnership. This type of partnership is governed both by the Commercial Code and the Indonesian Civil Code of 1847, as amended (13).

Investments in Indonesia may be structured as a joint venture company between two parties who may be an individual or any legally constituted organization, including a corporation. Foreign parties may invest in joint ventures but Indonesian shareholders must own a minimum capital investment of 5 percent. A joint venture company that has at least 51 percent Indonesian ownership is treated as a domestic corporation for many purposes. The government can grant a license for 30 years with possible extension for another 30 years. Appropriate applications and documentation including articles of incorporation must be submitted to the Investment Coordinating Board (19). Numerous permits and licenses are required. It is also usual to include a requirement in the articles of incorporation for an annual public accountant audit (9).

A limited liability company must have minimum capital of Rp. 20 million, which is approximately US $3,000, a minimum of 25 shares and a minimum of two shareholders. Capital must be denominated in rupiah but foreign investment may also be stated in a foreign currency to establish future capital repatriation rights. At the time of incorporation at least half of the capital must be paid in. Liability is limited to paid in or subscribed capital. Capital shares are permitted to be common, preferred or founders' shares but may not bear a fixed rate of return. Classes of shares may have special, conditional or limited voting rights and profit participations (19).

Shareholders have the rights to elect directors, elect the board of supervisors, make policy decisions and declare dividends. A board of supervisors, which is to oversee on behalf of the shareholders the work of the directors, is required for each corporation with powers specified in the articles of incorporation.

An annual general meeting of shareholders is required at which financial statements are considered and approved. The directors, the board of supervisors or the shareholders may call special shareholder meetings. In general the rights of shareholders are to have one vote for each share. This may be restricted in the articles of incorporation. Directors and board of supervisors' members are prohibited from acting as proxies at shareholder meetings (19).

The payment of dividends from current profits when the company has accumulated losses is not addressed in the law. The Ministry of Justice, however, prefers a restriction in company articles of incorporation that allows dividends only out of profits after past losses have been covered (20). Further a capital reserve of 20 percent of issued capital must be set up from net profits.

An annual statutory audit must be conducted by public accountants registered with the Indonesian Association of Accountants for public corporations. Companies which issue promissory notes, utilize public funds, or have assets over Rp. 50 billion are also required to have an annual public accountant audit, as are companies in certain sectors including banking, insurance, underwriting and stockbrokerage (9).

Any business in Indonesia is required to maintain accounting records such that rights and obligations of the business can be known. Such records should be kept in Bahasa, Indonesia, except where government authorities are notified and agree to keeping the records in English (chapter 11, 1). Businesses must prepare financial statements in accordance with Indonesian Accounting Standards. Financial statements and records must be kept on file in compliance with the tax law for 10 years. Further, businesses that are required by law to have an annual audit must file annual financial statements with appropriate government agencies (1).

The country's accounting professional body is the Indonesian Institute of Accountants. The Institute performs much of the regulatory process for accountants and accounting. Half of the membership estimated to be 5,000 in 1999 is in government service. Auditors of all except government-owned companies must be registered with the Institute. The Institute is responsible for generally accepted auditing standards. These were reissued in 1994 and follow in most respects the standards of the American Institute of Certified Public Accountants. Government auditors are responsible for government majority-owned companies. The set of government audit standards followed by these auditors differs in nature and purpose from an audit prepared under generally accepted auditing standards (3).

In the past the Institute has had less influence. But as the economy has grown and developed, the need for better cross-border comparability and consistency has become evident. Indonesian Accounting Standards were revamped in 1994. The improvement process clearly has accelerated since 1997. Indonesian accounting standards currently are promulgated by the Committee on Financial Standards of the Institute. When this committee issues a Statement of Financial Accounting Standard, the Institute must approve (Deloitte Touche Tohmatsu, 2001a, 2).

Prior to 1994, Indonesian accounting standards had been based roughly on the American standards. Beginning in 1994, the Committee on Financial Standards indicated that henceforth standards would be based on the International Accounting Standards. The Deloitte Touche Tohmatsu IAS Plus Web site observed in its January 2001 country update: "The Financial Accounting Standards Board of the Indonesian Institute of Accountants is continuing its policy of harmonizing Indonesian Financial Accounting Standards with IAS (1).

Thirty-five accounting standards were issued in 1994 to update and improve reporting prior issuances. These standards followed International Accounting Standards with few local adjustments. Twenty standards were issued in the following two years. These were standards developed by the Indonesian committee and did not necessarily follow

International Accounting Standards (Price Waterhouse Coopers, 2000, chapter 12, 1).

In their present activities, the Committee has issued 10 standards that are updates of prior standards or are new. Most seem to be following International Accounting Standards. Three standards became effective for years beginning on or after January 2000.

Indonesia, it does appear, has been harmonizing its accounting standards with International Accounting Standards. There remain a number of areas of difference. A report in 2001 from the International Forum on Accountancy Development (IFAD) is indicative of the work still to be accomplished.

The IFAD was created in response to the Asian financial crisis as a working group of many of the international organizations interested in global improvements in accounting. Their stated mission is "to improve market security and transparency, and financial stability on a global basis" (IFAD, 1). Among groups associated with this forum are the International Federation of Accountants, IOSCO, OECD, UNCTAD, the World Bank and the large international accounting firms (Deloitte Touche Tohmatsu, 2001g, 1).

The IFAD-sponsored study was designed to gauge the alignment of written national accounting standards in 53 countries with International Accounting Standards including interpretations issued by the IAS Standing Interpretations Committee. Rules effective for reporting periods ending on December 31, 2000 were used in the study (Nobes, 2000, 1).

Sixty accounting measures were used to make the comparisons. For each country, partners in large accounting firms were asked to benchmark local written accounting rules against the applicable International Accounting Standard or Interpretation. GDP for the 53 countries selected totaled to 95 percent of the world's GNP. The respondents were asked to identify nonalignment where national rules would not permit the international treatment because of inconsistent rules or would not require the international treatment because of missing or permissive rules (1).

The survey summary for Indonesia listed 21 instances in which respondents reported differences between Indonesian and international standards. These covered 13 International Accounting Standards and three interpretations (55). Reasons for these differences generally fell into four categories: an absence of specific Indonesian rules; no specific Indonesian rules for certain required disclosures; and inconsistencies between the two sets of rules.

MALAYSIA

Malaysia, situated in Southeast Asia, was created in 1963 by the merging of Malaya, Singapore, Sabah and Sarawak. Singapore seceded in 1965. The country has developed rapidly in part because of its stable government. The land mass of Malaysia consists of Peninsular Malaysia, at the South tip of the Asian mainland and East Malaysia on the island of Borneo. Approximately four-fifths of the country is made up of tropical rain forests and average rainfall is 107 inches per year.

The government is a form of constitutional monarchy with a bicameral Parliament consisting of a Senate and a House of Representatives. The chief of state is the paramount ruler elected for a five-year term from and by the hereditary rulers of nine of the states, which were the original Malay sultanates. Today each is headed by hereditary rulers who are regarded as constitutional heads of their states.

There are within the country a total of 13 states and the two federal territories of Kuala Lumpur and Labuan (CIA, 2001b, 5). The remaining four states are headed by governors appointed for fixed terms as constitutional heads of state. Each state has a constitution and elects a legislative assembly for the state. There is a chief minister for each state. The Federal Constitution sets out the powers of the states and of the federal government. The Constitution was approved in 1957 and amended in 1963 (Price Waterhouse Coopers, 2000, chapter 1, 3).

The nation's legal system is based in the British system of law and upon English common law. Legal affairs brought before the High Court can be appealed to a Court of Appeal and, as the court of last resort, the Federal Court. In each state, there are Syariah courts that try offenses against Islamic law (3).

The head of government is the prime minister. The 193 members of the House of Representatives are elected every five years. The prime minister is the leader of the party that achieves a plurality within the House of Representatives. The prime minister with approval of the chief of state appoints the cabinet members. The 69 members of the Senate are appointed, 43 by the paramount ruler and 26 by the state legislatures (CIA, 2000b, 5).

The population was estimated at 21,793,000 persons in July 2000. Fifty-eight percent are Malay and other indigenous people; Chinese 26 percent, Indian 7 percent and 9 percent other ethnic groups. Virtually all of the world's major religions have followers in Malaysia, but more than 50 percent of the population follows the Islamic faith.

English is taught as a second language in schools and is widely used for business pursuits. The official language is Bahasa Melayu. The country has people who speak the Chinese dialects of Cantonese, Mandarin, Hokkien, and among other languages Hakka, Hainan, Foochow, Tamil, Telugu, Malyalam, Panjabi and Thai (3, 4).

The country has a relatively high standard of living. There is a comprehensive public healthcare system throughout the country with mobile health service, rural clinics and hospitals in every major town. Specialist services are available in the larger urban centers. Life expectancy at birth is 69.5 years for males and 74.3 years for females (Price Waterhouse Coopers, 2000, chapter 1, 4).

Education is free to students from age 7 to 15. This is extended to age 19 for pupils who meet required academic standards. The numbers of students who continue their education into secondary schools and training institutes increased from 84 percent to more than 92 percent in 1997. The literacy rate improved from 85 percent in 1990 to 93 percent by 1997. There are 13 universities and a large number of technical and vocational institutions in the country (14).

The Malaysian economy is mixed with an active private sector, consisting of both indigenous and multinational business entities, and a public sector that maintains extensive involvement in business. The Asian financial crisis created the worst recession since independence. Tight capital controls were imposed in 1998. However, rapid economic recovery was made by 1999 and controls were relaxed. GDP grew in that year by 5 percent owing to a dynamic export sector and fiscal stimulus from increased government spending. A large export surplus allowed financial reserves to be built up to $31 billion by the end of 1999. The inflation rate for 1998 was estimated at 7 to 8 percent. Unemployment rates have been in the 3 percent or less range. Growth in total GDP is predicted to continue in the 5 to 6 percent range in the immediate years ahead. Clouding the future is the lack of reforms in the corporate sector for what is seen as lack of competitiveness and high corporate debt levels (CIA, 2000b, 6).

Per capita GDP was estimated at $10,700 in 1999. The national GDP was made up of 12 percent in the agricultural sector, 46 percent in the industrial sector and 42 percent in the services sector. The labor force was employed in manufacturing 27 percent, agriculture, forestry and fisheries 16 percent, local trade and tourism 17 percent, services 15 percent, government 10 percent and construction 9 percent (7). Industrial production growth is estimated at 8.5 percent. The currency is the ringgit (RM), which had an exchange rate to the US $1 of 3.8 in January 2000, 3.8 in 1999, 3.9 in 1998, 2.8 in 1997, 2.5 in 1996 and 2.5 in 1995 (8).

The government has adopted a policy of privatization such that by 2020 the private sector is expected to be the dominant force. The government seeks to attract foreign investments to aid in the development of the industrial sector. The framework of industry in the country can be viewed as three tiered. In the first tier, domestic small businesses in the past specialized in light industry, wholesale and retail trading and distribution. These indigenous businesses have advanced toward small to medium-sized industries. This was assisted by government actions to protect domestic businesses in these sectors. The second group consists of large corporations, many listed on the stock exchange, which have shareholders who are in the main institutional investors, including large holdings by government trust agencies. In the third tier are operations within the country of multinational corporations that are owned by foreign parent organizations (Price Waterhouse Coopers, 2000, chapter 2, 1).

A national development policy begun in 1991 is directed at restructuring the society to reduce the identification of race in economic functions and to erase poverty. Specific targets have been set for the distribution of ownership and for participation in the business and commercial sectors of the economy. These targets are 30 percent Malay and other indigenous Malaysian groups, 40 percent other Malaysians, primarily those of Chinese and Indian extractions, and 30 percent foreign investors.

The government intends to bring about the planned redistributions of wealth in a framework of a strong growing economy. Thus, high annual growth rates are important goals for the government. Government planners recognize that foreign investments are needed to reach these economic and social goals. Specifics of the goals are set forth in a series of plans. The five-year plan from 1991 to 1996 was designed to sustain the momentum of growth and to achieve more balanced development within the country. The plan for 1996 to 2000 emphasized export-oriented manufacturing in order to increase the foreign exchange earnings and reduce trade deficits. The five-year plan beyond 2000 is expected to be directed at upgrading infrastructures in rural areas and developing science and technology bases (2).

Within the constraints of its planning, the government has been pursuing a privatization program. Many government-owned entities have been privatized and many are now listed on the Kuala Lumpur Stock Exchange. The government has also been dispersing industry throughout the country in lieu of concentrating industry in urban areas. Industries which locate in less developed areas receive tax incentives. There are also incentives for industry investments in which local products are exported, for investments that use Malaysian mineral and agricultural resources, and for investments that transfer technology into Malaysia. Free trade zones have been established throughout Malaysia for the manufacture and trading of export-oriented goods. Specialized financing institutions have been established to provide financing for industry and for exports. A one-stop type of agency, the Malaysian Industrial Development Authority, is operating to provide all required licensing and regulatory approvals for new industrial investments (4).

The government has no policy or legislation concerning competition. It is clear that the government is not against competition, but the government does actively participate in business and does protect specific infant industries. The country does not have antimonopoly or antitrust laws. Monopolies are found in various sectors and are thought to be in the public interest.

Current foreign exchange controls are relatively liberal. As noted above, foreign investments are encouraged provided they have proper financing arrangements. If loans from abroad reach the RM 5 million level, approval from the Controller of Foreign Exchange is required. A company controlled by nonresidents must have approval for domestic source loans in excess of RM 10 million. Loans that do not exceed three times the company's share capital are generally approved. Foreign capital is not specifically restricted. Remittances or transfers abroad are not restricted but control forms must be filed for transfers over RM 100,000. Repatriation of capital, dividends, royalties or service fees are not restricted. However, prior approval of the Controller of Foreign Exchange is required when a resident wishes to pay from domestic credit, foreign sources for foreign securities, foreign immovable property, foreign lending or deposits and the like (chapter 6, 4–5).

The government has used systems of tariffs and import licensing to protect industry sectors in early development stages. In manufacturing, a well-established licensing system is used to prevent new entrants into markets thought to be saturated. It is reported that these systems are in decline as the government trend is to competition (5). The Ministry of Domestic Trade and Consumer Affairs sets forth and administers policies and procedures to provide a favorable economic environment for domestic businesses, including providing adequate protection of local industries. Foreign interests must apply to the Secretariat to the Wholesale and Retail Trade Committee for permission to participate in domestic wholesale or retail trade. Any business in the wholesale or retail sector that has foreign-owner participation must incorporate under the Companies Act 1965. Such foreign ownership may not exceed 30 percent, with the balance of the ownership made up of Malaysian citizens (7).

Restrictions on foreign ownership of resources in Malaysia are thought necessary by the government in order to meet its ownership and redistribution of wealth goals. The Industrial Coordination Act 1975, for example, requires all manufacturing companies, except those with less than RM 2.5 million in capital or less than 75 employees, to apply to the Malaysian Industrial Development Authority for approval to begin or to expand existing operations. The 1975 Act sets out ownership conditions and restrictions for permission to manufacture.

For companies that export at least 80 percent of their production there are no equity restrictions. If less than 80 percent of production is exported, foreign equity ownership percentages permitted declines with declining proportions of exports. For example, if a manufacturing company exports 30 percent or less of its product, foreign equity ownership can be a maximum of 30 percent (5). Up to 51 percent of foreign ownership is allowed for projects that manufacture products considered priority or high technology for the domestic market (6).

The government has a Foreign Investment Committee charged with responsibility to regulate acquisitions, mergers and takeovers that involve foreign and Malaysian ownership interests in sectors other than manufacturing including wholesale and retail trade. All proposed ownership transfers of Malaysian resources that exceed RM 5 million must be approved by this Committee (6).

The Securities Commission Act 1993 and the Futures Industry Act 1993 placed regulation of the securities and futures industries under the Securities Commission. The Commission performs the licensing, monitoring, and regulation of the markets and market participants in Malaysia. The basis of regulation of the markets in the past has been merit. Since 1996, the basis of regulation has shifted to one of full and accurate disclosure with significant penalties for misrepresentation. The new tact of regulation is to provide the investing public with full disclosure of information needed to make investment decisions on a timely basis (chapter 7, 8–10).

The Ministry of Domestic Trade and Consumer Affairs is charged with regulating trade practices so that the rights and interests of consumers will be protected. Under this Ministry, the Registrar of Companies administers the Companies Act, including the registration of all companies doing business in Malaysia. The Registrar's files are open for public inspection. Another agency within the Ministry, the Registrar of Businesses administers the Business Registration Act. All partnerships and sole proprietorships must register with this agency (5).

The forms of business used in Malaysia, aside from government-owned entities, include sole proprietorships, partnerships, unincorporated joint ventures, foreign company branches and companies. Only a Malaysian citizen may operate a business as a sole proprietorship. Both the sole proprietorship and partnerships have unlimited liability for business obligations. Partners have joint and several liability for the obligations of their partnership. A partnership agreement may be oral but should preferably be a written document, which should set out the rights, duties, and obligations of the partners. Corporations as well as individuals may be partners. If the partnership is for profit, no more than 20 partners are permitted, with exception to this rule made for certain professional partnerships (chapter 10, 14).

Malaysia has not legislated regulations for joint ventures specifically. Joint ventures may be organized by creating a separate corporation or by creating a partnership to carry out the project. The regulations pertaining to the chosen organizational form, of course, must be followed. In the past, the Registrar of Companies allowed only branches of foreign companies that had government or quasi-government contracts to register to carry on business in Malaysia. Price Waterhouse Coopers (2000) reports that in recent times foreign branches without such contracts have been accepted to carry on business in Malaysia (15). To register, a foreign branch must file a certified copy of the incorporation documents for its parent corporation; a certified copy of the parent's company charter or articles of incorporation with bylaws; a listing of parent company directors with details for each; location of the branch registered office in Malaysia; a memorandum of appointment or similar document naming a Malaysian resident who is authorized to take notices served on the company and who will act as the company's agent in Malaysia (16).

Companies incorporated in Malaysia may be public or private in nature. In the case of a private company, the articles of association must restrict the right to transfer shares, limit shareholders to no more than 50 persons, and prohibit the offering of shares or debentures for sale to the public. If a private company has no more than 20 shareholders, it qualifies as an exempt private company. Exempt companies need not file annual audited financial statements with the Company Registrar. Exempt companies may also make loans to directors or affiliated companies, a practice prohibited for public companies. A public company is one that does not meet the restrictions for a private company (3).

The Malaysian Companies Act of 1965 governs corporations. Application must first be made to the Registrar of Companies to reserve a company name. A memorandum of association together with the proposed company bylaws is then filed to request incorporation. A standard form of articles of incorporation complete with bylaws is contained in the Companies Act of 1965. This standard form may be used or specific articles may be submitted so long as the requirements of the Act are not violated. Upon acceptance, the Registrar issues a certificate of incorporation. All information filed with the Registrar is available for public viewing (3).

Minimum shares in a corporation's equity are two, except where wholly owned by another corporation in which case only one share is required. Shares may be denominated in any amount, usually with a nominal or par value of RM 1 each. Shares may be ordinary voting shares with no restrictions on dividends or preferred shares with no voting rights and preferential treatment to dividends. Voting rights of ordinary shares, defined as not-preference shares, is required to be one vote for each share. Share capital total may be in any amount. Issued shares may not exceed total authorized shares. Dividends may not be paid from company capital. Court approval is needed to reduce company capital (5).

A company must have a minimum of two directors who must be residents in Malaysia. Directors are not required by law to own shares. Directors are commonly appointed by shareholders to hold office for a

set term specified in the bylaws. Directors have the responsibility to operate the company and may appoint one or more of their number to act
as managing directors. The Chairman may be elected from and by the
Board of Directors. A company secretary, who is a natural person resident in Malaysia, is required. The company secretary may be a director.
The secretary is commonly responsible for assuring that the company
complies with company laws. The company secretary must be a member
of a professional recognized body such as the Malaysian Institute of
Chartered Secretaries and Administrators, the Malaysian Bar Council,
the Malaysian Association of Certified Public Accountants or similar organizations (8).

An annual shareholders' meeting must be held at which the usual
business includes approval of the company's accounts and the reports
of directors and auditors, declaration of dividends, election of directors
and the appointment of company auditors. Dividends may only be paid
out of profits (9).

In the past, share transfers were made by submitting to the company
a transfer form signed by both transferor and transferee. Once approved
by company directors, new stock certificates were issued to the new
shareholder. For nonlisted companies this process is still in force. However for all companies listed on the Kuala Lumpur Stock Exchange, a
new scrip-less stock transfer system was set up in 1997 by which share
transfers are made by electronic means (6).

The Kuala Lumpur Stock Exchange has approximately 450 companies
listed on its main board and 276 on the second board. Companies on the
main board are larger and older than those on the second board. Equity
and debt securities are traded on the Kuala Lumpur Stock Exchange. The
Exchange also handles futures trading.

Malaysian companies are required to maintain accounting and related
records such that company transactions and its financial position can
properly be determined. A true and fair profit and loss account and
balance sheets are required to be made and kept for audit. Every transaction must be properly recorded within 60 days after being completed.
These records should normally be kept at the registered company office
in Malaysia or in another place in Malaysia approved by Directors.
Should the records be kept outside of Malaysia, financial statements and
reports must be sent to a place in Malaysia and in sufficient detail to
allow a true and fair profit-and-loss account and balance sheet to be
made. Records of transactions and operations may be kept by making
entries in a bound book or in any permanent manner. The records must
be retained for seven years.

An annual report must be filed with the Registrar of Companies that
includes shareholders lists, summaries of issued share capital, details of
directors, managers, secretary and auditors. The return must include the

latest audited financial statements, unless exempt. Tax authorities generally require that audited financials required under the Companies Act be filed with company annual tax reports (chapter 12, 2).

Audit of company accounts must be carried out by an auditor approved by the Minister of Finance. To be approved, the auditor must be a resident Malaysian citizen who is a member of the Malaysian Institute of Accountants. Once appointed, the auditor may only resign at the annual meeting, unless he is not the only auditor of the company. The auditor is required to give his opinion as to whether the accounts give a true and fair view of the state of affairs, results and source and application of funds of the company in accordance with the Companies Act of 1965. He must also give his opinion about whether the accounting and related records required by the Companies Act have been properly prepared in accordance with the requirements set forth in the Act. If applicable, the auditor must give his opinion on whether consolidated accounts have been kept in accordance with the Companies Act (3). The auditor is required to prepare a report in writing to the Registrar of Companies when any of the provisions of the Act have not been properly followed (4).

The Malaysian Institute of Accountants, created by the Accountants Act of 1967, regulates the accounting profession. Membership in the Institute is open to all members of other specified accountancy bodies, including the Malaysian Association of Certified Public Accountants, which dates from 1958. The Malaysian Association conducts the professional accounting examinations. From October 1997, the Institute recognized in their entirety the Codified International Standards on Auditing as generally accepted auditing standards in Malaysia. Prior to that date, international auditing guidelines accepted for use in Malaysia and Malaysian Auditing Guidelines issued by the Institute and the Association were used as authoritative auditing guidance. The Institute will issue technical bulletins on auditing after public exposure for at least six months as Recommended Practice Guides (4).

The Financial Reporting Act 1997 named the Malaysian Accounting Standards Board as the organization responsible for establishing accounting standards for financial reporting in Malaysia. The Act gave the Board the authority to promulgate accounting standards. The Board came into operation at the same time as the Financial Reporting Foundation whose purpose is to provide funding for the Board. The Foundation also makes its views known to the Board and reviews the performance of the Board (chapter 13, 1).

The Act specifically places the force and authority of the statute behind the standards set by the board. Any accounts kept and financial reports made in accordance with any law administered by the Securities Commission, Bank Negara Malaysia and the Registrar of Companies are required to comply with Board-approved standards. According to the IAS PLUS Country Update on Malaysia prepared by Deloitte Touche Tohmatsu (2001c, 1), the Malaysian Accounting Standards Board intends to carry on a policy of international harmonization of Malaysian standards with international standards and concepts and with other national standards so that Malaysian standards are compatible in all significant aspects. In a transition, the Board adopted 24 of the existing accounting standards previously issued for Malaysia which is in the process of reviewing and replacing each within a new series of standards (1). In early 2000, there were a total of 21 new Malaysian standards issued. And 10 of the 24 transitional prior standards were still in force. There were a number of exposure drafts open on a number of important topics including: Provisions, Contingent Liabilities and Contingent Assets; Segment Reporting; Financial Instruments Disclosure and Presentation; Impairment of Assets; Financial Reporting by Unit Trust; Property Development Activities; and Goodwill (2, 3).

The survey of 53 countries' written accounting rules as compared to International Accounting Standards, conducted in 2000 under the auspices of the International Forum on Accountancy Development that is described in more detail in the Indonesian section of this Chapter, indicates 20 instances in which respondents reported differences between Malaysian and international standards. These differences included 12 International Accounting Standards and one interpretation. These differences were in three categories: an absence of specific Malaysian rules— 11 cases; no specific rules requiring disclosure—4 cases; and inconsistencies between the two sets of rules—5 cases (Nobes, 2001, 105).

THE PHILIPPINES

The Philippines gained independence from the United States in 1946. Forty years later in 1986, democratic political institutions were restored. A new constitution was ratified in 1987 which guarantees the following basic rights to all investors and enterprises. Assets will be free from expropriation without just compensation. Profits, capital gains and dividends may be remitted to other countries in line with monetary authority guidelines. Proceeds from selling or liquidation of assets can be repatriated. Investors may obtain sufficient foreign exchange to meet principal and interest payments for foreign obligations (Ernst & Young International, 1999, 5).

The country participates as a full member in the Multilateral Investment Guarantee Agency that insures investments made through the agency against losses caused by government restrictions on currency transfers or conversions, expropriation by government, war, revolution or civil disturbance. Foreign investors are insured against contract repudiation by the host government and against losses from political causes (5).

The Constitution provides for three separate and equal branches: a bicameral legislature made up of the House of Representatives and the Senate; an executive headed by the president; and a judiciary with the Supreme Court as final arbiter of laws of the land. The president, who is head of the government and chief of state, is elected for a six-year term of office along with the vice president. There are 260 representatives in the House of Representatives who are elected every three years as compared to the Senate which has 24 senators elected every six years. The court system is made up of the Supreme Court, Court of Appeals, regional trial courts, a Court of Tax Appeals and various metropolitan, municipal and family trial and circuit courts (99).

Until recently the government had a protectionist orientation. The current government policy is to have free operation of market forces, to have a level business-playing field that will encourage the free interplay of market forces. Policies call for decreasing government intervention and prohibiting cartels and monopolies. The laws and regulations of the business environment have been revised to this end (5). Planning for economic growth centers on development of an infrastructure that will integrate markets not only within the country but also with the rest of the world (8). Monopolies in various industries have been dismantled and competition introduced. Industries deregulated in recent years are the telecommunications, airline, mining, shipping and oil industries. The finance industry, retail trade and the energy sectors have all been liberalized so that increased participation has been opened (9).

The government is a republic with 73 provinces and 61 chartered cities. The legal system is based on Spanish and Anglo-American laws. There is a bicameral legislature with a 24-seat Senate and 221-seat House of Representatives with an additional 50 seats appointed by the president. The president and vice president are elected on separate tickets by popular vote for a term of six years. The Supreme Court justices have four-year terms and are appointed by the president upon the recommendation of the Judicial and Bar Council (3).

The population was estimated to be in excess of 81 million in 2000. Of these, 91 percent are said to be Christian Malay while 4 percent are Muslim Malay. While the official language is Filipino, there are 87 languages spoken in the Philippines. English is universal as the language of business, schools and government (98).

The country has a 95 percent literacy rate (CIA, 2001d, 1–3). Of the total labor force in 1998, 40 percent was engaged in agriculture, 19 percent in government and social services, 18 percent in services, 10 percent in manufacturing and 6 percent in construction. Total GDP was composed of 20 percent agriculture, 32 percent industrial, and 48 percent in services (6). The unemployment rate was 9.6 percent in 1998.

The currency unit is the Philippine peso. The exchange rate was approximately 40 to US $1 from 1998 to 2000. In 1997 the exchange rate was 29 to $1, and in 1996, 26 to $1 (7). There were two stock exchanges until 1992 when the two merged to form the Philippine Stock Exchange (Ernst & Young International, 1999, 12).

The Philippine economy deteriorated as a result of the Asian financial crisis and poor weather conditions. In 1998 the economy declined by a half percent after having grown by 5 percent in 1997. The economy recovered to a 2.9 percent growth rate in 1999. The government made a number of economic reforms during this period. The tax system was overhauled. Deregulation and privatization of the economy moved forward. There were improvements made in the infrastructure (4).

Organizing a business entity in the Philippines may take the form of a sole proprietorship, branch, representative office or regional headquarters. The sole proprietorship is open to all, foreign or domestic owners. Applicable Philippine laws must be observed. Foreigners who wish to use the sole proprietorship form must register their total capital with the central bank and seek approval of appropriate government agencies to operate. Since sole proprietorships have unlimited liability, only small-scale operations would seem to be appropriate for this organizational form.

A partnership may be either general or limited. The partnership form is a separate legal entity from its owners. In a general partnership all members are personally liable for all partnership obligations. In the limited partnership form, at least one partner must have unlimited liability while the remaining partners are liable only up to the amount of their partnership contributions. A partnership that has at least P 3,000 in capital is required to register with the Securities Exchange Commission, which administers partnership laws. The general partnership is dissolved upon the death of a partner (41). Partnerships with capital over P 3,000 are required to register with the Securities and Exchange Commission. Partnerships with less capital than the P 3,000 are not required to register (46).

Foreign corporations may elect to establish a corporate branch within the Philippines. Liabilities of branches are the responsibility of the foreign corporation. To cover the potential liability, P 100,000 in securities must be deposited with the Securities and Exchange Commission within 60 days after a license to operate the branch is issued. Should gross income exceed P 5 in any year, a deposit of additional securities must be made that is equal to 2 percent of the increase in annual gross income (46). Operation and liquidation of a branch is similar to that of a corporation. Essentially the same fees are paid to establish a branch as would be paid for establishing a corporation (42).

A representative office of a foreign corporation may also operate in the Philippines but it is restricted to information and promotional activities or may be used to facilitate orders for the foreign corporation. The representative office may not earn income from within the Philippines. A regional headquarters may also be operated from the Philippines for business activities directed from the regional headquarters elsewhere in the Asia Pacific region. Such activities may take the form of supervision, communications and coordinating the firm's affiliates outside of the Philippines. Such regional headquarters may not in any way participate in the management of entities within the Philippines. As the representative office, the regional headquarters may not earn income. Operating expenses of at least $50,000 annually must be remitted from the home corporations for either a regional headquarters or a representative office. At application for registration a total of $30,000 of the annual required minimum must be remitted to the Securities Exchange Commission. Upon registration approval an additional $20,000 must be remitted directly to the representative or regional headquarters office (42).

Foreign corporations are also authorized to operate within the Philippines by incorporating a subsidiary. The subsidiary is viewed as separate from the parent foreign corporation and may enter into contracts that are considered arms-length. The parent's liability is limited to its investment in the Philippine subsidiary. Foreign ownership of the subsidiary may with some exceptions be 100 percent. The corporation is considered a Filipino corporation if foreign ownership is limited to no more than 40 percent.

Private corporations may be formed in the Philippines under authority of the Corporation Code. Such corporations are viewed as separate legal entities with liability of owners limited to paid in or subscribed capital. This legal veil may be disregarded if the corporate entity is used contrary to public good. Corporate shares are transferable so long as rights of creditors and other shareholders are not impaired. The private corporation must have between 5 and 15 individuals founding the corporation. The majority of the founders must be resident in the Philippines. There are no limits set on numbers of shareholders (43).

The registration and operations of domestic corporations must meet the requirements set by the Securities and Exchange Commission under the Corporation Code. To register a corporation, founders submit proposed articles of incorporation and required information to the SEC. With the exception of more than 40 percent owned foreign corporations, minimum paid up capital stock must be at least P 5,000. No minimum is set on authorized capital stock, but subscriptions must cover at least 25 percent of the authorized capital stock total at incorporation, and a minimum of 25 percent of this must be paid in at time of incorporation. For corporations which have more than 40 percent foreign ownership, paid in capital must be at least US $200,000. Or, if the corporation employs more than 50 people or is in advanced technology as determined by the Department of Science and Technology, minimum capital paid in is US $100,000 at time of incorporation.

Corporate shares may be issued with par or no-par value and may be divided into classes in which property rights and voting rights may differ. Separate classes of stock may be set up which can only be purchased by citizens of the Philippines (45).

The board of directors, elected by shareholders, exercises corporate powers. Board members must own at least one capital share. A majority of the board must be resident in the Philippines. A corporate secretary is required to be a resident citizen. The board selects corporate officers. Only Philippine citizens may hold key corporate management positions (45).

Both the Corporate Code and the National Internal Revenue Code have requirements that govern business accounting and reporting in the Philippines (90). Companies that have more than 20 shareholders and all public companies are subject to the rules of the Securities and Exchange Commission (Deloitte Touche Tohmatsu, 2001d, 1). There are also additional requirements set for regulated companies such as banks, finance companies, insurance companies, investment houses and public utilities which require that financial reports be submitted to appropriate agencies on an annual, quarterly and monthly basis (Ernst & Young International, 1999, 89).

All business entities in the Philippines which pay internal revenue tax are required by the National Internal Revenue Code to keep account books in English, Spanish or the native tongue of their locality. A journal and ledger with subsidiary records are required. For businesses subject to value-added tax a subsidiary sales journal and purchase journal are required. Prior to use such books must be registered with the Bureau of Internal Revenue and after use must be retained for at least three years at the entity's principal place of business in the Philippines. Corporations must also have on file at the principal office in the Philippines minutes of shareholder and board of directors meetings, records of all business transactions including stock transactions. Shareholders are authorized to inspect these records (89).

Companies are required to file financial statements with their annual income tax returns. The SEC also requires that annual audited financial statements be filed with that agency by corporations that have capital of P 50,000 or more and by corporations where assets or gross revenues are P 500,000 or more (48). Foreign corporation branches must file annual audited financial statements with the SEC. Regulated companies, such as banks, insurance companies and the like, are also obligated to file annual audited financial statements with respective regulatory agencies in addition to the Securities and Exchange Commission (48).

Sole proprietorships, partnerships or corporations that have gross quarterly sales, earnings, receipts or output over P 150,000 must file audited financials with their annual income tax returns with the Bureau of Internal Revenue (48).

Required financial statements consist of a balance sheet, income statement, statement of retained earnings and cash flow statement and must be in comparative form with the prior year (3). The Accounting Standards Council of the Philippines Institute of Certified Public Accountants prescribes generally accepted accounting principles (GAAP) for the Philippines. And, after endorsement and approval by the government agencies, the Board of Accountancy and the Professional Regulation Commission, the Council's Statements of Financial Accounting Standards form a major part of the rules and regulations that must be followed by all Philippine certified public accountants (Deloitte Touche Tohmatsu, 2001d). Businesses in areas under supervision of government agencies have additional accounting rules and disclosures must be made in annual reports. In fact, it is usually the practice for such government regulators to issue regulation manuals and circulars (Ernst & Young International, 1999, 90).

The accounting profession is regulated and licensed by the Board of Accountancy, which is part of the Professional Regulation Commission. The Board is responsible for supervision, regulation and control of accountancy in the Philippines including administration of the CPA examination, registration of CPAs, continuing professional education, standardization and regulation of accounting education in the Philippines. The certificate of registration is originally issued after a candidate has passed the CPA licensing examination and must be renewed every three years provided that the CPA has earned 120 hours of continuing professional education in the prior three years (94).

The Auditing Standards and Practices Council has responsibility for issuing auditing standards. Organized in 1986, the Council has representatives from the SEC, public accounting firms, the Philippines Institute of Certified Public Accountants, the Board of Accountancy and others (94).

All CPAs in the Philippines must be members of the Philippines Institute (94). Accountants concerned with promoting high professional and ethical standards, developing accountancy education, and advancing the science of accounting, founded the Institute in 1929. The Institute integrated Philippine accountants over the years and now has eight regions with chapters that cover all areas of the nation. Membership is grouped into four sections: education, commercial/industry, government and public practice. The organization publishes the monthly *Accounting Times* and the quarterly *Accountant's Journal* (Philippines Institute of Certified Public Accountants, 2001, 1).

Among its many actions to improve accountancy, the Institute disseminates exposure drafts, bulletins and releases from the Accounting Standards Council and the Auditing Standards and Practice Council. The Institute also represents the country in the world accountancy bodies. The Institute's Web page declares that the Institute is active among international accounting organizations. And that chief among these are the International Federation of Accountants and the International Accounting Standards Committee, which seek to develop and enhance the worldwide accountancy profession functioning under harmonized standards (3).

The Accounting Standards Council of the Philippines Institute of Certified Public Accountants is pursuing its policy on harmonization of Philippine standards with International Accounting Standards (IAS). The policy of the Council is to review all IAS and to adopt IAS so that compliance with the Philippine standards would automatically mean compliance with IAS. The Council has an ongoing project to replace existing Philippine standards with the appropriate IAS (Deloitte Touche Tohmatsu, 2001d, 2).

The harmonization process seems to be rapidly taking shape. However, as indicated elsewhere in this book, an International Forum for Accountancy Development–sponsored study was conducted to compare written national accounting standards against IAS, including interpretations, in the Philippines, as one of 53 countries. The rules effective for reporting periods ending on December 31, 2000 were used in the study (Nobes, 2000, 1).

Respondent CPAs were asked to identify nonalignment where national rules would not permit the international treatment because of inconsistent rules or would not require the international treatment because of missing or permissive rules (1). The survey summary for the Philippines listed 21 instances in which differences were reported between Philippine SFASs and international accounting standards. These involved 12 International Accounting Standards and one interpretation. Reasons for the differences fell into three categories: Philippine accounting standards differ from IAS because of the lack of specific Philippine rules in eight cases; there are no specific rules in the Philippines that require disclosures by IAS in four cases; and inconsistencies between the two sets of standards in nine cases (Nobes, 2000, 83).

THAILAND

The unified Thai kingdom dates from the mid-fourteenth century. The country has never been under the control of a European power. Until

1939 the country was known as Siam. The present form of democratically elected government, a constitutional monarchy, dates from the bloodless revolution in 1932. A new constitution went into force in 1997, which is designed to update the prior constitution that dates from the 1939 era. The head of state is the king. The bicameral legislative system has a National Assembly consisting of Senate and House. The king appoints members of the Senate for six-year terms. House members are elected by popular vote for four-year terms. The prime minster and cabinet are appointed by the king from the House majority party.

Thailand has 76 provinces that are divided into four regions: the North, the Central, the Northeast and the South. The legal system stems from the Napoleonic Code with Court of the First Instant, Court of Appeals and Supreme Court. The political subdivisions consist of the province, district, town and village. There are seventy-six provinces (CIA, 2001f, 15).

The population is estimated to be in excess of 61 million with 5.5 million living in the Bangkok metropolitan area. The literacy rate is estimated at 94 percent. Thai is the national language. English is spoken by a majority of the population and by government officials (10). Ninety-five percent of the population follows Buddhism, while just under 4 percent are followers of the Muslim faith (4).

Fifty-four percent of the populace is engaged in agriculture, 15 percent in industry and 31 percent in the service sector. Agriculture accounted for 12 percent of the GDP, industry 39 percent and services 49 percent (6–7).

From 1985 to 1995, Thailand averaged nearly 9 percent annual growth. The currency crisis in 1997 disclosed substantial weakness in the financial sector and the government was forced to float the baht, the national currency. The baht had long been pegged at 25 to the U.S. dollar. In January 1998 the currency reached its low point of 56 to the dollar, and was 37 to the dollar in January 2000. The economy contracted by nearly 10 percent in 1998. Numerous bankruptcies ensued, banks closed and prices soared. Unemployment became widespread (6).

The Diamonds (2000, 16) reported that Thai companies have defaulted on $300 billion of Eurobond borrowings. The economy began a recovery in 1999 with a 4-percent expansion. The government has cooperated with the IMF adhering to a mandated recovery program. New bankruptcy and foreclosure laws were passed. A recovery in the region has boosted exports and fiscal stimulus has raised domestic demand. However, the financial sector has made slow progress toward recovery (CIA, 2000e, 6). In 2000, the private banking sector had an enormous external debt of $64.1 billion. The prices on the Bangkok Stock Exchange continue at historic lows (8).

Per capita income doubled from 1986 to 1991 to 41,021 baht. The daily minimum wage in Bangkok and nearby provinces is 94 baht or $2.59. In outlying provinces wages range from 94 baht ($2.11) to 107 baht ($2.41) (Diamond and Diamond, 2000, 16). The unemployment rate in 1998 was estimated at 4.5 percent. The population below the poverty line in the same year was an estimated 12.5 percent (CIA, 2000e, 7).

Import permits are seldom required but a certificate of payment must be presented for goods exceeding 10,000 baht, or about $225, before clearing customs. Foreign trade transactions can be invoiced in baht or approved hard currencies. Exports require a certificate of exportation prior to clearing customs. Foreign currency received by exporters in exchange for exported goods must be sold or transferred to an authorized bank within seven days of receipt which must be within three months following the date of export. Exchange delays can take up to three months (16–17).

Forms of business permitted in Thailand include limited liability companies, partnerships, joint ventures, and branches of foreign corporations. The partnership forms may be unregistered ordinary partnerships where partners all are jointly and indefinitely liable for partnership obligations. Registered ordinary partnerships may be formed which limit liability of partners to two years after leaving the partnership. In limited partnerships, there must be at least one partner with unlimited liability but remaining partners may have liability limited to their contributions if they are nonmanaging partners. The joint venture form is not available in the separate legal entity form in Thailand but may be used for tax purposes. Branches of foreign companies are permitted but they must have government approval (Ernst and Young, 1990, 19–20).

The limited liability company is the most popular form with both domestic and foreign investors. Public companies are permitted under the Public Companies Act of 1978. The Civil and Commercial Code allows private companies to be formed. Public companies have in the past faced severe restrictions including the requirement that the public company have more than 100 shareholders and at least 50 percent of total shares must be held by shareholders who each hold no more than .6 percent of the total stock. The public company was not permitted to have more than 10 percent of its shares held by one entity. These restrictions have been eliminated and according to the Diamonds "The Thai limited liability company is equivalent to a Western corporation" (Diamond and Diamond, 2000, 11).

For foreign investors, who obtain a promotion certificate from the Board of Investment, the limited liability company is preferred over other alternatives. The foreign ownership investment level permitted varies with the type of investment. For agricultural, mining, fishing or service sector investment, a Thai national must own at least 51 percent of the registered capital. Should the capital investment exceed 1 billion baht, foreign investors may own all of the shares initially with Thai nationals controlling 51 percent of the shares within five years. For investments in manufacturing when the products are primarily for the domestic market, at least 51 percent of the registered capital must be owned by Thai nationals. If at least 80 percent of the production is exported, foreigners are permitted to own the entire registered capital. The Board of Investment can eliminate the foreign ownership restriction on a case-by-case basis (11).

Company-formation application is made to the Central Registry Office in Bangkok or at the Companies Registry office in a province where the corporation is to be located. One of the promoters must be a Thai national. After a certificate of registration is issued an initial meeting of all subscribers is required. A minimum of 25 percent of the subscription price must be paid in at time of registration, 100 percent for bearer shares. Minutes of this initial meeting must be forwarded to the Registry office on the day following the meeting. A summary of all registration documents must be published in the *Government Gazette*. Upon registration the following must be filed with the Registry: a Memorandum of Association, the Certificate of Business Registration, a certificate which indicates the registered capital, a listing of directors, and the address of the head office. A listing of shareholders together with their nationalities are also required. The Board of Directors may have any number of resident or nonresident members but only Thai resident directors can make binding company decisions (13).

In the face of the financial and economic crisis, the Ministry of Finance and the Bank of Thailand loosened the rules for foreign ownership of banks. Investors from other nations may now hold all of the capital stock of financing institutions including banks for a period of 10 years. After that 10-year period, the foreign holdings of the entity must be progressively reduced until it is no higher than 49 percent (1).

The Investment Promotion Law now permits any part of the entire country to function as a free trade zone. Any location in Thailand can be designated as an export processing zone in which imports may be assembled or manufactured for re-export. Income tax and import/export duty exemptions are available for these areas. Free trade zones are under the governance of the Industrial Estate Authority of Thailand. Five such zones have been established with a number of new zones expected (16).

Records and books of accounts must be kept by each Thai company at its registered office in Thailand. There is generally a required 10-year holding period for these records. An annual audit by a licensed independent auditor is required for Thai companies. Audited annual reports must be presented to shareholders at their annual meeting for approval. After approval the audited reports must be filed with the Ministry of Commerce (Ernst and Young, 1990, 19–20). Audited financials must also accompany the annual income tax returns filed by each company with the Revenue Department, as corporate income tax is based on audited financial statements after any necessary adjustments (Ernst & Young, 2001d, 2).

Auditors are licensed and governed by the Institute of Certified Accountants and Auditors of Thailand and the Board of Supervision of Auditing Practice. The Board is an arm of the Ministry of Commerce and is responsible for regulating the auditing profession in Thailand. The Board issues practice licenses to qualified auditors and can for cause cancel those licenses. In order to qualify, applicants must pass in one sitting all parts of a board-administered examination. Those eligible to sit for the examination must hold a baccalaureate degree with adequate accounting content. Applicants for practice licenses must be at least twenty years old, citizens of Thailand, and have 2,000 hours or more of public accounting experience in the prior two years (Akathaporn et al., 1993, 260, 261).

Auditing practitioners are expected to follow the Code of Ethics of the Institute. Should a licensed auditor not audit at least five companies in each year, the Institute offers a series of seminars that must be attended in order to maintain the license to audit company financials (261).

The Institute of Certified Accountants and Auditors of Thailand (2001a, 1), the only organization for the accounting profession in Thailand, was founded in 1948 as the Institute of Certified Accountants of Thailand. In recognition that the membership was made up of both certified auditors and general accountants from the private and public sectors, the name was changed in 1965 to its present form. Current membership is comprised of professional accountants from the government and private sectors and includes certified auditors, accountants and accounting educators. There are currently 7,300 members composed of ordinary annual members, ordinary life members, individual technical activities members and institutional technical activities members.

The Institute's purposes include promoting the honor and unity of its members; promoting standards of the accounting profession; promoting knowledge exchange and information dissemination in accounting; and to promoting and cooperating in activities which are of benefit to the public, except that these activities must not be related to politics (2). To carry out their mission, the Institute is active on a number of fronts.

Starting in 1994, chapters of the Institute have been established in all the major provinces of the nation. Currently there are nine chapters, all designed to provide support and development to the profession as is provided in Bangkok (4).

A number of technical committees operate that include: Accounting Standards, Auditing Standards and Computerized Auditing, Government Accounting and Auditing Standards, Internal Auditing, Financial Analysis and Consultation, Taxation and Business Laws, Management

Accounting and Information Technology Management, Definition of Accounting Terminology and Development of the Accounting Profession and Continuing Education (2). The *Accountants' Journal* is published by the Institute to disseminate knowledge and technical information on accounting (4).

The Institute maintains rather extensive training and educational facilities. A Training Center for the Auditing Profession was opened in 1995 in Bangkok for the purpose of training accountants who seek to sit for the examination to become certified auditors. The Institute is also active in upgrading accounting instructors in Thailand. A curriculum has been developed to prepare instructors to teach in higher educational institutions and junior colleges, and, indeed, in the Institute's own training programs. Training for accounting instruction will also take place at the Northeast region's Nakhonratchasima Chapter of the Institute. This program is designed to train instructors from the entire region (5).

In addition to auditing standards, the Institute publishes technical papers and promulgates the accounting standards that constitute generally accepted accounting principles for the nation (4). The Accounting Act of 2000 provides that accounting standards issued by the Institute and approved by the Accounting Supervisory Board of the Ministry of Commerce carry the weight of law in Thailand. Therefore, not abiding by the accounting standards is a criminal offense.

The Institute is also working at the international level to promote the service of its members to regional and international businesses. It is an active member of global accounting organizations such as the International Federation of Accountants, the International Accounting Standards Committee, the Confederation of Asian and Pacific Accountants, ASEAN Federation of Accounting and the Institute of Internal Auditors (5). To enhance Thailand's position in global markets, the Institute has set a policy that its various technical committees when developing Thailand standards use the appropriate international standards as guidelines (4).

The movement toward harmonization with International Accounting Standards is being strongly continued. Eight Thailand Accounting Standards were issued by the Institute to become effective on January 1, 2000. Although the new standards are based on International Accounting Standards, they do not necessarily adopt all of the provisions contained in the international standards.

The harmonization with international standards process seems to be well advanced. Yet, the International Accounting Standards have not been adopted in complete form in a number of instances. The October 2000 Country Update from IAS PLUS indicated: "There are no Thai Standards in a number of important areas addressed by IAS. . . . There are also some differences between Thai standards and IAS" (Deloitte Touche Tohmatsu, 2001f, 2).

The survey of 53 countries' written accounting rules as compared to International Accounting Standards, conducted in 2000 under the auspices of the International Forum on Accountancy Development, that is described in more detail in the Indonesian section of this chapter, indicates 10 instances in which respondents reported differences between Thai and international standards. These differences included nine International Accounting Standards and one interpretation. These differences were in two categories: an absence of specific Thai rules—5 cases, and inconsistencies between the two sets of rules—5 cases (Nobes, 2001, 105).

Chapter 6

Accounting and Business Environments among Island Economies

The island economies of Fiji, Vanuatu and Papua New Guinea are studied in this Chapter. They were selected to represent the business and accounting environments in small island jurisdictions in the Pacific Ocean. Each nation state has developed and enacted laws and regulations that apply to business organizations and to accountants within their jurisdictions. They have developed institutions to seek to attain their governmental plans and aims. Investors, accountants and auditors operate in these environs and must conduct their business and themselves accordingly.

FIJI

Fiji became independent from the British in 1970 after having been a colony since 1874. There were two military coups in 1987. A constitution enacted in 1990 favored the native Melanesians. This led to out migration of the Indian community with a resulting population loss. This caused economic problems. The outmigration also resulted in the Melanesians becoming the majority of the electorate. Constitutional changes since then have made control of Fiji more equitable between the ethnic groups. The latest constitutional amendments enacted in 1997 discontinued racial prescriptions for voting. The elections in 1999, the first where open voting was followed, are reported to have been democratic, free and peaceful (CIA, 2000, 1).

The government is a republic with four divisions and one dependency, Rotuma. The executive branch of the government consists of the president who is chief of state, a vice president, prime minister, deputy prime minister and a cabinet. There is a Presidential Council that advises the president and a Great Council of Chiefs that consists of the highest ranked in the traditional system. The Great Council elects the president for a term of five years. The president appoints the prime minister (5).

The legislature is a bicameral Parliament with a Senate and House of Representatives. The Senate consists of 32 seats of which 14 are appointed by the Great Council of Chiefs, 9 are appointed by the prime minister, 8 are appointed by the leader of the opposition and one is appointed by the council of Rotuma. The House of Representatives has 71 seats of which 23 are reserved for ethnic Fijians, 19 are reserved for ethnic Indians, 3 are reserved for other ethnic groups, one is reserved for the Rotuman constituency within the whole of Fiji and 25 seats are openly elected. Members serve five-year terms.

The Fiji legal system is based on the British system of jurisprudence. Most aspects of the legal system have been codified, but many areas still depend on British common law. A system of courts was set up in the 1990 constitution with the Supreme Court the final appellate court. The president appoints Supreme Court members (5).

The country's currency is the Fijian dollar, for which the rate of exchange was US $1 at 1.97 in January 2000, at 1.97 in 1999, at 1.99 in 1998, at 1.44 in 1997, at 1.40 in 1996 and 1.41 in 1995 (7). The Fiji dollar is valued against a basket of currencies appropriate to its trading partners and patterns (11).

The population of Fiji was estimated to be 833,000 in 2000. The population total was made up of 51 percent Fijian, 44 percent Indian and 5 percent other. The Fijians are reported to be mainly Christian while the Indians are mainly Hindu with about 8 percent of the population being Muslim (2).

English is the official language and is widely understood and spoken. Fijian and Hindustani are also spoken within the ethic groups. The country's literacy rate is approximately 92 percent.

The work force is estimated at 235,000 persons. By occupation the work force was occupied in subsistence agriculture 67 percent, as wage earners 18 percent and as salary earners 15 percent in 1987. The unemployment rate in 1997 was estimated at 6 percent. GDP per capita in 1999 was estimated as $7,300. The composition of the GDP was approximately 16.5 percent in agriculture, 25.5 percent in industry and 58 percent in services (6).

Although there is a large subsistence sector, Fiji is one of the most developed of the Pacific island economies. The major sources of foreign exchange for the economy are sugar exports and the growing tourist trade. There are approximately 300,000 tourists per year. The real growth rate in 1999 was a robust 7.8 percent, having recovered from low world sugar prices and internal disputes in 1997 as well as a drought in 1998

(6). KPMG reported that the country's real GDP growth rate was 1.6 percent in 1993, 3.9 percent in 1994, 2.1 percent in 1995, 3.1 percent in 1996 and a negative 1.6 percent in 1997 (KPMG International, 2001a, 1).

Exports from Fiji in 1996 were: Australia, 27 percent of total exports; New Zealand, 12.1 percent; United Kingdom, 14 percent; other Pacific islands, 9.3 percent; and the United States, 8.2 percent (2).

The standard of living in Fiji is high when compared to other developing countries. This is especially true in the urban areas. The educational system is well advanced. Primary and secondary schools are government operated and are based on the New Zealand curriculum of education. There are a number of post-secondary educational institutions in the country including the University of the South Pacific, the Fiji School of Medicine and the Fiji School of Agriculture. There are two training colleges for primary teachers and the Fiji Institute of Technology, which provides industrial training (Price Waterhouse Coopers, 2000, chapters 1, 3).

The Native Land Trust Board Ordinance of 1940 was enacted to protect the interests of Fijian landowners. This ordinance vested all Fijian land to the Native Land Trust Board, which still administers the land. Fijians own 84 percent of the land in communal tenure. Land may only be sold to the government, but certain areas that are not currently needed by Fijians may be leased. The government owns 7 percent of the land. Government land may not be sold except in exceptional circumstances. Government land, which becomes available, is generally publicly advertised. Leases of government land by the Lands Department or by the Native Land Trust Board are permitted for periods of up to 99 years. Rent is generally reassessed after 25 years. Such leases also require land improvements within specified time periods. If land is needed for purposes that are beneficial to Fiji, consideration can be had on a case-by-case basis. Approximately 10 percent of total land area is freehold land. This land is negotiable (3).

The economy of Fiji is private market oriented but must be considered a mixed economy. The government does operate or control through its agencies the major public utilities including postal, telegraph and telephone, water and electricity. The government also owns the National Bank of Fiji and the Fiji Sugar Corporation, which mills all of the sugar cane produced in Fiji. Indian Fiji citizens represent a substantial portion of the business and commercial expertise in the country. The government encourages indigenous Fijians to enter the business and commercial sectors (chapter 2, 1).

The Suva stock exchange has only four companies listed. The government has indicated that it has instituted new policies in order to move the economy toward exports and toward an outward orientation. In line with this objective, the government has been deregulating areas of the economy. License controls on imports are being replaced with tariffs. Price controls on many goods have been removed and exist now on selected essential commodities. In other actions, it seeks to incorporate selected government entities with the intention of eventual privatization (2). Foreign investments that will be in Fiji's interest are encouraged. Government approval is needed for foreign investments in Fiji. Such investments generally take the form of branches of a foreign corporation or incorporating a local company. Borrowing by nonresidents in the local economy is available but generally restricted to an amount equal to shareholders' equity (3). Government permission is needed to make remittances, including capital remittances, in or out of Fiji. The exchange control approval is controlled by the Ministry of Finance through the Reserve Bank of Fiji under the Control Act. There are restrictions on the repatriation of profits out of Fiji but waiver of these restrictions is available in some cases (4). The government controls acquisitions and mergers under the Exchange Control Act. Overseas investors are generally discouraged from obtaining a controlling interest in an established local business (chapter 6, 1). An investment in Fiji by a nonresident must have prior approval of the Reserve Bank of Fiji and approved investments made must be registered with the bank (2).

Business forms authorized in Fiji are similar to those found elsewhere and include sole proprietorship, partnerships, joint venture, branches of a foreign company and a company incorporated in Fiji. Sole proprietors or partnerships need not register their business name unless the name of the business is the same as the names of all partners or of the proprietor. Registration of the name, if required, must be with the Registrar of Companies within one month of beginning business. If registration is required, additional information must also be provided to the Registrar: business name; the general nature of the business; principal place of business; and the names of the partners or proprietor. Limited liability partnerships are not authorized. The Partnership Act governs partnerships including the relationships among partners and with those doing business with the partnership (chapter 9, 7).

Two or more entities or individuals may associate to carry out a joint venture to complete a business project of limited duration. The joint venture may be undertaken in the form of a partnership or by creating a company for the venture. If a partnership, the partnership laws together with appropriate partnership agreements will govern the conduct of the venture. Where a separate company is used as the vehicle for the joint venture, separate agreements among the parties are commonly made to document the arrangements special to the venture. The financial, accounting and legal considerations remain the same as for any other partnership or corporation (7).

Any foreign company that does business as a branch in Fiji must comply with the Companies Act. The same annual license fees as local companies must be paid. Within 30 days of beginning the business, the Registrar of Companies must be provided with a copy of the company's articles of incorporation or similar documents; the full address of registered or principal office of the company; names, addresses, nationalities and occupations of company directors; and names and addresses of one or more Fiji residents who is authorized to accept service of process and other notices for the company. Each year a copy of company financial statements must be filed with the Registrar in the same form as for local Fiji companies. Each company must post conspicuously at every business site within Fiji and on all invoices, letterhead and company notices the following information: the company's name, its country of incorporation and a statement that the company has limited liability (8).

The Companies Act, which is based on the United Kingdom Companies Acts, governs all Fiji corporations. Companies limited by guarantee and unlimited liability companies may be formed under this act. Nearly all companies, however, take the form of limited liability companies where liability of shareholders is limited to any amounts unpaid for shares held. Such companies must have the word "limited" in their company name (2).

Companies may be private or public. For a private company, bylaws must restrict the right to transfer shares; the number of shareholders must not exceed 50; and company shares or debentures may not be offered for sale to the public. The minimum number of shareholders is two. A private company need not file annual accounts with the Registrar of Companies.

A public company needs at least seven people who subscribe their names to the charter and bylaws of the proposed company and who each subscribe to purchase at least one share in the proposed company. There is no upper limit on the number of shareholders for the public company. The memorandum and articles of association are filed with the Registrar of Companies. Upon approval the Registrar issues a certificate of incorporation. Following the date of incorporation, a return gives details of shares allotted, names of directors and managers, and the location of the company registered office. In addition a public company must hold a statutory meeting of its shareholders and file the required report and a prospectus with the Registrar. There are no restrictions as to nationality or residence of additional shareholders. Nonresidents must receive Exchange control approval for purchase of shares (4).

A company may have different classes of stock, for example common or ordinary shares, preferred stock or redeemable preferred shares. The shares may be freely transferred. A prospectus that contains company details and terms of the offer is required for sale of shares or debentures. Company boards of directors must consist of at least three directors for a public company two of whom must reside in Fiji or for a private company at least two directors, one of whom resides in Fiji. A company secretary who is resident in Fiji must be appointed for each company. Annual meetings of shareholders must be held. Such meetings need not be in Fiji. Each shareholder has the right of one vote and is entitled to attend the general meeting or appoint a proxy to attend and vote for the shareholder.

At the annual general meeting, directors must present a directors' report, an income statement and balance sheet together with the auditors' report, if one has been made. Information in the accounting records and reports must comply with the Companies Act provisions. The law requires that each shareholder must be sent a copy of the accounting reports with supporting documentation. There are no limitations on revaluation of assets or on the payment of dividends. An annual return must be filed with the Registrar of Companies with details on share capital, indebtedness, shareholder listings with details of share transfers and updated information on directors and company secretary. A copy of the most recent audited financial statements must accompany this return.

Every company in Fiji must maintain proper books of account in English. These records must allow reports to be drawn that disclose a true and fair view of company affairs. In particular, the books must disclose all money sums received and expended together with source or purpose, sales and purchases of goods and all company assets and liabilities. They must also include a register of debentures, a register of charges, a register of members of the company, minute books of shareholder and directors' meetings, a register of company directors and secretaries, and a register of shareholdings of company directors (chapter 11, 2).

An authorized officer residing in Fiji must be designated as the company representative who is responsible for carrying out all duties and obligations of the company under the Fiji Tax Act. Such designation must be reported to the Commissioner of Inland Revenue (5).

Every public company and private company whose shares are held by a public company must appoint independent auditors each year at the annual meeting of shareholders and must have the accounts of the company audited. Foreign companies that establish a place of business in Fiji must, within 30 days of such commencement, register as a branch of a foreign company with the Registrar of Companies. The branch is required to file annual reports in the same manner as a Fiji corporation (KPMG International, 2001a, 3). A private company is not required to appoint independent auditors unless required in company articles of incorporation. The Registrar of Companies at his own discretion may require an auditor to be appointed for a private company.

The independent auditor must hold a certificate of public practice from the Fiji Institute of Accountants (Price Waterhouse Coopers, 2000, Doing Business and Investing in: Fiji, 1997, chapter 9, 6). Auditors' duties are set forth in the Companies Act of 1983. The Act does not specify audit practices or procedures that must be used. The company auditor is granted the right of access at all times to accounting and other records as well as the right to have company officers provide records and information necessary in the course of the audit (chapter 11, 3).

Reporting for financial accounting purposes is not required to conform to tax reporting requirements. The tax authorities do not require that audited financial statements be submitted with the income tax returns. Where such audited statements are available, they are commonly submitted with the tax return (4).

The Fiji Institute of Accountants was established in 1972 as the professional accountant's body. Accountants with qualifying overseas credentials may be members of the Institute. Local qualifications for membership require the completion of a degree course at the University of the South Pacific in Suva and requisite practical experience.

The Institute is an associate member of the International Accounting Standards Committee and a member of the Confederation of Asian and Pacific Accountants. The Institute is responsible for the issuance of accounting standards and statements of auditing practice. International Accounting Standards, standards from the United Kingdom, Australia and New Zealand are also acceptable in Fiji where the Institute does not provide guidance. The Institute's auditing practice statements are comparable to the International Auditing Standards. Both Fiji auditing and accounting standards are contained in the members' handbook (chapter 12, 1).

Fiji accounting standards are similar to International Accounting Standards. The Institute being an associate member of the International Accounting Standards Committee can be expected to be fully cognizant of the trend to harmonization of national accounting standards with the international standards. And, it can be expected to adopt or harmonize its standards accordingly (6).

PAPUA NEW GUINEA

Papua New Guinea attained independence in 1975. A constitution was adopted that inaugurated a parliamentary democracy based on the Westminster model but with one chamber. Local government councils and provincial governments in 19 provinces have constitutions similar to the national constitution. Most provincial funding consists largely of grants from the national government. Most of the provincial governments also operate businesses within their province (Price Waterhouse Coopers,

2000, Doing Business and Investing in: Papua New Guinea, 1998, chapter 1).

The country's laws are based on the common-law system of England and Australia. The Supreme Court of Appeal sits in the capital, Port Moresby. Business and commercial laws are also based on the English and Australian systems. However, the 1997 Companies Act was based largely on New Zealand and Canadian laws. Population totals are ap proximately 3.9 million with 85 percent living in rural areas in clan or village communities. There has been a marked drift of population toward urban areas in recent years. The road network is in the early stages of development so that most travel is by air or sea (chapter 1).

The official language of business and government is English. Pidgin is the language understood and used by a majority. An estimated 52 percent of adults are literate. Education is not compulsory in Papua New Guinea, and only about 73 percent of children attended school in 1996. High schools enrolled about 12 percent of those eligible. Subsistence agriculture is the principal economic activity of most of the country's citizens. In the 1970s the cash economy grew rapidly as a result of development of primary export industries and expanding public services. By the 1990s the economy was relatively static as resource prices turned down. The effects of the Asian financial crisis of the late 1990s resulted in loss of the logging export market.

The currency unit is the kina for which the rate of exchange is based on a basket of currencies of the country's major trading partners. The kina has declined in value significantly since October 1994 when it was floated (chapter 1).

The economy is based on the market system and private enterprise. Agriculture, mining and petroleum are the largest segments of the economy. Overseas investors own most of the larger industrial and commercial enterprises in whole or in part. Investments by nationals are primarily in agriculture. The stated aim of government policy is to increase local ownership either in the private sector or lacking that, by government-owned or -controlled companies. This policy is being carried out by taking minority shareholdings in major agricultural, mining and industrial projects, among other actions. The government hopes that this will be a better approach to fostering local economic development through local ownership and local participation in businesses. If private parties cannot accomplish this, then the government has shown that it is willing to take control in economic sectors where necessary to bring about its aims and the desired types of development (chapter 2).

Both labor and government welcome foreign investment as a means to create employment opportunities and economic development. There has not been a movement toward nationalization. Government policy is to use government corporations in priority areas where private investment is not available. The government tends to enter into partnerships with foreign investors who can provide necessary skills in the areas considered to be in the national interest.

The government has set aside certain prescribed business areas that may only be owned and operated by local citizens or by nationally owned business units. Most major development projects involve the public sector as a joint venture with private investors providing both project management and the largest investment. Few in the local labor market have the necessary education and skills for senior management positions. A training levy has been implemented that is designed to encourage employers to devote a percentage of payrolls for training local citizens. There are no specific general trade barriers but local handicrafts and crops are protected by import restrictions (chapter 2).

Foreign investments in addition to being subject to all local business, company and other laws are specifically supervised by government departments. Goods, primarily food items, that affect the cost of living of local citizens are subject to price controls. The Department of Finance regulates imports and exports. Specific industry legislation has been enacted for a wide range of businesses, such as banking, copra, forestry, insurance, mining and petroleum (chapter 6).

Foreign corporations may establish business in the country by means of a branch, which must be registered with the Registrar of Companies of Papua New Guinea. Documents required include a certified copy of the proof of incorporation of the overseas corporation; a certified copy of the corporation's charter, articles of incorporation or like documents; details of all corporation directors; principal place of overseas company's business outside Papua New Guinea; and a designated person within Papua New Guinea authorized to receive documents in behalf of the overseas company. When registered, the branch must comply with the requirements of the Company Act, and annual reports must be filed with the Registrar. The reports must include annual audited financial statements for both the branch and the parent overseas companies. Company information filed with the Registrar must be kept up to date as to a number of particulars including corporate directors, shareholders, numbers of full-time and part-time employees and the resident agent.

Other forms of business organization permitted in Papua New Guinea are also similar to those encountered in other countries of the world. A sole proprietor may operate a business albeit with unlimited liability. Partnerships may be formed for most business purposes. Partners have unlimited liability to third parties for partnership obligations. The partnership agreement and the Partnership Act govern the relationships of the partners. If the business name is different than the names of persons in the partnership, the partnership name must be registered with the Registrar of Companies. If partnerships or sole proprietorships do not have a principal residence in the country, an agent who is a resident must be appointed. Joint ventures are permitted to be organized as either partnerships or corporations and must adhere to the appropriate regulations (chapter 9).

The Companies Act of 1998 permits single individuals to register a corporation, either alone or with others. A company limited by shares is the form commonly chosen by incorporators. Liability of the shareholders is limited to paid-in or subscribed capital contributions. Other forms permitted but not often used are companies with liability limited by guarantee, with liability limited by both shares and guarantee and companies with unlimited liability. Limited (or Ltd) must appear in the name of all companies. The Act provides that a company may either be an exempt company or a reporting company. An exempt company may not have more than K 5 million in assets at any time. It may have at most 25 shareholders and no more than 100 employees. A reporting company is designated as any other company except an exempt company. Reporting companies include an overseas company or a subsidiary or branch of a foreign corporation. The reporting company category also includes an issuer company that allots shares by registered prospectus and has no less than 25 shareholders. An overseas company or an issuer company may not own an exempt company (chapter 9).

Incorporation filings with the Registrar of Companies must include a corporation registration application; specifics on each proposed director with a certificate that each is qualified for appointment; specifics on each subscribing shareholder indicating the class and number of shares subscribed; proof of reservation of the company name; specifics about the company secretary, if any; and a proposed constitution, if any. The public may inspect all documents filed with the Registrar.

Although optional, company constitutions are required for certain corporate actions to be taken. Among these are issuances of more than one class of shares, the right to indemnify directors, and the authority to repurchase shares or to provide financing for purchase of the company's own shares. When the Registrar believes that all aspects of the Companies Act have been complied with, a certificate of incorporation is issued (chapter 9).

The Securities Act governs public issuance of stock or debt instruments. Prior to offering shares or debentures to the public, a proper prospectus must be issued and filed with the Registrar. There is no limit on the number of shares that can be sold. The issuance of no-par shares is not permitted. Nor can a nominal share value be used. Common, preferred and redeemable preferred shares are allowed if the company constitution permits. Unless restrictions are made in the constitution, shares may be transferred freely. If transfer of shares will be to nonresidents, the Investment Promotion Authority must approve. There is no established securities market in the country.

The Act provides that a corporation may not hold the shares of its parent or holding company. The company's own shares may be repurchased or the company may give financing to purchase its own shares, if allowed in the company constitution (chapter 9).

Shareholders at a general meeting are responsible for electing company directors, who then are responsible for company operations. At least one member of the board of directors must be a natural person who resides in Papua New Guinea. Each director must inform the board of directors of any interests the director has in company shares or in transactions with the company. At their option, company directors may appoint a company secretary. Directors should have one vote each as is the usual practice. Meetings of directors are not regulated in the statute but minute books of all directors' and shareholders' meetings must be kept and must be signed by the meeting chairperson.

Meetings of shareholders may be the annual general meeting or special meetings. There must be a general meeting held each calendar year but no later than six months after the balance sheet date nor later than 15 months after the prior general meeting. Special meetings require shareholder notice including specification of the nature of the business to be considered. In the annual general meeting, shareholders generally receive the annual accounts and the directors' report on the annual accounts. They also hold election of directors, appoint company auditors and declare any dividends for the year.

Auditors who are elected are required to agree to the appointment in writing. Exempt companies or other classes of companies exempted by the Registrar after giving notice in the National Gazette are not required to appoint auditors. Company auditors must carry out their duties in accordance with the Companies Act. Such duties may not be restricted by contract with the company or company shareholders.

Shortly after the annual meeting, the company must file its annual return with the Registrar of Companies together with a copy of the audited financial statements for the year, and a company declaration of company solvency. Details of shareholders, directors, registered charges among other matters must be included in the annual report to the registrar (chapter 9).

Before declaring dividends, a company must meet a solvency test. That is, it must be able to pay all debts as they come due in the ordinary course of business and the value of company assets must be larger than all stated and contingent liabilities.

The Companies Act specifies that books of accounting must be kept that will correctly record and explain company transactions. Such records must allow the financial position of the company to be determined within reasonable accuracy and must enable the company financial statements to be properly audited. Financial statements are required to be in compliance with generally accepted accounting practice (chapter 11).

Accounting records must be maintained in written form or be readily converted into written form. The current and prior 10 completed accounting period records must ordinarily be housed at the company's registered Papua New Guinea office. If company records are housed overseas, sufficient records must be sent to the registered office at intervals not to exceed six months. In addition to the books of account, other required company records must be maintained in similar fashion, including shareholders registers, minute books and the like (chapter 11).

The auditor must complete the company audit within five months after the statement date. Each shareholder must be sent an annual report that includes the audited financial statements at least seven days before the annual shareholders' meeting.

The Parliament granted the Accountants Registration Board of Papua New Guinea authority to regulate accountancy practice in Papua New Guinea, to determine qualifications of accountants to be registered, to register qualified accountants, and after registration to oversee as necessary the activities of the accountants. The Act empowered the board to adopt standards and rules it deems necessary to control the accountancy profession. The Board has drawn up rules only for the minimum registration qualifications for those persons applying to practice accounting in Papua New Guinea for a fee (chapter 11).

The Papua New Guinea Association of Accountants promotes the profession and its interests. The membership of the Association is said to come from suitably qualified local accountants and expatriates.

Neither the Accountants Registration Board nor the Association has codified auditing procedures or standards to be used in the country. In practice, auditors follow the International Auditing Guidelines (chapter 11).

The Companies Act requires auditors to give details in their report if the company under audit does not follow the requirements of the Act. The Companies Act of 1997 established a Papua New Guinea Accounting Standards Board. Financial statements prepared for distribution and reported on by accounting firms must conform to International Accounting Standards approved by the Accounting Standards Board. Some exceptions are available for exempt companies. The statements must include a balance sheet, profit and loss account, statement of cash flow, notes to the financial statements, and a statement of movements in equity.

By 1998, Papua New Guinea had adopted 32 of the 34 International Accounting Standards then available. In addition, three local standards were issued: PNG Accounting Standard No. 1, Profit and Loss statement; PNG Accounting Standard No. 2, Materiality in financial statements and

PNG Accounting Standard No. 3, Accounting for plantations (chapter 12).

Association members who have responsibilities for financial statements are required to apply the accounting standards adopted by the Association. Material departures from the promulgated standards of the Association call for disclosure and reference in the audit report. Should the auditor consider the departure to be unjustified and that the financial statements do not present a true and fair view, the report should be qualified. Any qualified audit report must be filed with the Registrar within seven days of completion (chapter 12).

VANUATU

Vanuatu consists of a chain of 80 islands covering 12,189 square miles and is situated 1,750 km northeast of Sydney, Australia. Ten of the islands have 90 percent of the total land area. British and French settled the New Hebrides islands in the nineteenth century and from 1906 the islands were administered as an Anglo-French Condominium (CIA, 2001, 2).

After 74 years of joint British and French rule, Vanuatu received independence in 1980 with the founding of the Republic. The country is a full member of the British Commonwealth, the French League of Nations, the United Nations as well as other world and regional bodies. The Asian Development Bank maintains regional headquarters in Port Vila (Moores Rowland, September 30, 1997, 2).

The Constitution provides for a parliamentary democracy with the president of the Republic as Head of State. The president is elected for a five-year term by the Electoral College, which is made up of all members of Parliament and the presidents of the regional councils, also known as the National Council of Chiefs. This Council also advises the government on matters of custom and land.

The unicameral legislative body, the Parliament, has 52 members elected for four-year terms. The prime minister is elected by the Parliament from its membership and is usually the leader of the majority party or majority coalition (2). There are at least four political parties plus independents represented in the Parliament. Political party affiliations are fluid and between the 1995 elections and 2000 there were four changes of government (CIA, 2001c, 5).

The country's judiciary consists of a magistrate's court and the Supreme Court headed by a Chief Justice. The Supreme Court may adjudicate all matters as a final court of appeal (Moores Rowland, September 30, 1997, 2). The president appoints the chief justice of the Supreme Court after consultations with the prime minister and the leader of the opposition. The president appoints the three other Supreme Court justices after consultation with the Judicial Service Commission (CIA, 2001, 5). The Vanuatu legal system is based on English law (KPMG International, 2001b, 2).

There are ten ministries with 40 departments in the central government. Various local areas of the country have local councils (CIA, 2001c, 2). The country is divided into the six provinces of Malampa, Penama, Sanma, Shefa, Tafea and Torba (4).

Although Vanuatu maintains a Permanent Mission to the United Nations, it does not have an embassy in the United States. Nor does the United States have an embassy in Vanuatu. The U.S. ambassador to Papua New Guinea is accredited to Vanuatu (CIA, 2001c, 5).

The population, which is predominantly Melanesian, was estimated at nearly 195,000 people in April 2001, with 35,000 residing in the capital, Port Vila (KPMG International, 2001b, 1). A majority of the population lacks access to a reliable supply of potable water. Life expectancy at birth is an average of 60.57 for the total population, or 59.23 years for males and 61.98 years for females. Over three quarters of the populace are Christians of various affiliations. There are 7.7 percent who have indigenous beliefs with the remainder holding other belief systems (CIA, 2001c, 2).

The official languages are English and French. Pidgin, also known as Bislama or Bichelama, is also spoken and is considered a national language. The literacy rate of the total population is estimated at 53 percent. Per capita GDP was estimated at $1,300 for 1999. The GDP was composed of 63 percent from services, 24 percent from agriculture and 13 percent from industry. The labor force was employed: 65 percent in agriculture, 32 percent in services and 3 percent in industry. The inflation rate in 1998 was estimated at 3.9 percent (6).

In 1986 the Parliament enacted the Companies Act that was modeled on the U.K. Companies Law. In 1992 an International Companies Act was passed that was modeled on the Bahamian and British Virgin Islands laws. These acts form the basis for regulation and governance of business organizations, both those that operate in the domestic economy and those that operate overseas (Diamond and Diamond, 2000, 18).

Small-scale agriculture provides a subsistence living for 65 percent of the populace. The mainstays of the small cash economy are fishing, offshore financial services and tourism. Approximately 50,000 visitors came to Vanuatu in 1997. Mineral deposits are negligible and the islands have no known oil sources. Small light industries sell their products primarily on the local market. Contributing to economic difficulties are long distances from international goods markets, relatively few export commodities and vulnerability to natural disasters. All have hindered economic growth. A severe earthquake followed by a tsunami occurred in November 1999, for example, causing extensive damage and leaving thousands homeless on the northern island of Pentecote (6).

Most of the industrial output is food and fish freezing, wood processing and meat canning. Agriculture export commodities consist of copra, beef, cocoa, timber and coffee, with copra being the most important. There are approximately 69,000 hectares of land devoted to coconut plantations. Exports totaled $33.8 million in 1998. Exports went 32 percent to Japan, 14 percent to Germany, 8 percent to Spain, 7 percent to New Caledonia and 2 percent to Australia. Imports are reported at $76.2 million in 1998. Imports came 52 percent from Japan, 20 percent from Australia, and smaller amounts from New Caledonia, Singapore, New Zealand and France (7).

The vatu is the country's currency. The value of the vatu is tied to a regional basket of currencies. Vanuatu does not have exchange controls. Funds can be held and transferred across the country's borders freely without seeking government approval and there are no restrictions regardless of the purpose for which the transactions are undertaken. Money can be freely invested and repatriated. Vatu exchange rates against the U.S. dollar were 129.76 to $1 in 1999, 127.5 in 1998, 115.87 in 1997, 111.72 in 1996 and 112.11 in 1995 (7).

The Vanuatu banking system consists of a Reserve Bank, the National Bank of Vanuatu, many international commercial banks, merchant banks, and a state-owned development bank. There is also a large offshore banking center. Most of the international commercial banks are authorized to conduct business both offshore with nonresidents and within Vanuatu, including with residents. Thus there is a global network of banks serving the islands and the offshore center (Moores Rowland, 2001, 3).

Beginning in the 1970s commercial laws were introduced that have added new economic dimensions. The laws were enacted to provide the infrastructure for development of offshore finance and banking activities. There followed a rapid increase of professionals and other support organizations in the capital city of Port Vila (2).

Although KPMG reports that government revenues mainly come from "custom import duties and a Value Added Tax (VAT) (KPMG International, 2001b, 2), the expanded offshore finance center does produce considerable government revenue because of the payment of business license fees, insurance, banking and trust company licenses, annual registration fees for all companies, stamp duties and other fees. These activities have been significant in providing foreign exchange to the country. The government places high priority on development of the offshore business and development of tourism in the country from which turnover taxes on hotels, licensed premises and casinos all produce government revenue. All forms of betting, albeit under strict controls, are permitted in Vanuatu (Moores Rowland, 2001, 2).

Incorporations in Vanuatu can be made using any recognized world currency. The country welcomes all forms of foreign investment so long as it contributes to the Vanuatu economy. There are no government restrictions on the maximum percentage of foreign ownership an entity may have. Most businesses are reported to be foreign owned (3). Another factor that adds to the appeal of the country is that no taxes are levied on capital gains, on personal income or on corporate income. There are no gift, estate or succession taxes. There are also no withholding taxes or double-taxation agreements with other countries (3). In fact, Vanuatu has no tax treaties with any other country (KPMG, 2001, 2).

Vanuatu does not restrict exports. And export duties are low. Full exemption from customs duties may be granted for favored projects both on capital goods and construction materials imported during start up and on raw materials or manufactured goods which are not locally available, so long as the product will be re-exported (CIA, 2001c, 3).

Entities which are formed for the purpose of conducting local business in Vanuatu are authorized by the Companies Act to use the following forms of business: sole proprietorship, partnership, branch of a foreign corporation, discretionary or unit trusts and local corporation. All businesses must obtain a business license in accordance with the Business Licenses Act. A proprietorship need not register the business name with a government agency so long as the business name is the name of the owner. Should this not be the case, under the Business Names Act, the proprietorship must register the business name with the Commissioner of Financial Services. Proprietorship owners have unlimited liability for business obligations (Price Waterhouse, 1992b, 42). There is no separate form of business for joint ventures in Vanuatu. Such affiliations may take any of the other acceptable forms for business entities.

Partnerships may be formed under the Partnership Regulation of 1975. They may be general or limited. In the general partnership, all partners have unlimited liability for partnership obligations. Whereas in the limited partnership, some partners may be considered limited partners whose liability for partnership obligations is limited to their contributions to the partnership. All partnerships must have at least one general partner. A limited partnership may not have more than 20 partners. Any limited partner is not authorized to withdraw his contributions during the life of the partnership and may not take part in partnership management. Limited partners may be natural persons or corporations. Limited partnerships must file with the Commissioner of Financial Services (Moores Rowland, 2001, 4).

Finance and business activities may be carried out by means of a trust. Assets can be transferred by means of a trust deed to a trustee who will administer the assets for the benefit of named beneficiaries. The trust need not be filed with a government agency. Nor are results of the trust administration required to be reported to government authorities (45).

A foreign company may establish a branch designed to conduct business in the domestic economy. A permit from the Finance Minister is required. A certified copy of the company Charter and Memorandum of Association written in English or French must be submitted with an application which indicates the nature and purpose of the business to be carried on in Vanuatu. The names of directors and the secretary of the company with information about their occupations and other corporate directorships must be provided with the application. The names and addresses of two natural persons resident in Vanuatu and authorized to accept documents and to act on behalf of the branch must be submitted with an application which indicates the nature and purpose of the business to be included. Once in operation, the parent overseas company must file branch annual reports with the Minister of Finance (Diamond and Diamond, 2001, 27).

There are three different classes of corporations that can be registered in Vanuatu, namely a local company, an overseas company and an exempt company. Any of these may be public or private companies. In a public company, at least seven shareholders and two directors are required. The minimum number of shareholders in a private company is two with a maximum of 50 shareholders permitted. Only one director is needed for a private company. Just one shareholder is needed when a private company is owned entirely by another corporation (42).

The local company form permits business to be conducted in the local domestic economy. Neither an overseas company nor an exempt company may conduct business within the local domestic economy. The overseas company is permitted to carry on business only outside of Vanuatu. An exempted company may carry on business only outside the country but such offshore activities may be directed from within Vanuatu (42).

The local company must obtain a business license from the Ministry of Finance prior to transacting business in the domestic economy. The company must be registered with the Commissioner of Financial Services together with required documentation in order to be incorporated (42). When a local corporation is formed to carry on normal trading business within the country, some offshore company provisions do not apply. The local company's file with the Commissioner of Financial Services is open for public inspection. If local company sales exceed the equivalent US $200,000, audited financial statements must be submitted to the Commissioner of Financial Services (Moores Rowland, 2001, 4).

The minister of finance grants a permit to operate an overseas company and incorporation when articles of incorporation and all related materials have been properly filed. At least two residents of Vanuatu must be agents in residence for the overseas company. The overseas company must file annual reports with the Commissioner of Financial Services but such statements do not require an audit (38, 42).

An exempted company must maintain a registered office in Vanuatu. The company must have at least one shareholder. One director and a corporate secretary are also required. All filings and documents pertaining to an exempted company are barred from public disclosure. An annual report must be filed with the Commissioner of Financial Services but it does not require audit (39).

All companies are required to maintain records and books of account such that a true and fair report can be made which explains the company's operations, financial condition and its transactions. These records must be maintained at the registered office of the company in Vanuatu. An exempt company may keep its accounting records overseas and may keep these records in any currency and in any language (Diamond and Diamond, 2000, 25).

All public companies and all private companies with sales that are over VT 2 million are required to appoint an auditor and to undergo an annual audit of their financial reports. The shareholders at their annual meeting make the appointment. Companies that operate under licenses for banking, trusts and insurance, including exempt companies, must also have their financials audited (40).

Most accountants in public practice in Vanuatu are members of the Institute of Chartered Accountants in Australia or of the New Zealand Society of Accountants with the Australian group being the largest. Vanuatu has not promulgated accounting or auditing standards. So long as the requirements of the Companies Act and the International Companies Act are upheld, companies are free to choose accounting practices and standards (53).

In practice, auditors are selected who are well qualified in another country, chiefly Australia or New Zealand. These professional accountants must uphold the accounting, auditing and ethical standards set by their professional organizations. Therefore, Vanuatu companies commonly follow the accepted practices and standards in the country in which their auditor is professionally affiliated. It is also common for accountants and auditors to follow International Accounting Standards and International Auditing Guidelines in countries such as Vanuatu where national standards have not been codified.

Part III

International Accounting Firms, Recovery and Growth

Chapter 7

The Role of the Firms among the Asian Tigers

The purpose of the present Chapter is to highlight the circumstances of the four jurisdictions known as the Asian Tigers, as they are fairing in the post-crisis world, and in particular to expose the facilitative role being played by the major international accounting firms. Toward those ends each jurisdiction will be dealt with individually beginning with Hong Kong and continuing with Singapore, South Korea and Taiwan. The implication is hardly that the accounting firms are the major force behind the real or potential recovery of the economies in question but rather on a somewhat less ambitious level that the firms do have services to offer that can impact the economies in a positive way. Since those economies all share an interest in international linkages, the role of the accounting firms in supporting such linkages will be explored.

HONG KONG

In the course of planning the nature and content of the present volume, omitting a discussion of Hong Kong was considered very seriously. The reasons behind such a consideration revolved around Hong Kong's new status as a part of the Peoples Republic of China. There were very real uncertainties with respect to that status, its nature and thus Hong Kong's role in the post 1997 global economy. However, as events have unfolded, it was felt that the omission of Hong Kong would leave a rather serious gap in the analysis.

The New Zealand Trade Development Board in describing Hong Kong's current economic status suggested that the jurisdiction is the world's freest economy (April 1999, 3). Beyond that it has been described as the world's most service-oriented economy and second most-competitive economy (3). Such descriptions in the post-1997 world are rather difficult to ignore. Hong Kong appears to have retained its economic significance.

"Hong Kong continued to rank as the fourth largest in terms of outward foreign direct investment in the world in 1996 . . . only less than that from the US, the UK and Germany" (3). Various developing countries in Southeast Asia have been receiving an increasing amount of capital from Hong Kong. Measured in terms of the cumulative amount on approval basis, Hong Kong is the largest investor in China, and ranks third in Indonesia, Taiwan, Thailand, Vietnam and the Philippines (3). Thus it is clear that Hong Kong has retained its position as an important regional business and financial power.

Indeed the jurisdiction's economy ranked among the world's top seven trading nations in 1997 and "is one of Asia's most dynamic economies with an international reputation as a major manufacturing and commercial center" (5). It possesses a sophisticated commercial infrastructure and is the world's busiest container terminal as well as a major transshipment point for goods traveling to and from China (5). It is well linked to the world's major cities through its telecommunications network.

In 1990 the Asian Tigers were said to "have been among the most spectacular performers in the world economy over the past 25 years, quadrupling their shares of world production and trade" (Noland, 1990, 15). At that time Hong Kong was a virtual city-state, owing a certain measure of its success to entrepot trade. Indeed trade has been central to the Hong Kong economy throughout its history as a British colony, which was founded as a trading outpost of the British Empire in the nineteenth century (Sung, 1988, 184).

However by the 1960s and 1970s Hong Kong had diversified its economy from a reliance upon entrepot trade for practically all of its exports to a position where "it was arguably the world's most dynamic center of light industry" (McKee, Lin and Chen, 1991, referring to *The Economist*, Survey of Hong Kong, 1989, 7). *The Economist* was of the opinion that Hong Kong had become "a minor industrial power in its own right" by the early 1970s (1989, 7). However the dawn of the 1990s found other jurisdictions able to produce various goods more cheaply than Hong Kong (McKee, Lin and Chen, 1991). Light manufacturing activity was shifting to locations within China (1991).

"Assuming a smooth transition in governance in 1997, Hong Kong's role as a catalyst to trade between the international economy and China should insure its ongoing economic vitality" (McKee and Garner, 1996b, 21). At the time that that prediction was made the Asian crisis had not emerged. The colony was described as an international financial center and a supplier of services to the international business community (21). That role generated some optimism since it was felt that through maintaining those functions, Hong Kong could be instrumental in strengthening trans-Pacific linkages as China expands its dealings with the developed world (21). Events appear to have supported that optimism where Hong Kong is concerned.

Hong Kong's manufacturing sector is led by various light manufacturing industries such as clothing, textiles, electronics, watches, clocks and plastics (New Zealand Trade Development Board, April 1999, 5). The production facilities for those industries are located in Special Economic Zones (SEZ's) in mainland China in order to take advantage of lower production costs. Beyond the light industries cited "There is also a well-established, albeit small, heavy industrial sector comprising shipbuilding and repair, aircraft engineering, and iron and steel rolling" (April 1999, 5). Manufacturers in Hong Kong are moving toward more sophisticated product lines, including consumer electronics and components for electronic and electrical industries.

Manufacturing activities notwithstanding, Hong Kong is predominantly a service economy and in 1996 nearly 85 percent of GDP was generated by services (KPMG, November 1998a). Trading services have been growing and Hong Kong has been a net exporter of services (New Zealand Trade Development Board, April 1999, 5). Indeed the surplus from trade in services increased by 6.5 percent in the first half of 1997 according to preliminary figures (5).

Not surprisingly, business-related services have been very significant in the service expansion. For example financial and business services which includes banking, insurance, real estate and a broad range of other professional services have enjoyed rapid expansion (6). Indeed, "Hong Kong's strategic location and its excellent communications network and efficient infrastructure has made it a hub for trade, finance and business services in the region" (6).

Certainly Hong Kong can be expected to be the ongoing host for various major international accounting firms. Such firms can be expected to provide many services to business clients with respect to dealings between China and the global economy. Bavishi (1991, 424) has reported that the Asia Pacific region is dominated by four major firms: Ernst & Young International, Coopers and Lybrand, Klynveld Peat Marwick and Goerdeler, and DRT International (Deloitte Ross Tohmatsu). Bavishi saw the growth of international accounting firms as closely related to the globalization of capital markets and suggested that "As investors worldwide increasingly invest in foreign securities, more comprehensive financial statements will be required, resulting in an increased demand for the auditing and other services of international accounting firms" (428).

Although what he has suggested has been occurring, it has been said that he has understated the international forces driving the growth and territorial expansion of the firms (McKee and Garner, 1996b, 85). "Through a wide range of service offerings, both traditional and new, they have joined the ranks of various service enterprises that are facilitating international business operations while also adding strength to the various domestic economies touched by their endeavors" (85). Hong Kong seems assured of an ongoing role in hosting major international accounting firms. Bavishi identified 192 partners, 147 of whom were members of the six largest firms (1991, Appendix B, 14).

Price Waterhouse Coopers professes to be the largest provider of professional business and financial advising services in Hong Kong, boasting more than 110 partners and a staff of 2,300 (November 1998). The firm claims to have both the commitment and the resources to provide an unmatched range of professional advice in Hong Kong, which they describe as the crossroads of Asia and the natural gateway to China (November 1998).

The firm in Hong Kong serves the major industries in the Asia Pacific region. "Our professional industry assurance and business advisory teams work alongside colleagues from management consulting and tax and legal services to deliver industry-focused solutions across all disciplines" (1999a). The firm focuses on 22 market sectors, organized into five key business units. The five units include financial services, technology, information, communications and entertainment industry, energy and mining, consumer/industrial products and property construction and development (1999a).

Among services offered by the firm are those related to assurance and business advisory, including assurance or compliance services, transaction support services, initial public offerings, global risk-management solutions and client accounting and audit of small and medium-sized entities (1999b). The firm also offers tax and legal services, financial advisory services and management consulting services (1999b).

Kreston International is another major accounting organization that is active in Hong Kong. The organization comprises a worldwide network of independent accounting firms. "The Kreston network has been established to facilitate the need of international companies to find reliable accounting services in the countries where their business is conducted" (Kreston International, 1999a).

Each firm in the network is independent and thus solely responsible for its work, its staff and its clients. "To insure local knowledge and understanding of current business laws, customs and conditions and their fiscal implications, international assignments will be coordinated by the Kreston firm in the client's country of origin" (1999a). Such assignments are completed by accountants who are nationals of the jurisdiction where the business is being housed. Kreston has member firms in Hong Kong, Korea, Singapore and Taiwan.

The network offers a wide range of services to its clients. Included are the usual auditing, accountancy, preparation of accounts and bookkeeping (1999b). It also does taxation compliance work for both companies and individuals, and taxation planning and consultancy for individuals, companies and other corporate bodies. It can advise companies on potential acquisitions and mergers, and on raising finance, as well as on offering their shares to the public and on selection or purchase of computers together with appropriate software and hardware (1999b).

It also deals with corporate recovery, insolvency, liquidations and receiverships (1999b). It can offer investment advice and actually manage investment portfolios. It offers consultancy on companies' internal systems and controls and assists with business and strategic planning. It can help with the recruitment of staff for clients, with company secretarial work, business valuations and personal financial planning (1999b). Clearly Kreston International has a service menu that compares favorably to those of the largest international accounting firms.

KPMG Peat Marwick is also active in Hong Kong, offering a service menu that includes auditing and accounting, taxation, management consulting, corporate financial secrecy, corporate services, management assurance services and executive search and selection (KPMG, November 1998b, 2). The firm is very involved in Hong Kong and quite cognizant of the ongoing significance of that jurisdiction. "As an important world financial center, Hong Kong has been a player in the global economy for decades, serving as a gateway to the entire Asia Pacific region" (KPMG, November 1998c).

KPMG suggests that thousands of international businesses have a valid interest in Hong Kong's change in status (November 1998c). "With a well established practice in Hong Kong and four burgeoning offices in China, KPMG will be among those businesses that feel the effects firsthand" (November 1998c). As seen by Marvin Cheung, KPMG's Senior Partner in Hong Kong, the jurisdiction "is attracting a lot of interest from mainland enterprises. They all want to establish a presence here and use it as a base for access to foreign capital, foreign stock exchanges and foreign investors" (November 1998c). Cheung predicted that that trend would accelerate after Hong Kong's return to China.

KPMG was one of the first accounting firms to enter the Chinese market (November 1998c). According to Cheung, "We have managed to look after our multinational clients in China satisfactorily and we have quite a good track record dealing with mainland Chinese enterprises as well" (November 1998c). He hopes that the firm can build on those foundations. Beyond an ongoing influx of mainland businesses, he sees only minor changes in the operation of the firm's business in Hong Kong.

It seems clear that Hong Kong continues to maintain its position as a major trading and financial center. It functions as a window on the world for China. Whatever fears may have been generated by its change in status appear to have been overpowered by its role in the region and beyond. Clearly the major accounting firms have a role in its ongoing success. By facilitating business dealings through it with China and by assisting multinational firms in their global dealings they serve to strengthen the local business service sector and contribute to Hong Kong's ongoing claim to be a major entrepot and offshore financial center.

SINGAPORE

As early as 1988 Singapore was recognized as a rather important service provider (Tucker and Sundberg, 1988, 117). "Located at the hub of South-East Asia along strategic waterways and lacking any significant natural resource endowments Singapore has developed as a regional centre, providing many services to neighboring countries" (117). The nation has also opted to encourage manufacturing for export (McKee and Garner, 1996b, 21).

Marcus Noland has reported the nation's progress in electronics and chemical industries and its attempts at attracting foreign direct investment in various additional sophisticated manufacturing activities (1990, 24). Noland thought that the nation might well gain from the contemplated changes in Hong Kong, citing efforts on the part of the government to encourage the nation's development as the international financial center of Southeast Asia, as an alternative to Hong Kong (26).

That Singapore has adopted an international perspective seems hardly surprising. "After its emergence early in the nineteenth century it quickly became a major link between Europe and Asia" (McKee and Garner, 1996b, 22). Its location at the entrance to the Straits of Malaca gave it a strategic significance. Thus it became significant both as a port for merchant shipping and as a naval base. As Elegant has pointed out it was "the chief Western stronghold in Asia" at the outset of World War II (1990, 172). He saw Singapore as unique among trading nations since, by 1987, its exports surpassed its gross domestic product and its total trade surpassed its domestic output of goods and services by a factor of three (176). Beyond its role as a regional processing center Singapore was a port for the Malaysian peninsula (176). According to Elegant its prosperity was based upon electronics, oil and entrepot trade (192).

Since gaining its independence from Great Britain in 1965 the nation has been a parliamentary republic. It possesses a common law legal system based largely upon English statutes. According to the New Zealand Trade Development Board the nation has the highest per capita GDP among all ASEAN countries (April 1998, 3). With a population of 3.1 million, the nation boasted a GDP at US $75 billion and an annual growth rate in GDP of 7.8 percent (1).

"Singapore companies are involved in many projects in South East Asia and Indo China" (3). Finance and business services account for 28 percent of GDP in 1997, followed by manufacturing at 26 percent, commerce at 20 percent, transport and communications at 12 percent and construction at 7 percent (3). The nation's major exports include machinery and equipment, mineral fuels, manufactured goods and chemicals (3). Its major export markets were the United States at 18 percent, Malaysia at 17 percent, Europe at 14 percent, Hong Kong at 9.6 percent and Japan at 7.1 percent (4).

The nation's "manufacturing sector is dominated by the production of electrical and electronic producers" (4). Other industries include transport equipment, petroleum products, fabricated metal products, paints, pharmaceuticals and other chemical products and printing and publishing (4–5).

Despite the financial and economic difficulties that emerged in the Asian region beginning in 1997, the New Zealand Trade Development Board found some basis for optimism in its 1998 assessment of prospects for Singapore. "Businesses that sell final products to the OECD markets, with revenues denominated in U.S. dollars should remain relatively healthy despite the regional slowdown" (7). The Board predicted continuing health for the manufacturing sector, supported by a growth in demand for electronics on the part of the United States and the European Union (7).

The Board was less optimistic vis-à-vis service offerings—"the hub-related services will be affected by the regional economic slowdown" (7). Retail trade was seen as remaining sluggish as a result of weak consumer sentiments and declines in visitor arrivals (7). "After almost a decade of continuous growth, the Singapore economy slid into technical recession in 1998, affected by events in Asia" (British Club, January, 1999). However, the British Club predicted a rapid recovery. It saw the nation's traditional strong sectors as including entrepot trade and shipping, and financial and business services and noted manufacturing and construction as key sectors as well (2).

It appears as though the nation has suffered as a result of the financial and economic difficulties that struck the Asian Pacific region in 1997 but that its functions in the global economy should underwrite its economic future. The nation's government seems willing to generate policies to support and encourage its international role.

According to a report issued by the state of Hawaii, "The development of Singapore as an international financial center and the regionalization of local operations to counter inherent internal limits to growth are major objectives of the government" (State of Hawaii, 1999, 1). That same report goes on to outline the nation's strategy for addressing competitive challenges. Included were increasing productivity, upgrading skills, improving infrastructure capabilities and offering a wide array of incentives to attract higher value-added industries providing leading-edge technologies (1999, 1). Although it seems doubtful that Singapore will successfully eclipse the role of Hong Kong, the nation should maintain a significant role in the global economy.

According to Walter and Dorothy Diamond (1998, 22), Singapore's growth rate was among the highest in the world, averaging 9 percent from 1988 to 1997, until the Asian currency crisis emerged. They pointed out that financial and business services were contributing more to the economy than manufacturing. The latter sector was contributing 28 percent of income, with wholesaling and retailing accounting for 20 percent in equal proportions. Commodity shipments accounted for roughly 25 percent, entrepot trade 10 percent and tourism 13 percent (1998, 22).

Singapore has also become a significant financial and business center (McKee, Garner and McKee, 2000). Indeed the nation has been seen as the banking center of Southeast Asia for some time (Diamond and Diamond, 1998, 26). It was said to be a sophisticated financial center for the entire region and the second most important financial center in the world (26).

According to Bavishi all of the then–Big Six accounting firms were active in Singapore in 1991. He noted 130 partners associated with the Big Six, and 30 additional partners associated with smaller firms. Among smaller firms represented were BDO, Dunwoody Robson, McGlaney and Pullen, Horwath International, Moores Rowland International, Summit International Associates, Inc. and TGI (1991, Appendix B, 19).

An example of how a major accounting firm might operate in Singapore can be seen in the case of KPMG. KPMG Singapore dates from 1941 and provides an extensive selection of services to both domestic and international clients (KPMG Singapore, 2000a). Services offered include assurance, tax, consulting and financial advisory services (2000a). Of course traditional accounting services are also available. The firm's client list is both domestic and international. "We understand that organizations are facing a range of significant business issues in the global and local marketplace, including information technology strategy, implementation and business transformation" (2000b).

The firm describes its consulting operations in Singapore as providing a range of integrated end-to-end solutions, involving elements of strategy, operations, package implementation, systems integration and outsourcing. Its service offerings cover a wide range of business concerns which include banking and finance consulting, financial management consulting, human resource consulting and information technology consulting. In addition the firm offers business advisory services and assistance with executive search and selection (2000b).

Of course banking and finance consulting is a rather significant service subset in Singapore, a jurisdiction enjoying global importance as an offshore financial center. The firm stands ready to assist with matters concerning banking and finance. More specifically it stands ready to assist with risk management and project management/information technology consulting (2000c). Beyond that it can assist the banking and finance community with market research, surveys, feasibility studies and investigations and can also offer seminars and training (2000c).

KPMG Singapore operates a business advisory group which offers financial and strategic advisory services to business (2000d, 1). Service offerings in that area include financial management advice, strategic management advice and corporate treasury services (2000d, 1–2). In the area of financial management the firm stands ready to assist with the development of effective financial strategy for businesses (2000d, 1). It can also assist with implementing financial and debt-restructuring exercises as well as with enhancing cash-flow management capabilities (2000d, 1). It stands willing to help in the design of effective budgeting and planning processes and in the evaluation of the adequacy of the corporate risk policy (2000d, 1–2). It can also assist with designing comprehensive costing processes.

In the area of strategic management the firm can advise on the formulation of strategic business plans and the development of integrated performance valuation and measurement systems (2000d, 2). It also assists in the implementation of corporate-restructuring programs as well as comprehensive business process improvement exercises (2000d, 2). It is also willing to help with government-assistance schemes (2000d, 2).

Corporate treasury services available from KPMG include the development of comprehensive integrated risk management and control systems and the identification and measurement of financial and nonfinancial risks. The firm can also analyze and value financial portfolios and can assist in conducting treasury risk analyses and developing hedging strategies (2000d, 2).

Moores Rowland International is also active in Singapore. Although not a member of the Big Five it sees itself as "one of the top 10 networks of independent accounting practices in the world" (1998b). It is composed of 140 independent accounting firms in 82 countries (1998b). The network embraces members in every region of the world working to make it both easier and more profitable for their clients to participate in international trade.

The organization offers assistance with business organization and tax structures in foreign countries (1998b). It can also help with due diligence and assurance engagements, and can aid in the acquisition of foreign subsidiaries. It stands prepared to help with legal and banking contracts abroad, as well as with international business information and advice concerning information technology. It also offers foreign market assessments and expert strategies (1998b).

SOUTH KOREA

From the perspective of the mid-1990s, the past performance and future prospects of the Republic of South Korea seemed rather impressive. As was the case with other newly industrialized nations in the region, Korea had cast its vote in the direction of export activities as the basis for its economy. Indeed export activity "Became an integral part of the government's efforts to promote the acquisition of technological capability more generally" (Westphal et al., 1984, 509). As pointed out elsewhere the exports concerned were capital goods and related services (McKee and Garner, 1996b, 81). The promotion of such exports was seen as a way to hasten the development of technology-intensive industries (Westphal et al., 1984, 509).

The leading export agents were the "Chaebol" which were large conglomerate business groups, dating from the 1970s (510). Those organizations as well as several large Korean construction firms were seen as among the world's largest international contractors (McKee and Garner, 1996, 81). The exports of the firms in question included "such things as technological knowledge, technical services, embodiment activity, training services, management services and marketing services (Westphal et al., 1984, 511).

To maintain and enhance their international interests, Korean concerns have become heavily involved in various export services (McKee and Garner, 1996b, 82). This is hardly surprising in a jurisdiction that has based its growth upon the export of manufactured goods and has begun exporting manufacturing technology as well (82). Westphal saw an "abundant international trade in the elements of technology, through transactions involving licenses, capital goods, direct investment, technical assistance and the like" (1990, 55). He was of the opinion that "the tacitness of much technology creates problems in communication over long distances and across social differences" because "peculiarities in local resources, institutions, and local technological practices cannot be comprehended without being experienced in some way" (55).

He saw major economies of scope vis-à-vis the application of many of the skills acquired from industrialization and producing an increase in transactions of domestic agents involving technology both in terms of frequency and specialization (55). He noted that "Additional externalities can result because demonstration effects from an initial entrant's investments to master new technology may greatly reduce costs for subsequent nearby entrants (55).

Westphal's insights were seen as applicable to various service categories aimed at supporting export activities (McKee and Garner, 1996b, 83). "The international transfer of technology cannot be accomplished without the assistance of various services geared to reduce institutional, legal and financial impediments" (83). As has been suggested in numerous emerging economies the varieties of services referred to are made available by service providers that have themselves become international in the course of serving the needs of their corporate clients (83).

In Korea where production for export was largely based upon domestic operations encouraged by government, external service cadres were said to be necessary (83). According to Chungsoo Kim, and Kihong Kim, the newly industrialized nations of Asia were seeing "areas of service trade where they may acquire international competitiveness" (1990, 182). Korea's service sector accounted for one-half of the workforce and 57 percent of GDP in 1987 (182). Nonetheless the Kims saw Korea's service sector as "characterized by labor intensive modes of production" which showed a fundamental difference from what they characterized as the capital intensive service sectors of industrialized countries (182). Those authors saw the nation's weak overall trade balance in services as attributable to its sectoral imbalance, suggesting that "much attention is being paid to the deregulation and internationalization of Korea's financial service industries" (183).

The New Zealand Trade Development Board has identified Korea as the world's 12th largest trading nation (June 1999a, 3). Its report explains that the nation "has moved from basic industries such as cement, fertilizer and industrial chemicals to automobiles, electronics, iron and steel and shipbuilding to computers and other high-technology products" (3).

The Asian financial crisis of 1997 found various large corporate entities (Chaebols) in financial trouble, in some cases ending in bankruptcy. "This signaled the beginning of a series of economic problems which culminated in the Korean government requesting a US $57 billion bailout from the IMF to avoid default on payment of short term foreign debts" (3).

The loan was granted with conditions requiring economic reform most especially the restructuring of the financial sector and the Chaebols. The government agreed to pass bills aimed at economic restructuring, particularly the opening up of the equity market to foreigners, the closure of ailing merchant banks, the sale of the two most heavily debt-burdened banks to foreign interests, the revision of corporate bankruptcy laws so as to hasten the departure of marginal enterprises and improving labor market flexibility reforms and the permitting of hostile mergers and acquisitions of domestic firms by foreign interests. The New Zealand Trade

Development Board saw such adjustments as resulting in a growing number of firms forced into insolvency and others into restructuring and downsizing (3).

Despite the recognition of the role of the Chaebols in the past success of the Korean economy, those organizations are now seen as largely responsible for the recent economic crisis (3). Chaebols "are involved in a wide range of activities from textiles and footwear to hi-tech semiconductors and micro electronics" (3). Their privileged position, together with government help and preferential access to capital, was seen as making it difficult for small to medium-sized Korean firms to expand (3).

The government has provided various incentives aimed at attracting foreign investment. In the realm of taxation, foreign firms operating in various high-tech sectors are given exemptions covering five years and discounts for three additional years. These concessions cover corporate income, property and land taxes (4). Sectors involved include information, electronics, bio-engineering, space engineering, medical science, environment and energy (4).

Two free-export zones have been established, "one in Masan in the south near Pusan Port and another in Iksan near Kunsan Port on the west coast" (4). The government also plans to set up "Free Investment Zones" (FIZ) where foreign direct investors in the high-tech sectors will get tax holidays of up to seven years and tax discounts of 50 percent for three additional years (4). "A pool of specialists will be located in the FIZ to give one-stop administrative services to foreign investors" (4). Existing free-export zones will be transformed into free-investment zones (4–5).

Among accounting firms active in Korea is Young Wha, a member of Ernst & Young International. Indeed the firm is one of Ernst & Young International's, International Council Country Members with direct access to "management policy making within the international organization" (Young Wha, 2000a).

Young Wha offers various auditing services to its clients. For corporations listed on the Korean Stock Exchange, it offers audits performed in accordance with Korean Securities Exchange Laws (2000b). It can also perform audits for private corporations in accordance with External Audit Law and can offer audits of government-invested corporations (2000b). Other statutory audits available include those of branch offices of foreign corporations for the purpose of remitting profits to their head offices "and those of foreign-invested corporations for the purpose of remitting dividends to their shareholders" (2000b).

The firm also offers various special audits. Included are those of joint venture companies, and those of Korean corporations wishing to list on an overseas stock exchange or issue debt instruments in international markets, as well as royalty audits and due diligence reviews and audits related to mergers and acquisitions (2000b). Others include those performed on behalf of the Ministry of Justice or court orders and audits of nonprofit organizations and charities and those required for obtaining or renewing certain business licenses (2000b). The firm can also perform information systems audits and audits related to financing through IBRD (2000b).

In the realm of domestic tax services the firm deals with both preparation and certification of corporate income tax returns (2000c). It represents clients in court on matters concerning refund claims or tax appeals and consults on tax regulations and procedures (2000c). It offers tax planning for minimizing tax liabilities on major transactions or contracts as well as to sole proprietorships pursuing incorporation (2000c). Indeed it deals in all tax-related filings and also offers international tax services (2000c).

The firm is also active in supplying general management consulting services and consulting services for government-owned enterprises (2000d). It works on the development of management goals and strategies and offers corporate finance services which include "M&A, restructurings and valuations" (2000d). It can conduct feasibility studies on new ventures and also offers marketing-related services, such as research, demand forecasts and strategic planning (2000d). It can design accounting systems and offers advice on accounting and auditing matters, as well as various forms of assistance with regard to establishing plans for projects (2000d). It can also provide performance evaluations of management and their operations (2000d).

Young Wha Consulting offers various major services to clients. In the realm of management strategy it can establish medium- and long-term management strategies and can provide a comprehensive analysis of management strategies (Young Wha Consulting, 2000). Beyond that it assists with the establishment of business strategies.

In the area of management innovation, the consulting arm of the firm deals with knowledge management and with business process and improvement (2000). It can assist with restructuring and right-sizing and can also help with system integration (2000). It also deals with change management, with strategic cost management and with supply chain management. The firm can also provide an analysis of organizational culture (2000).

The consulting arm of the firm is also active in information technology consulting. In that regard it works with the establishment, analysis and evaluation of information systems and also offers methodology consulting (2000). It deals with the construction of IT systems and provides consultation on ERP-related packages (2000). It also deals with the construction of accounting information systems as well as with information system audits (2000). It can also provide assistance with system security.

The firm also offers an array of accounting consultation services and executive search and compensation consulting. Included are such services as the valuation of stock prices and net worth, the design and evaluation of internal accounting control systems and the establishment of internal accounting policies and procedures (2000d). The firm also offers assistance with managerial accounting, such as cost accounting and budgeting (2000). It can also provide assistance in the preparation of financial projections and with due diligence reviews and can provide consultations on going public (2000). It offers advice and consultation on a selection of accounting related issues and can assist with executive recruitment. The firm also does compensation surveys and studies (2000). Young Wha stands ready to offer services to Korean companies investing overseas and to foreign companies investing in Korea (2000).

KPMG San Tong & Co. is another major accounting organization active in Korea. That firm offers traditional accounting services such as audit/attestation, international services, accounting services and M&A due diligence (KPMG San Tong & Co., 2000, 1). The firm is also an active supplier of tax and legal services. Beyond such matters it deals with management consulting. Included in such services are matters of strategic financial management and performance improvement as well as business process reengineering, information technology and SAP implementation (1). The firm offers assistance to businesses in various fields, including banking and finance, building and construction and energy and natural resources (1). It can also assist in areas such as healthcare and life science, industrial production and information, communications and entertainment, as well as insurance and retail and consumer products (1). It can also assist clients in the government sector (1).

Bavishi (1991, 424) reported that the world's 16 largest accounting firms boasted 250 partners in Korea of whom 139 were affiliated with the then big six. If the services available through the organizations alluded to above are any indication, accounting firms are major players in the Korean economy.

TAIWAN

According to the New Zealand Trade Development Board the Taiwanese economy has gone through three separate phases in its development (December 1998, 3). The 1950s marked an era during which growth was encouraged in agriculture and import-substituting industries, notably textiles and cement. Up to 1965 the nation was also enjoying substantial assistance from the United States (3). "The second phase of development started in the 1960s...involving mainly low-technology, light industry and the assembly of imported raw materials and parts for consumers goods and machinery" (3–4).

The third phase of the development process saw industries becoming more capital-intensive with the emphasis on high-technology activities (4). Taiwan was identified as "the world's third largest supplier of computer hardware" and was also seen as putting emphasis on software development (4). The nation was also considered as seeking to become a regional service center (4).

As late as 1990 Chungsoo Kim and Kihong Kim suggested that the service sector in Taiwan was the smallest among the newly industrialized economies of the region (184). Indeed "in every major service trade it has registered a chronic deficit" and "does not appear to have a strong across the board international competitiveness in service trade" (184).

The New Zealand Trade Development Board identified the production value of the service industry as US $176 billion in 1997, a figure accounting for 62.4 percent of GDP (4). This they attributed to the fact that finance, insurance, real estate and commerce have grown rapidly as a result of government liberalization policies (4). Indeed the government was said to have promised "to open up such fields as finance, transportation, warehousing and telecommunications to overseas business" (4).

Chin-ru Chang agreed that "The rapid growth in service industries was due to the implementation of financial openness" (1996). Chang went on to explain that the nation "has eased interest rate control, lifted credit and exchange controls, removed trade barriers, and allowed more foreign access to capital markets" (1996). According to Chang "international enterprises such as banks, lawyers, advertising companies, insurance organizations, [and] consulting firms are coming in floods" (1996). It has been suggested that as new high-tech industries develop and worker's earnings increase, coupled with expanding urbanization, more workers will be needed in service pursuits (New Zealand Trade Development Board, December 1998, 4). Indeed the service sector was seen becoming the central pillar of future economic growth.

Despite this appraisal of the nation's service sector, manufacturing, especially the export-oriented variety, holds a significant place in the Taiwanese economy. Taiwan's manufacturing economy is dominated by small firms (Naughton, 1997, 30). In Taiwan small firms have learned to export and engage in other international dealings (30).

According to the New Zealand Trade and Development Board, the manufacturing sector in Taiwan is dominated by the production of machinery, telecommunications equipment, petrochemicals and plastics, electronics and personal computers, including notebook computers and accessories (4). In 1997 the nation's foreign trade totaled US $208.9 billion which made it one of the world's top 12 trading jurisdictions (8).

"Direct foreign investment . . . is encouraged . . . for projects, which are considered strategic or vital to economic development" with emphasis on export-oriented heavy industry and high technology (13). Foreign companies are permitted to establish subsidiaries or joint ventures and enjoy the same tax incentives as local firms for approved projects (13). "Foreign investment is prohibited in government monopolies . . . public utilities and specified strategic industries, and is restricted in service industries including the financial sector" (14).

Incentives for government-approved projects include a five-year tax holiday, accelerated depreciation of equipment employed in research and development, subsidies to reduce pressure from loan interest and the provision of government land and exemption from import duties (14). Ventures that are socially desirable but possess low profitability may be entitled to government support for up to 35 percent of initial financing and investments in backward areas are taxed at lower rates (14).

In an article on November 24, 1998 Christopher Bodeen pointed out that the nation's economy was forecast to grow at 5.3 percent in that year, down from 6.8 percent in the previous year (1998, 1). He attributed that to a 7.4 percent drop in exports (1). The nation's resiliency was attributed to the kind of flexibility and adaptability displayed by the labor market (2). "The island's economic backbone is made up of small businesses many of them exporters, which unlike Japan's hulking corporations, must react quickly to survive" (2).

Certainly the Asian financial and economic crisis had some impact upon Taiwan. Writing in 1998 James K. Larson pointed out that the nation has averaged an annual growth rate in GDP of about 9 percent over a 30-year period (1998, 3). Larson suggests that export growth was even more rapid and provided the impetus for industrialization. He suggested that "Sources of GDP show the steady growth of Taiwan's economy, even through the Asian crisis" (3).

Larson suggests that the economy of Taiwan is closely linked to that of other Asian nations, "for the last three years, growth in Taiwan has been fueled by increasing consumption and exports, while investment fell slightly" (7). Larson saw the nation to be vulnerable to a decline in exports, "especially since many of its largest trading partners are Asian nations" (7). He pointed out that Taiwan is a major investor in China, Thailand, Indonesia, the Philippines, Malaysia and Vietnam and asked if there were signs that Taiwan was heading for troubles similar to those of its neighbors (7).

It seems clear that Taiwan's economic potential is very much dependent upon successful ongoing international relationships and linkages. Baring a major unanticipated change in its relationship to mainland China its need for continuing international linkages can be expected to retain its importance. Since it seems much less involved with major international corporate players than are many newly industrialized economies, it seems as though it may have much to gain from various international business service suppliers. If such suppliers can effectively assist the large numbers of relatively small to medium-sized Taiwanese businesses operating internationally, the gains should be almost self-evident.

The major international accounting firms are certainly in a position to supply various facilitative services to the business community in Taiwan. Various major accounting firms are active in the country. As Bavishi has pointed out, accountants unaffiliated with the Big Six have a larger presence in the country than do the then–Big Six (1991, 424).

Moore Stephens, P.C. is among the major international accounting firms active in Taiwan where it operates in Kaohsiung, Taipei and Taichung. The firm's mission statement reads, "To advise clients on evaluating and utilizing the resources necessary to maximize their profitability while maintaining an environment that promotes personal satisfactions and well-being" (2000a).

Beyond traditional accounting and auditing services the firm offers tax services to corporations, partnerships and individuals (2000b). It also offers business management consulting, computer consulting and not-for-profit consulting, as well as Internet consulting. It can assist with corporate, partnership and individual federal, state and local income tax review and planning. Other planning assistances offered include strategic planning, estate planning and financial planning, management and reporting, whether corporate or personal (2000b).

The firm also offers insurance and brokerage accounting services, IPO financial reporting and compliance services and litigation services (2000b). It can assist with executive search, multi-employer benefit plans and retirement planning. It also deals with mergers and acquisitions, investment analysis and reinsurance services. Its menu also includes outsourcing services and payroll and bookkeeping services (2000b).

Morison International Asia Pacific (MIAP) is another large international accounting firm active in Taiwan where it offers a rather extensive array of business and professional services (1999a). "Today through an integrated network of offices, the staff of MIAP pool their in-depth knowledge, experience and expertise to assist clients' business challenges" (1999b). On an ongoing basis the firm is engaged in developing and complementing strategies to improve business performance or promote business opportunities. It also identifies new markets and cross-border opportunities, and can use information technology for competitive advantage, and for meeting audit and tax requirements (1999b).

Mindsnell Group International (MGI) was established in 1947 and is an association of 180-plus independent accounting and consulting firms in over 68 countries, including Taiwan. "Through this alliance, members offer clients services and information regarding worldwide business practices, taxation, accounting and strategic alliance opportunities" (2000a, 1).

Prominent among services offered by MGI is a strategic alliance program to help midsized companies entering the international market (2000a, 1). Among the program's benefits are expanding operations to new consumer and production centers (2). Additional benefits include capitalizing on scale economies, reducing labor costs significantly and identifying and obtaining financial resources (2). "The Strategic Alliance Program promotes international trade and supports business opportunities on a local, state and national level" (2).

The program can help in identifying business opportunities and locating potential partners (2). It can create financial projections and business plans for projects and can also determine financial structures and project capital needs (2). It can negotiate with banks and other financial institutions and can identify "creative solutions and corporate structures to implement international transactions" (2). It can also coordinate an alliance that is practical and efficient (2).

"MGI firms assist clients with the following strategic alliance opportunities: technology transfers, manufacturing sender license, trademark licenses, factory representation, factory vendors, joint venture and mergers and acquisitions" (2). The facilitative business potential for such activities both domestically and in the global economy seems assured.

MGI firms offer various consulting services to businesses requiring help during periods of development and growth. They can assist with the establishment of accounting, management and control procedures and can also advise with respect to wage and salary levels (3). They can also help in the selection and implementation of computer software and with the design of management information systems (3). In addition they can offer help with projections, budgets and strategic planning (3).

DFK International is an international network of independent accounting firms that is represented in Taiwan. Its member firms are in a position to serve clients on a world wide basis (DFK International, 2000a). The organization is represented in 67 countries, through 50 member firms with 261 offices (2000a).

Its clients are engaged in a broad range of business and other activities both within particular countries and internationally (2000b). Clients come from both public and private sectors and represent a wide range of industries as well as nonprofit organizations (2000b). Clients can choose from a wide menu of service offerings ranging from traditional audit, accounting and various forms of tax assistance throughout the gamete of business services. In the financial sphere offerings include management consulting, reports for share issues, forecasts and budgets and restructuring studies (2000b). Other services available include assistance

with acquisitions and mergers, systems reviews, receiverships and liquidations and litigation support (2000b).

Assistance is also available with corporate secretarial services, trustee
and executorship, executive recruitment and technical communications
and updates (2000b). The organization can also help with information
technology consulting and personal financial services (2000b).

Chapter 8

The Firms in Emerging Nations

In this Chapter the emphasis turns to the cohort of emerging nations that were selected to be studied. Those include Indonesia, Malaysia, the Philippines and Thailand. The approach will be parallel to that of the preceding chapter. In the case of each nation a brief overview of the economy will be followed by evidence of the service offerings of selected major accounting firms. The intent is to highlight the facilitative role of the accounting firms most especially as it pertains to international business and economic linkages.

INDONESIA

From the vantage point of 1996, Indonesia was seen as potentially a force to be reckoned with (McKee and Garner, 1996b, 25). Elegant saw the nation as impressive in terms of both size and diversity (1990, 219). He described the nation as the world's sixth largest political entity and the fifth largest producer in OPEC (219). Three-quarters of its exports were agricultural and mineral but almost one-fifth were manufactured goods (1990, 219).

Prior to the advent of the Asian crisis it appeared as though a certain amount of optimism seemed warranted. Certainly the nation appeared to be forging an important regional economic niche in Asia. Unfortunately at the dawn of the new century the nation had been wracked by economic, financial and political crises, the negative overspills from which are still of some concern.

In January of 1998, the New Zealand Trade Development Board described the nation's trilogy of goals as economic stability, economic growth and the equitable distribution of development gains (7). In an update on Southeast Asia, that same organization pointed to the strengths of the Indonesian market as suggested in the meeting of the ASEAN Trade Commissioners in Bangkok (New Zealand Trade Development Board, June 2000, 1). Among suggested strengths was the nation's crucial role in the regional economy due to its size (1). Beyond that the report suggested that confidence is back as displayed by new business being initiated (1). In addition money for trading is available either from offshore resources, international sources or from pockets of wealth within the economy (1).

On the downside the report saw corporate restructuring as very slow with limited access to expansion capital (1). Democracy was described as finding its feet with many power factions emerging (1). Many regions are described as replete with risks which include poor justice and law enforcement and personal safety (1).

Speaking in Jakarta in January 2000, U.S. Treasury Secretary Lawrence Summers cited four lessons from the Asian crisis relevant for Indonesia. First among those was the need for sound macro-economic policy followed by the need for financial restructuring. The final two requirements cited were the need for the rule of law and the need for strong political leadership (January 20, 2000, 3). Summers saw macro-economic stability in Indonesia as an impressive achievement but criticized the failure of the nation to move forward aggressively with restructuring and institutional reform that he felt prevented a full expansion (3).

Summers saw inflation as down but felt that growth was less than it could be. Suggesting that a new democratic government had brought with it some inevitable uncertainty, he still saw the need for a real prospect that uncertainty and what he called "logjammed reform" would draw to a close (3). He called for the "demonstration of willingness to see foreign investors as a crucial part of a solution to Indonesia's corporate and financial debt problems, and not a part of the problem" (5). In that regard he suggested that experience around the world indicates that foreign banks can be a significant aid to financial reform, as suppliers of capital and more importantly as suppliers of resilience, diversification and knowledge (3). It seems as though the major international accounting firms may also have much to offer vis-à-vis the last mentioned considerations.

Writing in September 1999, Gary Dean described an economy hardly receptive of what Summers was to suggest. He saw the Indonesian economy dominated by state actors, following a lengthy tradition of economic nationalism whereby the state had attempted to have a part in all aspects of economic activity (1). He saw private capitalism as having been viewed with suspicion and referred to what he called a "Quasi-socialist Indonesian constitution" (1). "Capitalism was, and probably still is to a large degree, equated with colonialism and exploitation, and collectivist ideas still enjoy widespread support" (1).

Citing a tradition of "Sultanism" Dean saw all power concentrated at the top and all resources "within reach of sultan's mandala are the personal property of the sultan" (2). He saw what he called contemporary Indonesian "Bapak-ism" as a mere continuation of that tradition (2). Indeed in spite of pockets of industrialization and "paper-thin modernist venues," the state and the people are predominantly traditional in outlook (2). Clearly if Dean's assessment was accurate much must be accomplished if the nation is to enjoy successful linkages to the world at large.

Hadi Soesastro has suggested that the recent crisis as it has impacted Indonesia has pointed to the importance of governance and a developmental strategy able to respond effectively to the challenges of globalization (July 10, 2000a, 2). In policy terms this speaks to how the nation can offer a creditable commitment to maintaining open economic policies and good governance (2).

In another context the same author states that the crisis in Indonesia has assumed a dynamic of its own (2000c, 1). According to him what began as a currency crisis in the third quarter of 1997 quickly became a deep financial crisis wielding wide-ranging economic and social impacts and in May of 1998 became a serious political crisis (2000c, 1). He described the result as "an economy in shambles, a serious political vacuum, and a highly polarized society" (2000c, 1).

Soesastro cited a reluctance on the part of President Soeharto to implement an agreement with the IMF which he suggested increases the uncertainty in markets vis-à-vis the nation's ability to overcome the crisis (3). He even suggested a regional concern with the possibility that the nation might disintegrate (3). He is of the opinion that economic concerns may be less acute than the political (3). "A possibly greater impact is whether Indonesia will continue with or reverse its internationally oriented economic policy, and whether it will disengage from regional economic cooperation activities" (3).

Bavishi reported Indonesia as having 74 partners in major international accounting firms (1991, Appendix). Of the partners in question 65 were based in Jakarta, the nation's capital. Of the remainder Yogyakarto and Surabuya had four each while the remaining partner was located in Medan. As noted elsewhere, given the size of the nation, such a concentration of accountants in Jakarta seems less than encouraging vis-à-vis development in other locations (McKee and Garner, 1996b, 96).

That view was based upon the premise that the services of the firms help to reinforce or facilitate linkages between business firms in the nation and the rest of the world. The potential for such linkages appears strongest in Jakarta and the possibility of their encouraging development elsewhere in the nation seemed hardly definite (96). As was stated, "it can hardly be assumed that the accounting firms are positioned to assert their influence in matters of economic integration within the domestic economy (96).

KPMG Indonesia is prominent among accounting firms in the nation. In Indonesia KPMG is partnered with Siddharta, Siddharta and Harsono and also with PT Siddharta Consulting Services. Of the domestic partner firms the former dates from 1957 while the latter was established in 1986 (KPMG Indonesia, 2000, 2).

The two domestic firms combined present themselves as one of the largest practices in Indonesia, offering services to multinational corporations, joint ventures and domestic companies across a wide range of business sectors (2). They claim to be providing a source of international expertise in the nation as well as access to the global network of KPMG (2).

Among service offerings are a wide range of assurance services. Assurance services as explained are composed primarily of auditing, accounting and information risk management. The firms follow a system based approach, driven by risk-assessment models (2). "This helps ensure that management goals and objectives are achieved efficiently, effectively, and economically" (2). They explain that accounting services are developed to help in the preparation and management of underlying records and that they specialize in outsourcing financial records (2).

Information and management services are mainly business support and compliance services, relating to information systems (2). They are designed to ensure that systems have adequate internal controls and security features and also that systems applications are implemented and employed effectively (3). Assurance related activities constitute a major component of the services provided by the firm. Recommendations for improving account systems, controls and other operational aspects of the business are made in a management letter at the conclusion of each audit (3).

The KPMG affiliates in Indonesia are also offering taxation and establishment services. Their offerings in the tax area consist mainly of compliance and advisory services. As part of their overall taxation services, their establishment division focuses on business advice concerning the establishment of a business in Indonesia (4). They will help in all aspects of the process from expatriate permits to advice on manpower reports (4).

According to the firm taxes are inherent in business operations, both from the perspective of costs and from the need for compliance with prevailing tax laws and regulations (4). In Indonesia significant penalties are exacted for noncompliance. Thus it is important for firms to ensure that their tax affairs are in order. KPMG and its local partner firms stand ready to provide assistance. They stand ready to supply their clients with

the knowledge needed to meet legislative obligations and business requirements. They offer a comprehensive range of tax services to both
businesses and individuals (4).

Financial advisory services are also available. Those consist primarily
of corporate finance and corporate recovery/restructuring (5). "The firm
provides a full range of corporate recovery and restructuring service and
corporate finance capability" (5). Their corporate finance team assists clients through all stages and types of transactions. Matters covered include
acquisitions, takeovers or mergers, as well as disposals and the identification of the business to be bought or sold. Also included are business
appraisals, valuations and advice on initial public offerings, not to mention share issues and floatations and project structured finance (6). These
services are offered by a team of executives, experienced in the capital
market, the securities industry and investment banking (6). Such expertise combined with an understanding of local business, legal and cultural
issues gives the firm the ability to facilitate the business operations of
clients in Indonesia.

In the realm of consulting service offerings range from human resources to business strategies as well as from information systems to
financial management (6). The aim is to assist clients to improve the
effectiveness and profitability of their operations (7). Assistance is available in corporate management which includes matters such as strategic
planning, organizational restructuring and economic assessment and
forecasting, as well as investment appraisal and feasibility (7). Also included is assistance with respect to supply chain management and improving overall effectiveness, efficiency and financial performance (7).

Assistance is also offered in the marketing area covering such matters
as market research and planning, forecasting of sales and market trends
and pricing, sales administration and customer service (7). Operations
management constitutes yet another area in which services are offered.
Among those are assistance with facilities planning and production
methods, as well as production and materials requirements (7). Help is
also offered concerning quality control, inventory management, distribution management and clerical productivity (7).

Service offerings in the area of human resource management include
personnel planning, executive selection and staff recruitment, performance appraisal, and personnel management systems. Beyond such matters assistance is offered vis-à-vis job evaluation and salary
administration and management training and development (7).

The firm also stands ready to assist in financial management. More
specifically it provides help with financial planning and budgeting, performance evaluation and control and responsibility accounting, as well
as product and service costing, capital expenditure and control, financial
analysis and financial management reporting (7–8).

In the area of system integration the firm offers assistance with information service strategy, operation strategy, system architecture and system selection and evaluation. Other related service offerings concern enterprise infrastructure technology review, enterprise resource planning, supply chain management and change management. Help is also available for custom application development, data warehousing, secure electronic commerce and enterprise system integration, as well as program or project assurance (8).

It seems clear that KPMG and its Indonesian partner firms stand ready to provide a wide array of facilitative services to business. In general their services are offered to assist organizations on four major issues. First of all the services offered are intended to assist organizations in making better informed decisions on strategy and policy issues related to change (7). Their second intent is to assist in establishing effective management structures supported by sound personnel policies (7). Third they are prepared to assist firms in ensuring that their management information systems cover the needs of the organization and utilize most efficiently the opportunities stemming from developments in the computer and related technology (7). Finally they help organizations to become more competitive through improving marketing, cutting manufacturing and distribution costs and enhancing the supply of timely and effective information (7).

Ernst & Young is another major international accounting firm active in Indonesia. Its member firm, Sarwok and Sandjaja, boasts a professional and support staff of 160, working out of Jakarta, but available anywhere in the country (Ernst & Young, 1998a). The firm offers five main areas of service. Those include assurance and advisory business services which embrace external audit, internal audit and information systems audit and consulting services (Koesoetjahjo, 2000, 2). Also included are corporate finance, comprising corporate finance and corporate recovery and insolvency and business services, comprising accounting services, new business entry, executive search and recruitment and Japanese Business Group (2). The fifth major service area is taxation, which includes corporate, personal and indirect tax return preparation, as well as international and local tax planning, assistance with audits, objections and appeals. The firm also provides advice on financing structures, indirect tax and customs duty advice, not to mention expatriate tax services, transfer pricing studies, tax diagnostic and due diligence reviews, together with advice on mergers and acquisitions (2)

The firm is currently offering services to a clientele in the neighborhood of 1,200, both local and international (2). Various industrial sectors are represented including agriculture, banking and finance, insurance, manufacturing, mining, oil and gas, petrochemicals, transportation and communications, construction and tourism (2).

An earlier publication reviewed the service offerings of Price Water-house in Indonesia (McKee and Garner, 1996b, 97). Since that time the firm in question has merged with Coopers & Lybrand. Since the Price Waterhouse offerings were discussed in some detail, there is little to be gained by reviewing them or those of the merged firm at this juncture. The extent of what major international accounting firms are doing or can do in Indonesia seems clear. The earlier publication expressed reservations concerning the potential impact of the firms throughout the nation, given the concentration of partners in Jakarta. In the present context that reservation continues to hold true.

MALAYSIA

According to the New Zealand Trade Development Board, Malaysia is well supplied with natural resources and is a major exporter of tin, rubber, palm oil and tropical hardwoods (July 1999, 4). Beyond those resources the nation has substantial reserves of petroleum and natural gas (4). The Malaysian economy had been anchored by agriculture, but in an effort to assist in economic recovery the government has been seeking to encourage overseas investment, thus resulting "in manufacturing now being the major driving force in the economy" (4).

Writing in 1991 Schlosstein identified Malaysia as Asia's least-industrialized economy (284). Despite that assessment the economy had been growing and was showing signs of transformation to middle in-come status as early as the 1970s (Tucker and Sundberg, 1988, 83). In 1993 Cragg suggested that the nation was enjoying one of the highest growth rates in per capita income, and was the world's largest producer of rubber, palm oil and tin (169). Cragg saw "good expansion potential with a shift to manufacturing exports . . . an increased demand for dis-cretionary consumer purchases and country-wide development of rural markets" (169).

The Pacific Basin Economic Council has suggested that "Over the course of four decades, Malaysia has undergone a dramatic transfor-mation to become one of East Asia's 'mini-dragons' " (1998, 1). They described the nation as having become "a world-class economy, export-ing such high-tech products as radio telephones, data-processing equip-ment, VCRs and electronic circuitry" (1). They identified the nation as the world's third largest producer and largest exporter of semiconduc-tors, and the largest exporter of room air conditioners, color TV tubes and VCRs (1).

It was suggested in an earlier investigation that Malaysia was relying to some extent upon foreign linkages to fuel its expansion (McKee and Garner, 1996b, 93). In that regard it was thought "that services designed to facilitate international business, including those offered through the international accounting firms, would be helpful where available" (93). It was suggested that in Malaysia's case the services available through accounting firms should facilitate international linkages and may also have a part to play in strengthening the domestic economy (93). Of course those relatively recent observations may well require adjustment in view of the crisis of 1997.

According to the Pacific Basin Economic Council, the political environment in the jurisdiction is highly favorable to both international and domestic business development (1998, 1). Cited among the best prospects for business with the United States were electronic components (1). In that regard it was pointed out that Malaysia is the world's third largest producer of semiconductor devices, surpassed only by the United States and Japan. The nation ranks third in the export of such devices and the electronic components sector was expected to expand (1).

Other strong prospects for U.S. business included aircraft and related services. The report explained that Malaysia Airlines was operating in excess of 90 aircraft, linking 57 international destinations on six continents not to mention 35 domestic locations (1). Prospects involving the airport and aircraft service industry were seen as promising in light of what has been mentioned above as well as the construction of a major new international airport at Sepang (1).

Computer software as well as computers and peripherals were also mentioned (2). "The current economic uptrend has caused more business sectors to upgrade computer systems. Growth has been fueled by the government's active role in promoting a technologically advanced economy" (2). The thrust of the report, with its predictions of extensive opportunities for U.S. business interests suggests the return of international confidence in the nation's economy.

The report also speaks of the nation's electronics industry which has grown to become the largest manufacturing sector (2). Predictions concerning such activities also speak well of the economy. "Because Malaysia's industrial policy encourages the industry to undertake greater technological upgrading and to move into the area of microelectronics and automated manufacturing, electronics industry production equipment should expand significantly in the next three years" (2).

Other areas cited included telecommunications equipment and industrial chemicals (2). The nation's telecommunications network "has grown and improved over the last decade as a result of the country's strong sustained economic growth" (2). The report stated that Malaysia was expected to invest US $6.5 billion in telecommunications infrastructure over the next five years (2). Franchising was also viewed with optimism by the report. That area of endeavor was receiving strong government support through the Franchising Development Unit which assists Malay entrepreneurs by connecting prospective purchasers with established franchisers from abroad and by developing the local franchising network (2).

Despite the setbacks engendered by the regional crisis of 1997, judging from the report featured above Malaysia has recovered and presents a positive picture vis-à-vis a rather sophisticated array of business opportunities involving U.S. business interests. The New Zealand Trade Development Board also appears to be optimistic (July 1999). This optimism exists in spite of the very real impacts of the crisis.

The Malaysian government introduced strong austerity measures designed to cut government and corporate sector spending, overhaul banking and financial sectors, raise productivity in both manufacturing and agriculture and cut dependence on imports while simultaneously increasing exports (July 1999, 4). Those measures were elected due to a 34 percent drop in the ringgit against the U.S. dollar in October of 1997, a major drop in the stock market and a slowing economy (July 1999, 4).

"Throughout the crisis the government and the banking system have remained stable, factors which set Malaysia apart from her immediate neighbors" (July 1999, 4). In order to stimulate trade and investment in various parts of the country and also to strengthen its relationship with its ASEAN neighbors, the nation has been the catalyst for establishing growth triangles in the region (5). Examples include the Indonesia, Malaysia, Thailand growth triangle with a particular focus on telecommunications and the Brunei, Indonesia, Malaysia, Philippines, East Asia Growth Area (5).

As mentioned earlier the government is promoting import substitution and beyond that a "Buy Malaysian" policy (7). It is encouraging firms to improve their productive efficiency, acquire technology and expand exports (7). Manufacturing license approvals are granted by the Malaysian Industrial Development Authority with preferences to joint-venture projects in which equity is held by Bumiputras (12). Preferences are also given to projects providing needed jobs and training for Malaysians, enhancing local technology and manufacturing expertise, having high local value-added and establishing export outlets for local products (12). There is also consideration given to projects that redress economic imbalances among the nation's ethnic groups (12). The government offers a variety of incentives aimed at attracting foreign investment (12).

The nation has created 13 free zones. Ten are free industrial zones, offering investors duty-free importing of raw materials, parts and materials. These feature minimal customs control and formalities. A free commercial zone is aimed at establishments engaged in training, breaking bulk, grading, recapping, relabelling and transit (13). The remaining two free zones are for trade in export products (13).

Beyond the free-zone concept various tax structures and incentive packages are aimed at attracting foreign investment, especially in manufacturing. Such incentives include reinvestment allowances and incentives for locating in the eastern corridor of Peninsular Malaysia, Sabah and Sarawak (13). Also included are research allowances for research and development companies and for companies conducting in-house research and development activities (13). Incentives also exist for forest plantation projects, for operational headquarters and regarding the petroleum income tax (13).

Malaysia has good air and sea transportation linkages and has greatly improved its domestic travel infrastructure. A North-South highway from the Thai border to Singapore, coupled with an ongoing program of road construction and improvement is improving domestic travel efficiency (16). A cheap and efficient transnational bus service is in place as is a long distance taxi service (17). Domestic air links are well developed, as are North-South and East-West rail services that facilitate the movement of shipping containers and cargo (17).

Bavishi reported a fairly strong presence on the part of major international accounting firms (1991, Appendix). According to him the nation boasted 159 partners, 77 percent of whom were concentrated in Kuala Lumpur. The remaining partners were scattered among various state capitals and regional centers. As was mentioned in another context "their positioning throughout the nation affords opportunities for strengthening economic and business endeavors and for providing national and international linkages" (McKee and Garner, 1996b, 96).

Among major international accounting firms Arthur Andersen professes to be the largest professional service organization active in Malaysia (1998). They offer their services through 13 locations in Peninsular Malaysia, with a staff of 1,000. The firm established its "Malaysian entity" with Samad & Company in 1990 and during that decade merged with Hanafiah, Rastan & Mohamad (1998).

The firm's headquarters in Kuala Lumpur is in close communication with Arthur Andersen client service teams throughout the world, which of course is one of the advantages that major international accounting firms bring to specific locations. That office acts as the overall integrator of services for Malaysian companies with overseas operations (1998). The firm offers a full range of integrated services for Malaysian companies and multinational corporations operating in Malaysia. Such services deal with audit, taxation, management and business problems (1998).

Ernst & Young is another major international accounting firm active in Malaysia. It sees itself as one of the leading professional service firms in the country, with its complement of 1,200 professionals and support staff, working out of 12 offices positioned throughout the country (1998b). The firm stands ready to provide expert advice on every business issue. With respect to accounting, that entails computer audits and security reviews, due diligence reviews and internal controls and system reviews.

The firm's Malaysian branch, Ernst & Young Malaysia, was established in 1909 and claims to be the country's first internationally linked public accounting firm (Ernst & Young, 1998b). They claim to possess a deep knowledge of the Malaysian business environment based upon their early presence. "We derive our professional strength from the diversity of our people who combine: Experience with innovation. Tradition with technology. Discipline with flexibility." Their attitude toward clients is clearly stated, "Our hands-on approach means that we work with you until you get results."

The firm has organized its professionals into multidisciplinary teams in accordance with the industry being served rather than the service being offered. Many of their professionals specialize in one or two industry sectors, which of course increases the significance of what they can offer. The firm designs "large-scale change programmes to revitalise the growth and profitability of large, diversified companies."

KPMG is also actively involved in Malaysia with offices in Kuala Lumpur and nine other locations. They offer a wide range of services. In the accounting area they offer audit and internal audit service, information risk management, accounting services and M&A due diligence (1998, 1). Their tax and legal services cover corporate/business tax, personal tax, international tax and indirect taxation. In the area of management consulting they can assist with strategic financial management, performance improvement, business process reengineering, SAP implementation and enabling technologies. In the corporate finance area they deal with fiduciary services, privatizations, executive search and selection, bid defense, valuation and securing finance.

Among business sectors that the firm stands ready to assist are banking and finance and building and construction, as well as energy and natural resources and health care and life science (1998, 1–2). They can also assist the industrial products sector, and information, communications and entertainment (2). They can assist in insurance, transportation, retail and consumer products and also business services (2). Beyond the private sector the firm stands ready to assist government agencies (2).

Price Waterhouse was also very active in Malaysia prior to its merger with Coopers & Lybrand. Its services in that nation were reviewed in some detail in an earlier investigation and need not be re-listed here (McKee and Garner, 1996b, 99–101).

THE PHILIPPINES

Writing in 1999 Chalongphob Sussangkarn et al. suggested that the crisis that is the justification for the present volume impacted the Phil-

ippines less severely than was the case with Thailand, Indonesia and
Malaysia (Sussangkarn, Flatters and Kittiprapas, 1999, 3–9). Indeed those
authors were of the opinion that the Philippines, while incurring some
of the contagion effects of the spreading crisis, weathered the crisis re-
markably well. Those most affected by the crisis were seen as the upper
and middle classes, living in urban areas and enjoying high levels of
participation in the formal sector.

According to the New Zealand Trade Development Board the nation
was one of the wealthiest in Asia during the 1950s but by the 1980s had
become one of the poorest—a result of poor economic management and
policies (February 2000a, 3). The Philippines have an abundance of natural resources ranging from timber to agricultural products, rubber and
minerals (3). The composition of GDP in 1998 saw agriculture, forestry
and fishing accounting for 19.75 percent (3). Other sectors included manufacturing at 21.83 percent, government and private services 16.80 percent, commerce and trade 17.15 percent and communications and
transport 4.51 percent (3).

The report alluded to provided further detail regarding the manufacturing and industry sector, the agriculture, fishing and forestry sector
and the service sector. It points out that manufacturing is dominated by
electronics, garments, footwear, food manufacturing, petroleum and coal
products and base metal production, with electronics and garments being the major generators of foreign exchange (3). Agriculture was cited
as employing about half of the nation's workforce (4), a fact that is in-
structive given the sector's share of GDP. The report points to the nation's success in developing light industries that have gained footholds
in the major world markets (4).

The service sector, including transportation and communications,
trade, finance, real estate and private and government services contributes roughly 45 percent of annual GDP (4). The report cites major areas
of service expansion to be tourism, computer services, advertising, financial services and institutions, transport and communications services,
housing and trade (5).

In another context the New Zealand Trade Development Board has
assessed the strengths and weaknesses of the Philippine market (June
2000, 3). Their appraisal was cast primarily in the context of the nation's
potential for commerce and business relations with New Zealand. The
report in question predicted that the Philippines market will remain stable and will offer opportunities to New Zealand exporters (3). It cited
credibility and image as the main concerns and suggested that political
tensions could possibly affect business momentum (3).

Among market strengths enjoyed by the Philippines the report cited
the existence of a growing middle class with rising incomes and the
growth momentum of the manufacturing sector (3). Beyond that it cred-

ited the nation as being resilient and having established institutions. Other positive notes included the Philippines' status as the world's third largest English-speaking nation as well as its use of western style business practices and its highly skilled and educated labor force (30).

Despite the list of positive elements the report saw weaknesses based upon a perception/image problem, reliance on the agricultural sector and inefficiencies and delays in implementing plans and projects (3). Other drawbacks cited include the nation being prone to natural disasters, deficiencies in infrastructure and direct airlinks, although the last mentioned issue may pertain to New Zealand (3).

It does seem as though the Philippines have much to gain from services available through major international accounting firms and other purveyors of facilitative business services. In 1991 Bavishi reported the nation as having 157 partners in the major international accounting firms, 141 of whom were located in Manila. It was suggested in another context that such a concentration may not be advantageous for the nation's overall development (McKee and Garner, 1996b, 97).

Deloitte Touche Tohmatsu is represented in the Philippines by C.L. Manabat & Company. Representatives of the firm act not just as advisors but as partners in assisting organizations in achieving their business objectives (Deloitte Touche Tohmatsu, 1999, 1). It offers audit, finance, consulting, outsourcing, tax and corporate advisory, management and business consulting services to a wide range of clients in various industries (1). Clients come from various service industries, manufacturing, commerce, agri-business and nonprofit organizations (2).

The firm has various objectives including providing clients with an array of services responsive to their needs and helping them in making choices and pursuing action that reflects shared values and vision (2). In addition the firm stands ready to build the capabilities of its client companies in managing change and achieving sustainable development, as well as to contribute to the growth of technology and organization development (2).

Among professional services offered by the firm are business consulting services (2). Those services are divided into three categories—general business advisory, financial advisory and business development and strategy (2–3). In the area of general business advisory services the firm can assist with business systems analysis and design, organizational restructuring, organization development and planning and visioning, corporate image enhancement and public relations (2–3).

Financial advisory service offerings include assistance with investment planning, financial restructuring for private and public placements and loan syndication (3). Service offerings in the area of business development and strategy include industry studies and market research, project development and implementation and corporate strategic planning (3).

The firm offers a broad range of tax and corporate services. Services listed include the organizing of business enterprises, labor and personnel relations and fiscal and nonfiscal incentives (3). The firm can also assist with trademark applications and registration of licensing agreements (3). In the area of taxation the firm can assist with real property taxation and local taxation as well as with income tax preparation and statutory returns (3). Other tax services offered include tax advisory and planning, tax audit and tax laws compliance evaluation and review of tax effects of alternative courses of action (3).

Assurance and advisory services include statutory audit, acquisition audit, internal audit, operations and management audit and fraud audit (3). Due diligence reviews and litigation support are also available (3). The firm is also active in the area of outsourcing. It assists with manpower sourcing and executive headhunting, payroll processing, bookkeeping services and business-center facilities.

In an earlier study the activities of Price Waterhouse in the Philippines were cited (McKee and Garner, 1996b, 100). That firm was providing a wide range of professional services (100). Beyond accountants the firm employed systems analysts, economists, human resources specialists, project development experts, industrial engineers and investment advisors (100). The firm was described as having structured itself as a wide ranging service supplier that was equipped to facilitate business in a variety of ways. It saw itself as helping the community at large as well as its clients and indeed had placed representatives in various professional, public and private organizations (100). It was quoted to the effect that its "professionals also participate in public hearings of issues involving tax, investment incentives and other business concerns" (Price Waterhouse, 1989c, 165). As noted in another context, involvements such as those described reinforce the firm's credibility while advancing its business interests and impacting the local economy (McKee and Garner, 1996b, 100).

What has been presented above in regard to Deloitte Touche Tohmatsu tends to reinforce perceptions gained from earlier discussions of Price Waterhouse. Major international accounting firms have much to offer with respect to the facilitation of economic and business activity.

THAILAND

It seems ironic that Thailand is generally seen as the origin of the financial and economic crises that ravished Southeast Asian nations beginning in 1997, considering a rather optimistic prognosis for that nation as late as 1996 (McKee and Garner, 1996b, 95). Writing in 1993 Claudia Cragg reported that Thailand was enjoying the highest growth rate in GDP in the Asian-Pacific Rim "at an average of nearly 10 percent per annum" (299). Thailand during the 1990s was increasingly being grouped with the Asian Tigers as a newly industrialized economy that was export led (McKee and Garner, 1996b, 95).

Cragg pointed to Thailand as becoming more and more involved in the global economy and "has started to become a major export platform for a number of companies that have relocated large-scale manufacturing facilities there" (1993, 312). According to her the international involvement in question revolved around manufacturing for export (313).

Evidence that the events of 1997 had exacted a toll on the nation's economy can be seen in a prediction of negative growth in the 6 percent range for 1998 (New Zealand Trade Development Board, July 1998, 3). In actuality "Real GDP contracted by . . . 8.0% in 1998" (APEC, August 29, 2000, 1).

The crisis is said to have had greater social impacts in urban areas where there was "particularly rapid employment reduction in the construction and manufacturing sectors as well as sharply increasing underemployment" (Sussangkarn, Flatters and Kittiprapas, 1999, 4). The Institute pointed out that the rural economy is also encountering growing unemployment, especially in agriculture (4). Services and commerce have registered employment increases but are simultaneously encountering underemployment (4). The crisis has impacted traditionally poor rural areas as well as Bangkok and other urban centers. In Bangkok unemployment and declining incomes have emerged, in large part caused by the collapse of the financial, manufacturing and construction sectors, causing large layoffs of both white collar and skilled workers (4). Rural areas have been hurt by reduced remittances and rising food costs (4).

According to the New Zealand Trade Development Board the government's eighth Five-Year Plan (1997–2001) placed emphasis upon various areas. Among its concerns were the development of the private sector, including industry and services, and further deregulation in trade, finance and industry accompanied by tax revisions aimed at encouraging domestic competitiveness (July 1998, 3). The plan also included national policies on environmental protection and pollution and increased government expenditures on the development of the infrastructure and health care (3). Land reform, improved education and government decentralization were also included (3).

In 1991 Bavishi credited Thailand with hosting 73 partners in major accounting firms. All of the partners were based in Bangkok. Prominent among major accounting firms active in the nation is Deloitte Touche Tohmatsu Jaiyos. Its service offerings include traditional audit and advisory, enterprise risk and corporate finance and restructuring, as well as resource solution and Japanese business services (2000c, 1). The firm also provides consulting services through Deloitte Consulting and deals with accounting and bookkeeping.

It lists among its clients major banks, companies listed on the stock exchange and more than 300 international enterprises as well as numerous medium-sized companies (1). Its clients come from a wide range of industries including banking and finance, manufacturing, utilities, transport and distribution, construction and hospitality (1).

In the area of audit and advisory services the firm assists clients to meet their statutory requirements and also acts as business advisors (2). "With professionals well versed in audit and accounting regulations and standards . . . we provide clients with assurance that their financial statements fairly present the financial position . . . and comply with the relevant rules and regulations in Thailand" (2). Through its global firm they keep abreast of International Accounting Standards (2). Expatriate professionals in the firm in Thailand provide knowledge and experience in areas related to international GAAP reporting and other matters related to international business operations (2).

With respect to tax matters the firm can assist with strategic tax planning and financing structures, as well as mergers and acquisitions and expatriate planning and tax compliance (3). They also provide corporate legal services and act as a liaison with the Revenue Department.

Enterprise risk services constitute another area of interest for the firm. In that area it identifies and quantifies present and future exposure and puts systematic risk management policies in place (3). It seeks to make risk management an explicit, integral part of everyday business (3). Their approach is designed to integrate people, objectives and processes in a cohesive risk framework (4).

With respect to resource solutions the firm provides a range of services designed to assist clients to effectively manage their people resources (5). They assist with the recruitment of qualified people to fill senior and middle management roles and also advise clients with respect to human resource needs, including compensation reviews, organizational reviews and performance assessment (5).

In the area of corporate finance they offer strategic advice and assistance concerning investment opportunities and give independent support and advice concerning mergers, disposals, refinancing, restructuring, joint ventures and other forms of strategic alliance and transactions (5). The firm stands ready to provide cross-border investment advice in various forms (5). They provide assessments of the strategic value of targets and advice on acquisition strategy (5). They assist with financial analysis and due diligence, transaction structuring and negotiations and completion (5–6). With respect to corporate restructuring the firm assists individuals, financial institutions, government agencies, creditors, debtors and multinational companies (6).

The importance of Japanese business to Thailand can be seen in the firm's practice of having a full-time Japanese expatriate partner in Thailand as head of their team charged with servicing Japanese companies (7). "Our Japanese Business Services team understands the needs of Japanese business and the requirements of the local Thai business environment" (7). The team offers experience over a wide range of industries which include banking and financial institutions, car manufacturing, machinery and equipment manufacturing, electrical/electronics manufacturing, chemical and pharmaceutical manufacturing, wholesale/trade distribution, and utilities (7). In fulfilling the needs of Japanese firms, the team works closely with Tohmatsu & Company, the firm's affiliate in Japan.

Arthur Andersen is another member of the Big Five active in Thailand. Arthur Andersen Thailand consists of several affiliated companies including SGV-NA Thalang & Co. Ltd., Arthur Andersen Business Advisory Ltd., Andersen Legal & Tax Ltd., and Executive Recruitment Services Ltd. (2000a, 1). The Andersen practice has moved beyond the Bangkok location of their head office and are represented in all regions of the country (1). The firm assists with assurance, business consulting, corporate finance business, human capital, legal services, outsourcing, risk consulting and tax services (2000b, 1–2).

Grant Thornton International is another major international firm active in Thailand. Grant Thornton Thailand provides a comprehensive range of business advisory services with the goal of helping growing entrepreneurial businesses achieve their ambitions locally, nationally and overseas (April 1998, 1). The firm offers services in the areas of auditing, accounting, taxation, and corporate recovery and restructuring, corporate secretarial services, tax and legal and recruitment (2000, 1).

Trade Partners Limited came into being in 1978 and offers services concerned with company incorporation, accounting and tax matters (2000a, 1). They claim to have incorporated in excess of 200 foreign companies in Thailand (1). The firm can assist in finding partners and shareholders as well as in all legal matters relative to the company's incorporation (2000b, 1). It provides managerial services on behalf of absentee directors and is also willing to assume responsibility for performing various duties on behalf of a director as required (2000b, 1). Legal services offered include establishing a company, reporting requirements and alien business law (1). Professional services offered include accounting, auditing and tax, as well as secretarial services, business consulting and acting as trustee on behalf of absentee directors (1).

European Accountants Co., Ltd., provide what they describe as "Affordable multilingual accounting services and financial management" in Thailand (1999–2000a, 1). That particular firm came into being with an eye to servicing a clientele presumably ill-suited to employing the services of the larger accounting firms. "[I]n January of 1996, European Accountants Co. Ltd. was established with the specific aim to assist the small to medium-size foreign owned local businesses or foreign representative offices with their financial management" (1).

Chapter 9

Accounting Firms and Development Prospects among Pacific Island States

No discussion of the role of major international accounting firms in the post-crisis Asia Pacific region would be complete without some attention to the island economies. For that reason this Chapter examines the situation in three island states, Papua New Guinea, Fiji and Vanuatu. Those nations will be discussed in a fashion parallel to that employed in the preceding two Chapters.

FIJI

The republic of Fiji comprises more than 300 islands, situated in the middle of the South Pacific approximately halfway between the Hawaiian Islands and Australia. Its two largest islands account for 87 percent of the land area and 93 percent of the population (NAI'A Cruises Fiji, 1998, 1). The nation's population is in the 800,000 range.

"The Bureau of Statistics indicates that by the year 2001 Fiji's population will have reached 843,000—a growth rate of 1.2 percent [per] year between 1991 and 2001" (Fiji Trade and Investment Board, 1999a, 1). More than 60 percent of the nation's population live in rural areas. Among urban centers, 205,695 people live in the greater Suva area, 51,302 in Lautoka, and 17,546 in Nadi (1). Other urban centers include Ba, Labasa, Sigatoka, Levula and Nausori (1).

Port facilities exist in Suva and Lautoka. The main island also houses most of the primary and secondary industrial development and a good deal of the tourist infrastructure (1999, 4). Economic activity on the second largest island Vanua Levu, is centered around sugar, logging, copra, fishing and tourism (1999a, 4).

"The present road system is well developed with a tar-sealed highway linking Suva and Lautoka along the southern/western sections of the island" (1999a, 4). Buses follow scheduled itineraries within and between cities, towns and other populated areas on Vita Lava and the other main islands (1999a, 4). Main commercial centers are linked by road, air or sea. Most international flights on trans-Pacific routes use Nadi International Airport. The nation enjoys regular service by airlines from Australia and New Zealand, while its national airline Air Pacific flies between Nadi, New Zealand, Australia, Japan, Republic of Korea and west coast United States, not to mention other countries of the South Pacific (1999a, 4). The nation also enjoys international shipping services through the main port of Suva with "wharf facilities . . . capable of handling large cargo and passenger vessels" (1999a, 4). Other ports of entry include Lautoka, Levuka and Savusava.

The nation gained its independence from Great Britain in 1970 but remained a member of the British Commonwealth. It was dismissed from the Commonwealth in 1987 following two bloodless coups. "The coups had a devastating effect on the Fijian economy. Fiji was thrown out of the Commonwealth, suffered an 11 percent decline in gross domestic product, and lost thousands of Indian professionals and their families to overseas emigration: Nearly 30,000 all told" (1999, 3).

Following a period of rather significant political adjustment, Fiji was "reembraced back into the Commonwealth following the Heads of Government meeting in Edinburgh in 1997" ("An Introduction to the Fiji Islands," 1999, 2). The nation is a democratic republic—a bicameral government based on the Westminster model (New Zealand Trade Development Board, March 1998, 3). Its legal system is also based upon English Common Law.

The nation traditionally has been a key economic power in the southwest Pacific (3). It recovered well from economic problems occasioned by the coups. "In 1996 Fiji's economic growth rate was 4.4% compared with 1.4% in 1995" (3). However, "The effect of the South East Asian crisis was hard felt by Fiji and in an effort to remain competitive in the region the government devalued the Fijian dollar by 20% in January of 1998" (An Introduction to the Fiji Islands, 1999, 3). Tourism was seen as the nation's major foreign currency earner (3). "The past ten years were a time of hardship for Fiji. The effects of the coups and Fiji's alienation from the international community were felt by a devalued dollar, tourism fell due to the negative impact associated with the coups, inflation was high, and wages were low" (3).

The government is making serious efforts to diversify the economic base and welcome foreign direct investment (3). Manufacturing, agriculture, fishing, timber, garments and gold mining are expanding (New Zealand Trade Development Board, March 1998, 3). Indeed, "Fiji is industrialising and now has a diverse and in some areas, internationally competitive manufacturing sector" (March 1998, 3). A recent source of expansion in manufacturing has been the garment industry (3).

"Fiji has an outward looking export oriented trade policy" (4). The government offers many incentives for investors, including such things as a 13-year income tax break, and trade-free zones ("An Introduction to the Fiji Islands," 1999, 3). In addition to export industries such as garments and footwear, manufacturing includes concrete, cement and other building materials for domestic and regional markets, as well as furniture, foods, processed timber for export and household products (Fiji Trade and Investment Board, 1999a, 6).

The government is active in promoting an outward looking development strategy for the nation. This can be seen in the mission statement of the Fiji Trade and Investment Board—"To be a dynamic force in the creation of economic wealth and prosperity for the people of Fiji, the Board will promote increased investment and export, stimulate the development of industries, ventures, or enterprises that enhance employment opportunities and facilitate economic development" (1999b, 1).

The Fiji Trade and Investment Board was established "in recognition of Fiji's need to generate more investment opportunities and to assist in fulfilling national development objectives" (1999b, 2). The Board is actually the first point of contact for those wishing to set up business in Fiji. It helps with procedures with respect to applications for work permits, tax concessions and the approval of companies to operate in the country (1999b, 2).

Among the Board's divisions is marketing, which is responsible for promotional activities. The projects division "Collects and appraises all requests by companies that wish to establish a business in Fiji, and advises those who need information about setting up business (1999b, 2). The Projects Implementation and Monitoring Division carries out strategic planning research to assist the Board in providing advice to government on economic policies designed to increase the level of investment in the nation. The Finance and Human Resource division controls finances and coordinates human resources activities. The Kalabo Tax Free Zone Division was established in 1997 to manage the operations of the new tax-free zone (1999b, 2).

Fiji was grouped by Te'o Fairbairn among Pacific states with a potential for attaining cumulative economic growth and structural diversification through the use of land, sea and tourist resources (1985, 46). While acknowledging that the economies in question had made progress through planning and a "considerable input of private foreign investment" (46), he attributed their positive performances to natural endowments. "The major factor underlying these growth performances has been successful export diversification through natural resource development" (48). In the case of Fiji it seems clear that the Fiji Trade and Investment Board has far broader objectives than what was alluded to by Fairbairn.

Although it seems clear that Fiji has been committed to attaining foreign investment and the diversification that such a policy should support, a robust pursuit of international service activities is somewhat less obvious. Tourism notwithstanding, outward-looking service activities do not appear to occupy a major position in the Fijian economy.

It is known that services that are traded internationally are quite significant in the growth possibilities of small economies (Amara, 1993a). Amara has suggested that such services can often do what primary and secondary pursuits have not done, by earning needed foreign exchange, not to mention domestic employment opportunities. She has presented evidence concerning the inputs of various services in the strengthening of selected Caribbean economies (1993b).

Of course locational factors, among other things, make comparisons between the Caribbean experience and the realities facing the Pacific Island economies in general, or more specifically Fiji, rather difficult. It has been conceded that there are very real limitations on the ability of the island mini states of the Pacific to improve their international linkages, not to mention their domestic economies, through service involvement, even though they could benefit from an expansion of service subsectors in their economies (McKee and Garner, 1996b, 108). This may well be true of Fiji. Nonetheless, various business services can strengthen domestic economies that have no involvement in dramatic service subsectors such as international tourism or offshore finance (1996, 108).

An example of such a service set would be the offerings of the major international accounting firms. Such firms "have grown in keeping with the needs of international business or perhaps more accurately in keeping with the needs of the international economy" (McKee and Garner, 1992, 72). The firms in question have demonstrated their willingness to establish themselves as warranted by the business needs of their clients. In cases where they located in emerging nations, they have been assisting those nations with linkages to the global economy, not to mention the strengthening of domestic economies (McKee, Garner and AbuAmara McKee, 1998 and 1999).

The major accounting firms have not had a heavy concentration in Fiji. Bavishi reported Fiji as hosting four partners in major accounting firms (1991). As mentioned elsewhere Price Waterhouse had two partners and a staff of 60 in Fiji (McKee and Garner, 1996b, 113). The services offered by that firm were similar to those offered in Papua New Guinea and thus need not be redetailed here. Whether a heavier concentration of accounting firms in Fiji would strengthen the nation's prospects remains to be seen. However some of the functions or services offered by the firms resemble some of the actions of the Fiji Trade and Investment Board.

PAPUA NEW GUINEA

Papua New Guinea (PNG) is located about 160 kilometers north of Australia and covers some 470,000 square kilometers. It is composed of the eastern half of the island of New Guinea and some 600 offshore islands. The nation's capital is Port Moresby, a city of 250,000 inhabitants. Lea is the main industrial center and the major port, boasting a population of 120,000. In all the population of the nation totaled some 4.3 million in the mid-1990s.

Papua New Guinea became an independent nation in 1975, as a parliamentary democracy and member of the British Commonwealth. "The legal system closely follows Australian law, which in turn is derived from the English legal system" (New Zealand Trade Development Board, June 1999, 3). Nonetheless in some circumstances, traditional law, predating colonialism, applies (3).

The nation is classified as a lower-middle-income country and more than 80 percent of the population live in rural environments, dependent upon subsistence agriculture. Its exports include copper ore, gold, oil, coffee, cocoa, lobster and forest products, with minerals and oil accounting for up to 80 percent of the total (4). Its principle export markets include Japan, Australia, the United States, Singapore and New Zealand (4). Thus it relies heavily upon exports within the Asian Pacific region.

Among the nation's principal imports are machinery and transportation equipment, manufactured goods, food, fuels and chemicals, which have as their principal sources Australia, Japan, the United Kingdom, the Netherlands and New Zealand (4). The need to import machinery and manufactured goods is hardly surprising in a nation of its size and level of material development. However food imports may be an area suggesting the need for import substitution.

As early as 1985 Te'o Fairbairn saw Papua New Guinea among the larger island countries of the Pacific with the best growth prospects (45). He predicted that such countries could expect major changes in social and economic life as "manifested through such avenues as the attainment of higher levels of social and welfare services; greater diversification of economic activity; stronger involvement in foreign capital; accelerated urbanization; and a further decline in subsistence activity" (45). If such a statement can be seen as a prescription rather than a prediction, it has certainly retained major relevance.

Transportation linkages between the nation's provinces have not been among its advantages. The New Zealand Trade Development Board reports that "With a world class new international and domestic airport in operation in Port Moresby, air travel has improved considerably" (June 1999, 6). The airport is linked to the capital city by a new road. However travel between provinces is accomplished mainly by air, sea or river, since few locations enjoy good road access (6). On the positive side change is occurring since the construction of new roads is being funded by aid from Australia, Korea and Japan (6).

The current authors are hardly on controversial ground in endorsing the need for further diversification of the nation's economy, not to mention its external linkages. According to the New Zealand Trade Development Board the nation suffered a GDP growth rate of minus 6.5 percent in 1988, while experiencing an inflation rate of 14.7 percent (June 1999, 1). Speaking more generally of the islands of the Pacific it has been suggested that "ongoing subsistence activities and indeed the cultures associated with them have long been recognized as impediments to material improvements in various locations" (McKee and Garner, 1996b, 104). Presumably improved domestic transportation linkages, coupled with economic diversification where possible, would certainly strengthen the nation's economy.

In another context it was suggested that services that are traded internationally are very important to the growth of small economies (Amara, 1993a and b). Such services can often accomplish what primary and secondary pursuits have been unable to do by earning needed foreign exchange and generating domestic employment opportunities. What offshore financial services can do in small jurisdictions is quite evident (McKee, Garner and AbuAmara McKee, 2000).

It might be overoptimistic to suggest that Papua New Guinea can meet desired developmental goals by becoming an offshore financial center. That field is already rather crowded. However, certain international business services may prove helpful in both domestic and international contexts. Notable among such services may be the facilitative activities of major international accounting firms and organizations.

As early as 1991 Bavishi reported that the major international accounting firms boasted 21 partners in Papua New Guinea, all but one of whom were associated with the then-Big Six. Fourteen of the partners were located in Port Moresby, the nation's capital. Of the remainder four were based in Lea, while Gorka, Mount Hazen and Rabaul each were hosting one partner. The parties to the recent Big Six merger, Coopers & Lybrand and Price Waterhouse accounted for nine and three partners respectively. Of the remainder KPMG had five partners, Deloitte Ross Tohmatsu International had two and Ernst & Young had one partner. Pannell Kerr Forster, with one partner, was the only non–Big Six firm represented (Bavishi, 1991, Appendix B, 19).

Although not a member of the Big Six at the time of Bavishi's investigation, Pannell Kerr Forster International Association (PFK) is among the top business advisory organizations, measured by turnover and quality (PKF International, 1995–1997). In 1996 the organization boasted over 150 firms in 111 countries. "Member firms of the Association are legally independent of one another and provide services to clients on the basis of qualified and uniform standards kept consistently by all PKF Member firms" (PKF International, 1995–1997).

Principle services provided include audit, accounting and corporate restructuring. In addition the organization provides corporate advice on matters including mergers, acquisitions, public listings and management buyouts. Management Consultancy services available include all aspects of financial consulting, human resources and information technology. The organization claims to have a "particular worldwide consulting pre-eminence . . . in hotels, leisure and tourism where offices . . . provide a co-ordinated service to hotel investors, owners and operators worldwide covering all aspects of feasibility planning, valuation and operation" (PKF International, 1995–1997).

Indeed in the realm of tourism the organization through its International Tourism Unit stands ready to offer high-level policy advice to both national governments and international agencies concerning all aspects of tourism policy and planning (PKF International, 1995–1997). The organization is also prepared to assist with tax matters. Although boasting only one partner in Papua New Guinea, that partner has access to the expertise to dispense the services detailed above.

Price Waterhouse was also active in Papua New Guinea. It seems clear that that firm was well aware of its potential for impacting host jurisdictions. It saw itself through its worldwide network of specialists as "particularly well placed to meet the changing needs of international business. It is uniquely equipped to advise in matters relating to international operations, not only in individual countries but on a regional or global basis" (Price Waterhouse, 1990b, 152) This excerpt from the firm's guide for Papua New Guinea speaks to the potential impact that it might have.

Price Waterhouse in Papua New Guinea was operating as a part of its Australian firm. Although it had only three partners and a total staff of 25, it did boast "a significant group of consultants engaged on management consulting assignments" (152). The offices in Port Moresby and Lae each had a resident audit partner, assisted by expatriates, audit personnel and local staff members with varying levels or stages of training and qualifications. As was suggested elsewhere it seems clear that the firm saw an advantage in training local staff and such a function was expected to have a positive impact on the local economy (McKee and Garner, 1996b, 111),

In its manual for Papua New Guinea the firm included a detailed statement of purpose that is illustrative of how a large accounting firm can relate to a host economy and the world at large (154). "From its intent to react quickly to the needs of clients to its desire to contribute to the development of its profession while playing a role in the wider community, it is clear that the firm intends a positive broad-based and expanding role in the economy of Papua New Guinea" (McKee and Garner, 1996b, 111). It hardly seems unrealistic to assume that Price Waterhouse Coopers and indeed other major international accounting firms and organizations share similar objectives.

The firm's intentions and indeed the scope of its role can be seen in its desire "To adopt a comprehensive and integrated multi-discipline approach to the provision of service, based on an understanding of the requirements of each client" and "to be part of a strong worldwide organization serving clients on an international basis" (153). Of course if such objectives were pursued by the Australian branch of the firm it seems logical that linkages between Papua New Guinea and Australia should be facilitated.

Price Waterhouse offered a rather broad menu of services in Papua New Guinea beyond its basic accounting and auditing services. Its offerings included taxation and exchange control, management consultancy, corporate reconstruction and insolvency, together with business advisory, corporate secretarial, government liaison and the recruitment of personnel and training (153–154). Certainly such a range of services should be expected to have very salutary impacts upon the economy.

The firm offers assistance with income tax planning, including international tax planning, the preparation of returns and advice on exchange controls (154). Of course to the extent that such services can be expected to be successful in attracting international clients, and presumably international financial capital, they should serve to improve linkages between Papua New Guinea and the global economy. Such an integration "may provide higher levels of needed foreign exchange, more employment opportunities in the domestic economy and presumably economic expansion" wherever they occur (McKee and Garner, 1992, 85). It has been suggested that such benefits may come in exchange for a reduction in economic sovereignty as the domestic economy gains a closer linkage to the global scene (McKee and Garner, 1996b, 112). It seems clear that planners in Papua New Guinea or other small economies experiencing such adjustments should appraise themselves of the costs and benefits on an ongoing basis.

The management consulting arm of the firm in Australia was Price Waterhouse Ururck, which offered a wide variety of services. "By making use of the worldwide network of Price Waterhouse, the firm is able to supplement the skills of its own consultants with the skills of other consultants in specialized areas and industries" (Price Waterhouse, 1990b, 154). The firm claimed to cover a majority of business functions, including general management, information technology, finance, manufacturing, marketing and matters related to human resources (154–155). As has been suggested elsewhere "where any international accounting firm offers such services it is involved in a fundamental way in matters that will impact not just its clients but also the economies that house those clients" (McKee and Garner, 1996b, 112).

In Papua New Guinea the firm offered its business advisory services to both small and large firms. It stood ready to assist firms entering the market in staff recruitment and in structuring activities to conform to local laws and regulations. It was also able to assist in business services vis-à-vis management decision making, forecasting and marketing (155). It arranged for the incorporation of subsidiaries, the registration of foreign companies, and for immigration clearance and work permits for expatriate personnel. It also prepared localization and training programs to be filed with the Department of Labour and Employment. Beyond such matters it assisted firms in establishing accounting systems and maintaining accounting records (155).

Price Waterhouse was also actively involved in assisting government and quasi-public agencies. "We are able to provide positive assistance in liaising with a wide range of government departments and instrumentalities, vital in setting up and maintaining a business operation in Papua New Guinea" (155). Whether Price Waterhouse or other major international accounting firms or organizations offer their services to smooth the way for foreign firms to set up operations in Papua New Guinea directly, or assist government agencies in their dealings with potential foreign business entrants, it seems reasonable to expect developmental impacts.

VANUATU

Formerly known as the New Hebrides and administered jointly by France and Great Britain, Vanuatu became an independent nation in 1980. The country is composed of about 80 islands, situated some 1,750 km northeast of Sydney, Australia. The nation's capital is Port Vila, which is situated on Efate Island. The population of the nation numbers about 140,000 with 20,000 living in the capital.

According to Walter and Dorothy Diamond, the backbone of Vanuatu's economy is agriculture, supplemented by tourism and offshore financial activities (1998, 14). Moores Rowland has described Vanuatu as a dualistic economy, with "a large smallholder subsistence agricultural sector and a small monetised sector" (September 30, 1997, 2). The monetized sector includes plantations, ranches and associated trading, as well as manufacturing, banking, shipping services and of course tourism (2).

"Nearly all domestic exports are primary goods, the principal ones being coconut products, beef, cocoa, coffee and timber" (2).

The Diamonds report that "Vanuatu's third national development plan, from 1992–1996, is supposed to conclude the Government's program of achieving economic self reliance" (1998, 14). According to those authors the third phase seemed to fill three gaps in the economy. The first gap was insufficient investment funds from domestic savings, which presumably could be alleviated by the Vanuatu Development Bank and the four commercial banks. The second was an imbalance of trade and the last was the failure to achieve a balanced budget (1998, 14).

In spite of those difficulties an FND report seems rather optimistic in its appraisal of the nation as an international financial center (1997–1998). The report points to the absence of income, capital gains and withholding taxes as well as estate duties. It explains that the nation has no exchange controls and no reporting requirements with respect to the movement of funds. In addition, funds can be held in most currencies and can easily be converted from one to another. FND declares Port Vila to have first-class international communications facilities. Their report also points to "Extensive financial, legal and banking expertise within the financial centre" (1997–1998, 1). The report describes the financial center as enjoying a reputation for successfully holding the integrity of its jurisdiction (1997–1998, 1).

It does appear that Vanuatu is in a position to improve its economic circumstances through encouraging its offshore financial activities. In spite of the difficulties referred to by the Diamonds, the economy is growing at a rate of 6 percent (1998, 14). According to those authors at least eight Far Eastern, European and American banks have branches in Vila and five trust companies offer financial management assistance (1998, 16). It would appear that major accounting firms may find the nation a good base from which to offer their international services.

Moores Rowland is quite prominent among major international accounting firms and organizations operating in Vanuatu. By its own assessment Moores Rowland International is the world's ninth largest accounting group, boasting 140 firms in 569 offices in more than 80 countries. The organization's South Pacific specialists are housed in Vanuatu. The firm is a founding member of the Vanuatu Financial Center Association (1998a). It offers accounting, auditing, management and consulting services to government, offshore clients, local businesses, and private individuals on a worldwide basis (1998a). It also provides wholesale company incorporation services to finance, legal and tax guidance professionals (1998a).

The firm was established in Port Vila in 1971 and describes itself as a central figure in the offshore financial centers of the Pacific (1998a). It identifies Vanuatu as the premiere Pacific tax haven and a major financial center for administering and managing offshore companies, trusts, banks, insurance companies and shipping regulation (1998a). Vanuatu is described as free of personal and corporate income taxes, estate and gift taxes. In addition it has no exchange controls and enjoys secure privacy provisions (1998a).

Moores Rowland offers a complete range of professional accounting services. In addition they assist with the incorporation of international companies, local companies, insurance companies and banks (1998b). They serve as a registered agent and keep a registered office address in the country of incorporation. They deal in all aspects of company and trust management, which includes bookkeeping, the establishment and management of bank accounts, and arranging for corporate credit cards. In addition they assist with corporate management and offer advice on corporate tax matters (1998b). Their subsidiaries and associate entities deal with trustee services, real estate sales and management, communication services, as well as banking and legal services (1998b).

Another major accounting firm operating in Vanuatu is BDO International. That firm deals with international company formation, as well as trust formation and trustee services. Beyond such matters it deals with the formation and management of offshore banks and captive insurance companies. The firm provides the traditional accounting and auditing services and offers a range of consulting services. Beyond such matters it can provide local investment advice and can also assist with funds management (BDO International, 1999).

Prior to its merger with Coopers & Lybrand, Price Waterhouse maintained an office in Vanuatu. "The Vanuatu practice is a part of the Price Waterhouse Australasian Firm and operates from an office in Port Vila. Clients over a wide range of Vanuatu are served from this office" (Price Waterhouse, 1992d, 63). The firm dated from 1972 when it was established "to provide professional auditing, accounting, management consulting and financial services to both local and international clients" (63). According to the firm it was able "to provide distinctive comprehensive service on an integrated basis to global clients with operations based in Vanuatu," by working with its offices around the world (64).

It seems clear that the major accounting firms have much to offer clients in Vanuatu and are in a position to influence the domestic economy of that jurisdiction as well. Indeed Moores Rowland has suggested a willingness to assist investors that have experienced difficulties resulting from the Asian crisis (Moores Rowland, 1998c, 1). That firm recognized the possible advantages offered to offshore financial centers in the Pacific. "Amid the turmoil of recent months, Asian investors, particularly those with exposure in Indonesia are turning to the Pacific offshore finance centers to base their holding companies and regional financing vehicles" (1998c, 1).

The firm explains that investors looking to establish a temporary base to weather the crisis have looked to safe havens such as Vanuatu (1998c, 1). "Enquiries from Indonesia have become regular daily events in our Port Vila office since late April" (1998c, 1). The firm further explains that the inquiries in question are mainly passive investors seeking to set up holding companies and trusts in order to safeguard assets for long-term family use "for will planning and to distance beneficial ownership from individuals for asset protection purposes" (1998c, 1). The firm has added a new range of opportunities for its Asian investors to its Web site. This of course suggests that Moores Rowland has actually found a means to benefit from the Asian crisis. It seems clear that Vanuatu as their host should also benefit. The firm summarizes the potential impact of its endeavors succinctly: "As our site develops, the end result will be an online service that simplifies the establishment of offshore entities from remote locations" (1998c, 1).

Certainly it cannot be said that jurisdictions like Vanuatu will succeed economically in some direct proportion to the presence of major international accounting firms or networks. Nonetheless, "It can be said that the firms are members of the cadre of services that facilitate international business operations in the world economy" (McKee and Garner, 1996b, 114). Clearly by extending their dealings to Vanuatu, they have certainly strengthened international linkages with that jurisdiction. Vanuatu and other offshore financial centers in the Pacific may have actually benefited from the Asian crisis if major accounting firms and other purveyors of facilitative services have been able to redirect international dealings through their economies.

Part IV

Implications for Recovery and Growth in the Pacific Basin

Chapter 10

From National to Global Accounting and Reporting Standards

In the past accounting, auditing and financial reporting standards were oriented primarily to national markets. Today, and increasingly in the future, it would seem, these standards need to be promulgated for transactions occurring in ever-wider markets. Capital formation and allocation is occurring within ever-wider borders as nations continue to group themselves into regional markets. Capital markets, which in prior times served smaller areas of the globe, now service extensive constituencies, with many having global reach. In an evolutionary process the capital markets of the world have become more interdependent and more competitive.

Capital flows and ownership have always to some extent transcended national borders. In recent times, capital moves with such rapidity and ease across many borders that the globe has virtually become the marketplace. Modern improvements in transportation, communication and technology have, of course, allowed the great strides that have resulted in the efficiencies of larger markets. Not the least of these efficiencies is in the capital markets.

Information needs are perhaps greater in the wider marketplace than they have been in past smaller arenas. Capital market participants seeking to buy and sell securities depend on information received from financial reports. With the exercise of user judgment, the reports must be indicative of prospects for future cash flows. Financial reports in order to be most useful for decision making must be as accurate, as free from misstatements made from error or intention, and as relevant as possible. They must also be reliable. And, because users make decisions about alternatives, ideally they need to be comparable from one company to another, from one country to another.

The development of accounting standards was in the past highly influenced by the needs of the society that gave rise to them. National standards seemed to have followed an evolutionary process. As the needs of business organizations and the economy grew, accounting and reporting standards changed and grew in response, taking different paths depending upon the society, its needs and organizational patterns.

Some countries have allocated capital through the use of large company combines; some through collecting the funds into large banking systems from which they are distributed to large corporations and other users; some have government-directed or cartel-directed allocation systems; and some use market-based stock markets. Each of these national systems of allocating funds to uses has given rise to accounting and reporting standards that were more or less appropriate to the needs of the nation in question.

As the global economy grows, larger amounts of capital are required for investments that can bring down unit costs and allow business organizations to compete in world markets. Such capital sums are often not available in many countries within the constraints of their historical national systems of capital accumulation and allocation. It should not be surprising that the accounting and reporting systems from nations which have capital market-based national systems are better suited to global use than are the systems of countries which use other arrangements such as the bank system or the combine system or the like.

Some countries, notably Japan, loaned or invested capital in widespread global markets, still using their national accounting and reporting arrangements, which had always been adequate for their intra-country needs. Because of the changed conditions in which they were operating, their internal country systems often proved to be inadequate for the information needs at hand.

Rapid technology advances and the liberalization of capital markets in recent times have also made the structure and stability of national markets vulnerable. The sheer volume of capital flows is immense. On a daily basis, the foreign exchange market is reported to be in excess of $1.2 trillion and the value of capital flows has become greater than the value of trade by a multiple of 10 to 1 (International Forum on Accountancy Development, 2001).

Adequate global standards are becoming an important imperative. In former Chairman of the U.S. Securities and Exchange Commission Arthur Levitt's opinion, "Global capital markets cannot work without uniform, high-quality financial reporting standards" (Levitt, 2001). He points out that information is necessary and is needed on a timely basis. A system of comparable, uniform and high-quality financial reporting is fundamental to efficient allocation of capital resources. In the past much of this allocation was done within countries. Today, the economies of the world have achieved what Levitt sees as "explosive" growth.

Most observers would agree with Levitt's statement that the American financial reporting system is not perfect, but it is one of the best in the world because it is "one of the most transparent and comprehensive disclosure regimes in the world. For this reason," he asserts, "the reporting system has inspired systemic confidence in U.S. markets—the sine qua non for capital formation" (1). The goal then should be a system of global accounting and reporting which is at least as good as the one which the United States currently has in place.

The fact that there is no such global system extant has, in the view of many observers, exacerbated recent economic and financial crises. First in importance among these crises is the Asian crisis in 1997–1998 in which, upon devaluation of the Thai currency, funds rapidly drained from most Southeast Asian countries. The rapidity and the volume of trading across global markets spread the problem in one country quickly to others much more quickly than at any time in the past. There are few constraints on the flow of funds across national borders. Capital can easily flow out of, or into, markets in minutes. With this speed and ease of movement, investors, whose perceptions may or may not be correct, can transfer a problem in one jurisdiction to another by capital flows.

Speaking of the 1997–1998 Asian financial crisis, Lynn Turner, U.S. Securities and Exchange Commission Chief Accountant, stated, "Lurking behind the events was financial reporting that inaccurately portrayed the economic reality" (Turner, 2001, 1). He describes balance sheets that did not include billions of dollars of debt, which caused banks to unknowingly continue loaning, or investing in entities from which there was virtually no hope of recovery. Banks included nonperforming loans, which were in many instances worthless, as though they were receivables in the ordinary course of business. The numbers and the reporting in the financial statements of both banks and clients did not in fact reflect reality. Turner believes that "Accounts failed to provide the information that investors needed—and auditing failed to detect the vulnerabilities" (1).

The problems leading up to the Asian crisis were, of course, many but surely include insufficient accounting and auditing rules and requirements as well as improper accounting and auditing. The crisis, it appears, has at least served the purpose of moving the process of achieving better laws and standards forward dramatically.

From the evidence in other chapters of this book, the more substantial the difficulties created within a country by the crisis, the more substantial were the changes in accounting and reporting, as well as regulatory reforms, within the affected countries. In the aftermath of this drastic financial crisis, a reform-like movement seems to have taken hold and seems to have moved the accounting and auditing scheme of things dramatically forward not only in many of the jurisdictions in question but on the international stage as well.

In response to the problems that arose in the Asian area in regards to inadequate auditing, The International Federation of Accountants has established a new section of its organization, which is to be known as the Forum of Firms. In January 2001, 23 international accountancy firms met in London as the Forum of Firms with the stated purpose of developing a Global Quality Standard for accounting firms that conduct transnational audits. The aim of this group is "to ensure consistent, high-quality auditing practices worldwide as a means of protecting the interests of cross-border investors and other economic decision-makers and of promoting financial market stability" (International Federation of Accountants, 2001, 1).

A substantial boost, it would appear, was given to the International Accounting Standards Committee (IASC), which, since its inception, has had as its primary goal the harmonization and then the convergence of national standards leading to a comprehensive global system of financial reporting. The IASC was founded in 1973 by an agreement made among 10 professional accountancy bodies from Australia, Canada, France, Germany, Japan, Mexico, the Netherlands, the United Kingdom, Ireland and the United States. The organization was an outgrowth and was sponsored by the accountancy bodies making up the membership of the International Federation of Accountants (IFAC). The IASC was a part-time volunteer board (Deloitte Touche Tohmatsu, 2001h).

In the years since the beginning of the IASC, the organization has gone through its own evolutionary processes. In its earliest years the IASC standards were more descriptive than prescriptive. The standards contained many alternative accounting treatments for the same type of transaction and, in fact, the standards may be described as an attempt to list best practices from competing elements.

As is abundantly clear in other chapters of this volume, countries from throughout the world, and certainly those represented in the IASC organization, each have a national accounting standard setting board or authority and in addition each have regulators and legislators who frequently have their own agendas. Across the various countries of the world, differing accounting procedures and standards are the rule rather than the exception. In order to pass an international accounting standard in its earlier years, IASC needed the agreement of a large majority if not the entirety of the committee.

In its middle years the IASC began to eliminate alternative treatments and strengthen many of its standards. The committee began to consider some of the more difficult accounting issues, which separated many of the national standards. A conceptual framework was also developed, modeled on the U.S. framework. Progress was made but too often the many permitted alternatives also remained. The tone of a number of the pronouncements reflected a change to a prescriptive positioning in place of the former descriptive approach.

A major continuing problem for the IASC and its standards has been the lack of enforcement behind the pronouncements. Unlike most national standards for which national enforcement powers have been marshaled by one method or another, there is no comparable organization to the U.S. Securities and Exchange Commission with global reach that can enforce the use of international standards across the entire world.

In an apparent move to seek an enforcement rubric, the IASC and the International Organization of Securities Commissions (IOSCO) joined forces and in 1993 agreed upon "components of a reasonable complete set of accounting standards (core standards) that would comprise a comprehensive body of principles for enterprises undertaking cross-border offerings and listings" (IASC, 2001, 1). The items in the proposed core standards were 40 in number. The IOSCO noted that a number of the core standards were already complete and were adequately codified in existing International Accounting Standards.

By July 1995, the two organizations agreed upon a work program that would, when completed, produce International Accounting Standards acceptable to IOSCO. The standards would then be endorsed by IOSCO to its member commissions as being acceptable for cross-border capital raising and listing purposes in all the world markets. The IASC set 1999 as a target for the completion of the project. In 1997, IASC indicated that it was committed to completion of the original content in the project by 1998 (1).

IAS 39, *Financial Instruments: Recognition and Measurement*, was the last standard completed in December 1998. A standard on investment property was all that remained unfinished from the original core standards. Standards for investment property had been included in IAS 25 that was superseded by IAS 39, which did not include the investment property standards. IASC agreed to prepare a new pronouncement on the subject of investment property and the standard was completed in March 2000 as IAS 40 (2).

Early in 1999 the IOSCO began detailed consideration of the ASC standards through a subcommittee of the IOSCO Technical Committee. The subcommittee's recommendation made in March 2000 was that IOSCO endorse the IASC Standards, now referred to as IASC 2000 Standards, for the purpose of multinational offerings and cross-border listings. In May 2000 the Presidents' Committee of IOSCO offered a resolution titled "Resolution Concerning the Use of IASC Standards for the Purpose of

Facilitating Multinational Securities Offerings and Cross-border Listings" (Technical Committee of the IOSCO, 2000, 1).

In the resolution, the Presidents' Committee notes that IOSCO has identified matters applicable within certain jurisdictions that may require different treatments from those prescribed in IASC 2000. Therefore, the Committee's recommendation was that IOSCO member commissions "permit incoming multinational issuers to use the IASC 2000 standards to prepare their financial statements for cross-border offerings and listings, as supplemented . . . where necessary to address outstanding substantive issues at a national or regional level" (2). The supplements referred to are covered in sections on reconciliation, disclosure and interpretation. Waivers were also covered as allowable in certain circumstances.

In essence, IOSCO recommended adoption of IASC 2000 and at the same time recognized that national commissions might need to provide for special circumstances requiring additional reporting codification because of conditions in the country in question. Detailed reconciliations to IAS may be needed in cases where national regulations or laws might require treatments that differ from IAS. The Committee also recognized that some jurisdictions would need to have additional disclosures not provided for in IAS. In addition, interpretations by the national commissions may be needed to specify a choice among IAS approved alternatives or to apply a particular treatment where the IAS is unclear or silent.

The IOSCO recommendations for use of IAS are applicable to incoming multinational issuers in making cross-border offerings and listings. What of the use of IAS as the national GAAP by domestic companies, either multinational or not? Perhaps the matter of national sovereignty was at issue in the wording of the recommendation. A number of countries studied in this volume have used IAS as the basis for their national standards. Such use appears to be increasing. And, as discussed elsewhere in this volume, nations such as Singapore are set to simply adopt IAS without an intervening national rubric.

Citing their past program of convergence accounting and financial reporting standards as a major factor, the IASC believes that the level of acceptability of IAS will dramatically increase in the years just ahead. This, in fact, does seem likely in many countries of the world. The European Commission has recommended that by 2005 all European listed companies be required to use IAS for their consolidated financial statements and accounts. Further, the Commission's communication states that member countries will be permitted to require the application of IAS for unlisted companies and for individual accounts as well (Commission of the European Communities, 2000). Ian Wright reports that the only European countries currently allowing companies to report using

IAS in place of applicable national standards are Austria, Belgium, Finland and Germany (Wright, 2001, 1).

In many countries, stock exchanges listing requirements or national securities legislation permit foreign companies that issue securities in those countries to prepare their consolidated financial statements using International Accounting Standards. In May 2001 there were 52 countries that allowed foreign companies listed on stock exchanges within their jurisdiction to report financial statements in accordance with IAS. The United States, one of these countries, requires that reconciliation between IAS and U.S. GAAP be included in a footnote (IASC, 2001b, Stock Exchanges That Allow IAS Financial Statements, 1).

The U.S. Securities and Exchange Commission issued a call for public comments about the broader concepts of shaping a global financial structure for the increasingly globalized capital markets, about the acceptability of IAS and about whether the U.S. required reconciliations between IAS and U.S. GAAP should continue. The Commission sought to receive responses from both domestic and foreign sources, which would indicate problem areas and areas of concern. In responding to this request, a joint letter was sent by the U.S. Financial Accounting Standards Board and the Trustees of the Financial Accounting Foundation, which is responsible for general oversight of the FASB. The general oversight does not extend to technical matters. A separate response was also sent by the FASB covering technical aspects.

The responses stated that the FASB was fully supportive and committed "to the objective of increasing international comparability while maintaining the highest quality accounting standards in the United States" (FASB, 2000, 1). The Board continues to actively seek to narrow the range of differences between the United States and other country standards as well as to narrow the differences between U.S. standards and IAS. The Board believes that it has an obligation to its domestic constituents to narrow differences and to aid in the convergence of IAS and national standards.

The FASB indicated that it had a leadership role to fulfill as international accounting standards evolved. It believes that the ideal outcome of these efforts will be a high-quality single set of standards that can be used worldwide for domestic as well as cross-border financial reporting.

As to allowing IAS to be used without reconciliation to U.S. GAAP, the board noted that there were substantial differences between the two sets of standards. To allow IAS to be used for registrants who list foreign securities on U.S. stock markets would open the door to comparability problems between domestic registrants who file using U.S. GAAP and foreign registrants who would be using IAS. This would also allow domestic users to question whether they too should be allowed to use IAS within the United States. The Board does not recommend using standards other than U.S. GAAP within the United States unless reconciliation to U.S. GAAP is provided by footnote to the financial statements (3).

IAS in the opinion of the FASB has important roles to play outside of the U.S. markets. The IASC is seen as important to evolving global standards and aiding the convergence of national and international standards. The IAS are seen serving emerging economies well as a basis to develop their own national standards. And, the IAS has an important role to play in the European Union as member states adopt the standards for their capital markets (4).

The Board also commented that there was a lack of a global financial reporting infrastructure that had been tested by actual use. Successful worldwide implementation will need all of the elements that are present in a successful national setting, in particular such relationships as are found between an enforcing body such as the SEC and the standard setters. The Board supports the restructuring of the IASC as a step toward a more adequate infrastructure (4).

The framework within which the IASC works was revamped effective April 1, 2001. The process was started in 1997 as IASC viewing the great increase in cross-border capital flows and the recurring financial crises, concluded that a convergence of national accounting standards and practices and comprehensive global standards was imperative. A Strategy Working Party was formed to study possible structures and strategies. The Working Party report with final recommendations was published in late 1999. The IASC Board approved the report and proposals in December 1999. The member organizations of IASC also approved in May 2000. On July 1, 2000 a new constitution became effective (Deloitte Touche Tohmatsu, 2001h, 1).

The IASC was reorganized into a not-for-profit Delaware corporation on March 8, 2001 with the name of the International Accounting Standards Committee Foundation. The Foundation has 19 Trustees who appoint, oversee and fund the newly created International Accounting Standards Board (IASB).

An initial nominating committee, which was chaired by the U.S. SEC Chairman Arthur Levitt, appointed the initial Trustees. They were drawn from throughout the globe: seven from Europe, six from North America, four from Asia Pacific and one each from Africa and South America. Paul A. Volcker, former chairman of the U.S. Federal Reserve Board was selected as the Trustees' Chairman.

The IASB is the primary body in the new organization and is empowered with sole responsibility for promulgating International Accounting Standards. The Board is constituted of 12 full-time and 2 part-time members. The structure also includes a Standing Interpretations Committee,

Advisory Council of from 20 to 30 members, and Steering Committees for major agenda projects (2).

The principal charges to the IASB are to develop and issue International Accounting Standards and Exposure Drafts and to approve Interpretations developed by the Standing Interpretations Committee. The Board will use Exposure Drafts for public comment before issuance of a final standard. On major projects a Draft Statement of Principles or similar document will generally be issued for public comments. Steering Committees will usually be formed to provide advice on major projects. The Board is required to consult with the Standards Advisory Council on agenda matters, work priorities and major projects. The bases for conclusions reached in setting Exposure Drafts and final Standards will be publicly issued. The Board must consider the need for field tests and public hearings for every project (3, 4).

Board members must be technically expert. Trustees are charged with the responsibility to see that no regional interests or particular constituency can dominate the board. To balance the board with members who have different perspectives and experience, no less than five members are required to have practicing auditor backgrounds, no less than three are required to have financial statement–preparation backgrounds, no less than three are required to be users of financial statements and at least one must have an academician's background. Sir David Tweedie, former Chairman of the U.K. Accounting Standards Board, was appointed as the first Chairman of the IASB (4).

The stage seems to be set for the evolution of national standards into global standards. The recurring financial crises, which have swept over large portions of the global economy, have jolted nations into action. It seems certain that nations are moving to converge national standards with IAS albeit in a less than direct fashion in many cases. Some countries, Indonesia and the United States as examples, seem to take steps toward convergence and then initiate separate national standards that do not appear to conform to IAS.

Another important question is how far national authorities, such as the U.S. Congress, will allow global standards to be adopted for their country's corporations and stock markets. How will national forces react as favored items are about to be or are changed? Will they intervene? How much will national governments and legislatures be willing to bear? The U.S. Congress has been notorious in its actions when standards were adopted or about to be adopted which were out of favor with Congress or congressional constituents. Dennis R. Beresford, former Chairman of the U.S. FASB from 1987 to 1997, describes intervention and interference by Congress with United States standard setters over the years. The record is dismal at best (Beresford, 2001, 73–86).

There remains much to do. There are a very large number of remaining differences between the various national standards and IAS. The prospective work program of the new IASB has benefited from lists of potential problem areas from the outgoing IASC, from IOSCO, from the U.S. FASB and many others. But the efficiency benefits would be great for a single set of high quality, comprehensive, and internationally comparable standards.

In a new beginning, the International Accounting Standards Board met on May 24, 2001 for an initial meeting with the chairs of eight leading national standard setting boards from Australia, Canada, France, Germany, Japan, New Zealand, the United States and the United Kingdom. This was to be the initial step in agreeing on a common standard-setting work program. The IASB has announced that its goal is "to reach a single set of high quality accounting standards supported by national bodies around the world" (IASB, 2001a, 1).

Paul Volker stated the expectations for the IASB as he announced the selection of members: "This group is exceptionally well qualified to ensure we reach the goal of globally accepted standards. The result should bring highly significant economic benefits to both the developed and emerging economies" (IASB, 2001b, 1).

Chapter 11

Accounting Services, Growth and Change in the Pacific Basin

A relatively recent publication sought to assess the role played by major international accounting firms in selected Pacific Basin jurisdictions (McKee and Garner, 1996b). The current volume has attempted to reassess the role of such firms in the light of the financial and economic crises that swept through the Pacific Basin beginning in 1997. Service menus offered by various accounting firms in the region have been reviewed in efforts to appraise their roles in ongoing business and economic dealings as the nations of the region recover. The intent has been to contribute to an understanding of how the services of the firms support both domestic and international business and economic dealings and thus have facilitated recovery efforts and can be expected to offer strength to international linkages on an ongoing basis.

This Chapter will summarize the economic circumstances of the various jurisdictions that have been discussed. It will also review selected specifics concerning the activities of accounting firms in those jurisdictions. For expository purposes those jurisdictions will be arranged in three groupings: the Asian Tigers, emerging nations and small island economies.

THE ASIAN TIGERS

The successes of the four jurisdictions in question as significant players in the global economy prior to the events of 1997 are well known at this point. Despite the change in the status of Hong Kong with respect to China, it can be said that the future economic strength of all four jurisdictions is closely linked to their ongoing ability to function effectively in the global economy. Whether the crises that have been referred to will have lasting impacts upon their ability to maintain their international linkages remains to be seen. Certainly the expertise that is available from the major international accounting firms and presumably other major business facilitators should have some bearing upon results.

In 1997 Hong Kong was ranked among the world's top seven trading nations and was identified as one of Asia's most dynamic economies, enjoying a reputation as a major manufacturing and commercial center (New Zealand Trade Development Board, April 1999, 5). Hong Kong has also been a net exporter of services, with the surplus from that activity having increased by 6.5 percent in the first half of 1997 according to preliminary figures (5). Significantly, business-related services such as financial and business services including banking, insurance, real estate and a broad range of other professional services have been prominent in that expansion (6). As stated in Chapter 7 the strategic location of Hong Kong, its excellent communications network and efficient infrastructure has made it a hub for trade, finance and business services in the region (6).

It seems clear that Hong Kong will retain its role as the host to major international accounting firms. Among such firms, Price Waterhouse Coopers claims to be the largest provider of professional business and financial advising services in Hong Kong (1998). That firm serves the major industries in the Asia Pacific region and in doing so is organized into five key business units, focused on 22 market sectors (1999a).

Kreston International is another major accounting organization active in Hong Kong and boasting a worldwide network of independent accounting firms and a service menu comparing favorably to those of the largest firms (1999a and b). That particular organization also boasts member firms in Korea, Singapore and Taiwan.

KPMG is also active in Hong Kong and has suggested that thousands of international businesses have valid interests in that jurisdiction's change in status (1998b). Indeed Marvin Cheung, the Senior Partner of KPMG in Hong Kong has pointed to a very strong interest on the part of mainland firms in establishing their presence in Hong Kong, as a place from which to access foreign investors (1998b). Cheung saw KPMG as effective in dealing with mainland firms, a circumstance that he hoped would set a foundation for his firm's future business expansion (1998b).

Of course Cheung's view suggests that Hong Kong was maintaining its position as a major trading and financial center and window on the world for China. As mentioned earlier in this volume (Chapter 7), "Whatever fears may have been generated by its change in status appear to have been overpowered by its role in the region and beyond." It seems quite clear that the major accounting firms have a role to perform in facilitating business dealings with China through Hong Kong. In addition by aiding multinational firms in their global dealings, the accounting firms add strength to Hong Kong's local business service sector and contribute to that jurisdiction retaining its claim to be a major entrepot and offshore financial center.

Like Hong Kong, Singapore is essentially a metropolitan complex, pursuing its economic well-being through an international perspective. Historically it served as a link between Europe and Asia since early in the nineteenth century. According to the New Zealand Trade Development Board Singapore companies are pursuing many projects in Southeast Asia and Indo China (April 1998, 3).

In 1997 finance and business services accounted for 28 percent of GDP (3). Major exports included machinery and equipment, mineral fuels, manufactured goods and chemicals, and major export markets were the United States, Malaysia, Europe, Hong Kong and Japan (3-4).

According to the New Zealand Trade Development Board, there appears to be some basis for optimism for the nation in the post–Asian crisis world. They based their judgment on the fact that businesses selling final products to OECD markets in exchange for U.S. dollars should sustain relative health, the regional slowdown notwithstanding (7). Thus they predicted ongoing health for manufacturing due to a growth in demand for electronics by the United States and the European Union (7).

Service pursuits in Singapore were given a much less optimistic prognosis—"hub-related services will be affected by the regional economic slowdown" (7). Retail trade was predicted to be sluggish due to weak consumer sentiments and declines in visitors (7). In fact the Singapore economy slid into technical recession in 1998 (British Club, January 1999, 2). Still the British Club predicted a rapid recovery, describing the nation's strong sectors as including entrepot trade and shipping and financial and business services, as well as the key sectors of manufacturing and construction (2). Although the nation suffered from the 1997 crisis, its functions in the global economy should underwrite its economic future. As suggested earlier (Chapter 7), "The development of Singapore as an international financial center and the regionalization of local operations to counter internal limits to growth are major objectives of the government" (State of Hawaii, 1999,1).

Among accounting organizations active in Singapore is Moores Rowland International. That organization is a network of 140 independent accounting firms operating in 82 countries (1998). It embraces member firms in every region of the world that stand prepared to assist clients to better participate in international trade. It offers assistance with business organization and tax structures in foreign countries and can also help with the organization of foreign subsidiaries (1998). It can help with legal and banking contracts abroad and with international business information and advice vis-à-vis information technology (1998). It can also offer foreign market assessments and export strategies (1998).

In South Korea the financial crisis of 1997 found various large corporate players (Chaebols) in financial trouble and on occasion bankrupt. Indeed the Chaebols are seen as largely responsible for the crisis (New Zealand Trade Development Board, June 1999, 3). As mentioned earlier, "Their privileged position, together with government help and preferential access to capital was seen as making it difficult for small to medium size Korea firms to expand."

Various incentives aimed at attracting foreign investment have been provided by the government. Sectors where such incentives are available include information, electronics, bio-engineering, space engineering, medical science, environment and energy (4). The nation has also established two free-trade zones and also plans to establish free-investment zones where foreign direct investors in high-tech sectors will get tax holidays of up to seven years and tax discounts of 50 percent for three additional years (4).

Young Wha is the member of Ernst & Young International in Korea. The firm offers a variety of auditing services to its clients. Among such services are statutory audits of branch offices of foreign corporations with an eye to remitting profits to their head offices as well as audits of foreign invested corporations for the purpose of remitting dividends to shareholders (2000b). The firm also offers audits for joint venture companies and Korean corporations wishing to list on an overseas stock exchange or issue debt instruments internationally.

Young Wha Consulting offers various services to clients, including assistance with management strategies, knowledge management and business process and improvement. The firm also deals with change management, strategic cost management and supply chain management (Young Wha Consulting, 2000). They are also involved in information technology consulting (2000). In addition they can assist Korean companies investing overseas and foreign companies investing in Korea (2000).

KPMG San Tong & Co., another major accounting organization active in Korea, offers a wide selection of services including traditional accounting, tax and management consulting, not to mention international services (KPMG San Tong & Co., 2000, 1). The firm offers services to businesses in various fields and can also assist clients in the government sector (1).

With respect to Taiwan the New Zealand Trade Development Board saw the service sector becoming the central pillar for future economic growth (December 1998, 4). This of course hardly negates the importance of manufacturing, since manufacturing exports hold a significant place in the nation's economy. As suggested earlier in Chapter 7, considerable export activity is carried on by small firms. The New Zealand Trade Development Board sees the manufacturing sector as dominated by the production of machinery, telecommunications equipment, petrochemicals and plastics, electronics and personal computers, including notebook computers and accessories (December 1998, 4).

In 1997 Taiwan's foreign trade made it one of the world's top 12 trading jurisdictions (8). In 1998 the nation's economy was forecast to grow at 5.3 percent in that year, compared to 6.8 percent in the previous year (Bodeen, November 24, 1998, 1). Bodeen cited a 7.4 percent drop in exports as the cause. Clearly the Asian financial and economic crises have impacted the nation. The data above seem significant in light of James K. Larson's observation that Taiwan had averaged a 9 percent growth rate in GDP over a 30-year period (1998, 3). Larson observed that export growth was even more rapid and actually provided the impetus for industrialization. According to him, "Sources of GDP show the steady growth of Taiwan's economy even through the Asian crisis" (3).

He suggested that the nation's economy is closely linked to that of other Asian nations and saw it to be vulnerable to a decline in exports "especially since many of its largest trading partners are Asian nations" (7). Clearly the nation's economic potential is quite dependent upon successful ongoing international linkages, a circumstance unlikely to change, barring a major adjustment in its relationship with mainland China. This international dependence seems to support the importance of international business service providers, especially since large numbers of the nation's export businesses are small to medium-sized. A role for major international accounting firms seems almost self-evident. They are in a position to supply various facilitative services to the nation's business community.

Moore Stephens, P.C. is among large accounting firms active in Taiwan. Beyond traditional audit and tax services the firm offers business management consulting, computer consulting and not-for-profit consulting, as well as Internet consulting (2000b). Another major accounting firm active in Taiwan is Morison International Asia Pacific. That firm offers an extensive array of services (1999a). On an ongoing basis it develops and complements strategies to improve business performance and/or promote business opportunities. It identifies new markets and cross-border opportunities and is able to employ information technology for competitive advantage as well as for meeting audit and tax requirements (1999b).

Midsnell Group International (MGI) is also active in Taiwan. It is a group of 180-plus independent accounting and consulting firms offering clients' services and information regarding worldwide business practices, taxation, accounting and strategic alliance opportunities (2000a, 1). They offer a strategic alliance program to assist midsized companies entering the international market (2000a, 1). The program can help in expanding operations to new consumer and production centers, can assist in capitalizing on scale economies, reducing labor costs and identifying and obtaining financial resources (2). As stated earlier in Chapter 7, "The Strategic Alliance Program promotes international trade and supports business opportunities on a local, state and national level" (2).

THE EMERGING NATIONS

The dawn of the twenty-first century has found Indonesia wracked by economic, financial and political crises, the negative overspill from which appear to be ongoing to some extent. Before the turn of the century the nation was described as having a trilogy of goals—economic stability, economic growth and the equitable distribution of gains from development (New Zealand Trade Development Board, January 1998, 7). In another context the same Board seemed somewhat optimistic, citing the nation's crucial role in the region due to its size, a return of confidence as evidenced by new business starts, and the availability of funds for trading either from international sources or domestic pockets of wealth (June 2000, 1). However the Board also noted a slowness in corporate restructuring with limited access to expansion capital, the emergence of political factions and regional risks due to poor justice, low enforcement and personal safety (1).

Speaking in Jakarta, Lawrence Summers, then U.S. Treasury Secretary, referred to four lessons from the Asian crisis relevant for Indonesia—a need for sound macro-economic policy, a need for financial restructuring, a need for the rule of law and a need for strong political leadership (January 20, 2000, 3). Summers called for the "demonstration of willingness, to see foreign investors as a crucial part of a solution to Indonesia's corporate and financial debt problems, and not a part of the problem" (5). He suggested that experience around the world indicates that foreign banks can be a significant help with financial reform, as suppliers of capital and more importantly as suppliers of resilience, diversification and knowledge (3).

According to Hadi Soesastro the recent crisis with respect to Indonesia has illustrated the importance of governance and a development strategy able to respond effectively to the challenges of globalization (2000a, 2). In another context Soesastro suggested that what began as a currency crisis in the third quarter of 1997 soon grew into a deep financial crisis with wide-ranging economic and social impacts and in May of 1998 became a serious political crisis (2000c, 1). He saw the result as "an economy in shambles, a serious political vacuum, and a highly polarized society" (2000c, 1).

He saw President Soeharto as reluctant to implement an agreement with the IMF, thus increasing the uncertainty in markets with respect to the nation's ability to overcome the crisis (2). He suggested a regional concern with the chance that the nation might disintegrate (3). He suggested that economic concerns may be less acute than the political and speculated as to whether the nation will continue or reverse its internationally oriented economic policy and whether it will disengage from activities aimed at economic cooperation (3).

It has been suggested that the major international accounting firms operating in Indonesia may be having their impacts blunted beyond Jakarta due to their heavy concentration in the capital (McKee and Garner, 1996b, 96). KPMG Indonesia operating with Siddharta, Siddharta and Harsino; and PT Siddharta Consulting Services as domestic partners is prominent among accounting firms in the nation (KPMG Indonesia, 2000, 2). The firms in consort offer services to multinational corporations, joint ventures and domestic companies covering a wide range of business services (2). They claim to be providing international expertise and access to the KPMG global network (2).

KPMG and its local partner firms stand prepared to provide a wide range of facilitative services. Their services are in general aimed at four major issues—(1) assisting organizations in making better strategy and policy decisions vis-à-vis change, (2) assisting in setting up effective management structures supported by sound personnel policies, (3) assisting firms in ensuring that their management information systems cover needs and use as efficiently as possible opportunities from developments in computer-related technology, and (4) assisting organizations to become more competitive by improving marketing, cutting manufacturing and distribution costs and enhancing the supply of timely and effective information (7).

Ernst & Young is active in the nation through its member firm, Sarwok and Sandjaja, working out of Jakarta but available nationwide (Ernst & Young, 1998a). The firm offers various services including insurance and advisory services, corporate finance, business services, Japanese Business Group and taxation (Koesoetjahjo, 2000, 2). The firm also provides customs-duty advice, expatriate tax services, transfer pricing studies among other forms of assistance. It boasts a local and international clientele in the neighborhood of 1,200, representing various industrial sectors including agriculture, banking and finance, insurance, manufacturing, mining, oil and gas, petrochemicals, transportation and communications, construction and tourism (2).

Reporting on Malaysia the New Zealand Trade Development Board commented that the nation is well supplied with natural resources and is a major exporter of tin, rubber, palm oil and tropical hardwoods (July 1999, 4). Malaysia has substantial reserves of petroleum and natural gas (4). The economy has been anchored by agriculture, but in order to assist in economic recovery the government has been encouraging overseas investment with the result that manufacturing is now the major driving force in the economy (4).

The Pacific Basin Economic Council described the nation as having become "a world-class economy, exporting such high-tech products as radio telephones, data-processing equipment, VCRs and electronic circuitry" (June 24, 1998, 1). They identified Malaysia as the world's third largest producer and largest exporter of semiconductors as well as the largest exporter of room air conditioners, color TV tubes and VCRs (1). Despite the setbacks engendered by the regional crisis of 1997 the nation seems to have recovered and presents a positive posture with respect to a sophisticated array of business opportunities involving U.S. business interests.

The New Zealand Trade Development Board appears somewhat optimistic despite the very real impact of the crisis (July 1999). Unlike neighboring nations, the government and the banking system of Malaysia remained stable throughout the crisis (1999, 4). The government is promoting import substitution and a "buy Malaysian" policy (7). It gives preferences to projects providing jobs and training to Malaysians, and enhancing local technology and manufacturing expertise (12). It also gives preference to operations having high local value added and establishing export outlets for local products (12). Special consideration is also given to projects to redress economic imbalances between ethnic groups (12). The government offers a variety of incentives intended to attract foreign investment and has created 13 free-trade zones (12–13).

Arthur Andersen is prominent among major accounting firms in Malaysia with a staff of 1,000 (1998). Its office in Kuala Lumpur acts as an integrator of services for Malaysian companies with overseas operations (1998). The firm boasts a full range of integrated services for both Malaysian companies and multinational corporations operating in the country. The services in question deal with audit, taxation, management and business problems (1998).

Ernst & Young is also active in Malaysia, with a staff of 1,200 professionals and support staff, operating out of 12 offices positioned throughout the country (1998). The firm offers expert advice on all business issues. It has organized its professionals into multidisciplinary teams relating to the industry being served rather than the service being offered. The firm designs large programs aimed at change and intended to revitalize the growth and profitability of large and diversified companies (1998).

KPMG is also active in the country with offices in the capital and nine other locations, offering a wide range of services covering accounting, tax and management consulting (1998,1). The firm can assist various business sectors including banking and finance, building and construction, as well as energy and natural resources and health care and life science (1998, 1–2). They can also assist the industrial products sector and information, communications and entertainment (2). They can assist in insurance, transportation, retail and consumer products and business services (2). They can also provide assistance to government agencies (2).

Some feel that the Philippines weathered the crisis of 1997 rather well as compared to Thailand, Indonesia and Malaysia (Sussangkarn, Flatters and Kittiprapas, 1999, 3–9). The nation is well endowed with natural resources, with agriculture, forestry and fishing accounting for 19.75 percent of GDP in 1998 (New Zealand Trade Development Board, February 2000a, 3). Other sectors included manufacturing at 21.93 percent, government and private services 16.80 percent, commerce and trade 17.15 percent, and communications and transport 4.51 percent (3). Agriculture accounted for about half of the nation's workforce despite a much smaller share of GDP. The report points to the nation's success in developing light industries that have gained footholds in major world markets and points to the service sector as contributing roughly 45 percent of GDP when the figures above are aggregated (4). Major areas of service expansion include tourism, computer services, advertising, financial services and institutions, transport and communications services, housing and trade (5).

Certainly the Philippines would appear to have much to gain from services offered by the major international accounting firms and other firms purveying facilitative business services. As noted elsewhere the accounting firms in question are concentrated in Manila (McKee and Garner, 1996b, 97). The operations of Deloitte Touche Tohmatsu through its local representative, C. L. Manabat & Company, serve as an example of what an accounting firm has to offer. That particular firm offers audit, finance, consulting, outsourcing, tax and corporate advisory, management and business consulting services to a wide range of clients in a variety of industries including various service industries, manufacturing, commerce, agri-business and nonprofit organizations (Deloitte Touche Tohmatsu, 1999, 1–2).

Although Thailand is generally recognized as the origin of the financial and economic crises of 1997, its economic situation appeared to be quite strong prior to the crisis (McKee and Garner, 1996b, 95). As mentioned earlier in this volume (Chapter 8), "Evidence that events of 1997 exacted a toll on the nation's economy can be seen in a prediction of negative growth in the six percent range for 1998". Actually the contraction in real GDP reached 8 percent in 1998 (APEC, August 29, 2000, 1).

The crisis has impacted poor rural areas as well as Bangkok and other urban areas (Sussangkarn, Flatters and Kittiprapas, 1999, 4). The government's eighth five-year plan (1997–2001) concerned itself with the development of the private sector, including both industry and services and also addressed deregulation in trade, finance and industry, accompanying those measures with tax revisions aimed at encouraging domestic competitiveness (New Zealand Trade Development Board, 1998, 3). Land reform, industrial improvements and government decentralization were also included (3).

Various major accounting firms are active in Thailand, among them Deloitte Touche Tohmatsu Jayios, whose service offerings include traditional audit and advisory, enterprise risk and corporate finance and restructuring, and also resource solutions and Japanese business services (Deloitte Touche Tohmatsu, 2000, 1). The firm also offers consulting services through Deloitte Consulting and deals with accounting and bookkeeping. Among its clients it lists major banks, companies listed on the stock exchange and more than 300 international enterprises and numerous medium-sized companies (1). The firm can provide cross-border investment advice in various forms (5).

Due to the importance of Japanese business the firm boasts a full-time Japanese expatriate partner as head of their team charged with servicing Japanese companies. In serving Japanese firms the team works closely with Tohmatsu & Company, the firm's affiliate in Japan. The team offers its experience over a wide range of industries.

Arthur Andersen is another major accounting firm active in the country where its operations have moved beyond Bangkok to all regions of the nation (2000a, 1). It can assist with insurance, business consulting, corporate finance, human capital, legal services, outsourcing, risk consulting and tax services (2000b, 1-2).

Grant Thornton International is yet another active competitor in Thailand where it provides a comprehensive range of business advisory services with the goal of helping growing entrepreneurial businesses realize their ambitions locally, nationally and overseas (April 1998). Service offerings cover auditing, accounting, taxation, and corporate recovery and restructuring, corporate secretarial services, tax and legal and recruitment (1999–2000, 1).

THE ISLAND NATIONS

Papua New Guinea has been an independent member of the British Commonwealth since 1975, functioning as a parliamentary democracy. It is a lower-middle-income country with in excess of 80 percent of its population dependent upon subsistence agriculture (New Zealand Trade Development Board, June 1999b, 4). Although the transportation infrastructure linking provinces is not strong, the country does have a new world class airport at Port Moresby (6). Inter-provincial travel is by air, sea or river due to few areas enjoying good road access (6).

Clearly the nation would be well advised to seek further diversity in its economy and stronger and more numerous external linkages. In 1998 the nation suffered a GDP growth rate of minus 6.5 percent while experiencing an inflation rate of 14.7 percent (1). Although it can hardly be suggested that the solution to the nation's developmental difficulties rests with business services, it does seem clear that certain international business services may be helpful in both domestic and international contexts. Among such services the facilitative capabilities of major international accounting firms appear to hold some promise.

Among accounting firms and organizations operating in the nation, Kerr Forster International Association is quite significant. In 1996 that organization boasted over 150 firms in 111 countries. "Member firms of the Association are legally independent of one another and provide services to clients on the basis of qualified and uniform standards kept consistently by all PKF Member firms" (PKF, 1995–1997). Among its service offerings PKF includes audit, accounting and corporate restructuring, as well as corporate advice on matters including mergers, acquisitions, public listings and management buyouts. Management consultancy offerings include all aspects of financial consulting, human resources and information technology. According to PKF they have "particular worldwide consulting pre-eminence in hotels, leisure and tourism where offices . . . provide a coordinated service to hotel investors, owners and operators worldwide covering all aspects of feasibility planning, valuation and operation" (PKF, 1995–1997).

Well before its merger with Coopers & Lybrand, Price Waterhouse was offering a wide selection of services beyond basic accounting and auditing in the country. Offerings included assistance with taxation and exchange control, management consultancy, corporate reconstruction and insolvency, as well as business advisory, corporate secretarial, government liaison and the recruitment and training of personnel (1990b, 153–154).

The firm's management consulting arm in Australia, Price Waterhouse Ururck, offered a variety of services as well. Indeed the firm claimed to cover a majority of business functions, which included general management, information technology, finance, manufacturing, marketing and matters related to human resources (154–155).

In Papua New Guinea the firm offered its advisory services to both large and small firms. It dealt with the incorporation of subsidiaries, the registration of foreign companies, and immigration and work permits for expatriate personnel. In addition it prepared localization and training programs to be filed with local authorities (155). Price Waterhouse was also actively involved in assisting government and quasi-public agencies.

Fiji is a republic, currently a member of the British Commonwealth, following a period of uncertainty caused by coups and ethnic unrest. Although it is composed of more than 300 islands, its two largest islands embrace 87 percent of the land area and 93 percent of a population of 800,000 (NAI'A Cruises Fiji, 1998). More than 200,000 live in the greater Suva area although more than 60 percent of the population are rural (Fiji Trade and Development Board, 1999a, 1).

Nadi International Airport accommodates most trans-Pacific flights, while international shipping services are available through the main port of Suva with "wharf facilities ... capable of handling large cargo and passenger vessels" (1999a, 4). The nation has been seen as a key economic power in the Southwest Pacific (New Zealand Trade Development Board, March 1998, 3).

Fiji recovered well from the economic problems precipitated by the coups; however, the nation was impacted by the Asian crisis (March 1998, 3; *An Introduction to the Fiji Islands*, 1999, 3). The government is seeking to diversify the economic base and welcome foreign direct investment (1999, 3). Various sectors of the economy including manufacturing, agriculture, fishing, timber, garments and gold mining are expanding (New Zealand Trade Development Board, March 1998, 3). The nation has an outward-looking, export-oriented trade policy (4). The government offers many incentives for investors, including such things as a 13-year income tax break, and trade-free zones (Introduction to the Fiji Islands, 1999, 3). The commitment to pursuing foreign investment and the diversity suggested by such a policy has not resulted in an energetic pursuit of international service activities. Although there is some international tourism, outward looking service activities do not seem to be playing a major role in the national economy.

Certainly there are limitations on the ability of the small island states of the Pacific to better international linkages and their domestic economies, through service involvements (McKee and Garner, 1996b, 108). Although such limitations may well apply to Fiji, various business services might well strengthen the nation's economy, despite having little to do with dramatic service subsectors such as international tourism or offshore finance (108). The major international accounting firms may constitute such a service subgroup. Such firms have not had heavy concentrations in Fiji but Price Waterhouse was reasonably active there (113). Since the services available through that firm were similar to those offered in Papua New Guinea, they need not be redetailed at this point.

Walter and Dorothy Diamond describe the backbone of Vanuatu's economy as agriculture, supplemented by tourism and offshore financial activities (1998, 14). According to Moores Rowland, Vanuatu is a dualistic economy with a large smallholder subsistence agricultural sector and a small monetized sector, composed of plantations, ranches and associated trading, as well as manufacturing, banking, shipping services and tourism (September 30, 1997). Domestic exports are primary goods (2).

According to the Diamonds the nation's economy is growing at a 6 percent rate (1998, 14). The nation boasts branches of at least eight Far Eastern, European and American banks, as well as five trust companies (16). Thus it would appear as though Vanuatu is in a position to improve its economic circumstances through encouraging its offshore financial activities. In such an environment the major accounting firms may see a good base from which to offer their international services.

Moores Rowland is prominent among major accounting firms and organizations in Vanuatu where it houses its South Pacific specialists (1998a). Its service offerings include accounting, auditing, management and consulting services to government, offshore clients, local businesses and private individuals (1998a). The firm also offers wholesale company incorporation services to finance, legal and tax guidance professionals (1998a). The firm identifies Vanuatu as the premiere Pacific tax haven and a major financial center for administering and managing offshore companies, trusts, banks, insurance companies and shipping regulation (1998a). Through subsidiaries and associate entities it deals with trustee services, real estate sales and management, communication services, as well as banking and legal services (1998b).

BDO International is also active in the country. That firm deals with international company formation, and also trust formation and management of offshore banks and captive insurance companies. BDO International offers traditional accounting and auditing services and a range of consulting services. It can also provide local investment advice and can assist with funds management (BDO, 1999).

Well before its merger with Coopers & Lybrand, Price Waterhouse operated an office in Vanuatu "to provide professional auditing, accounting, management consulting and financial services to both local and international clients" (Price Waterhouse, 1992, 63). Clearly the major accounting firms have much to offer in Vanuatu and are in a position to actually influence the nation's domestic economy.

Moores Rowland stands prepared to assist investors that have experienced difficulties as a result of the Asian crisis (1998c, 1). The firm explains "Amid the turmoil of recent months, Asian investors, particularly those with exposure to Indonesia, are turning to the Pacific offshore financial centers to base their holding companies and regional financing vehicles" (1998c, 1). According to the firm Vanuatu seems to be a safe haven for investors seeking a temporary base in which to weather the crisis (1998c, 1). The firm has added a new range of opportunities for its Asian investors to its Web site. Thus it has actually found a way to benefit from the crisis. Of course Vanuatu stands to benefit as well by hosting them.

Chapter 12

A Final Overview

It was clear in an earlier investigation that accounting services were significant in economies at various levels of development throughout the pre-crisis Asia Pacific region (McKee and Garner, 1996b). The importance of such service groups has sustained itself in both crisis and recovery in the economies reviewed in the present volume. The accounting firms have retained a significant presence in the region and stand equipped to service business clients and government agencies in a variety of ways aimed at both domestic concerns and multinational operations. Such service capabilities have been shown to extend well beyond the international accounting firms, known as the Big Five, to include various others which are formidable competitors in their own right.

The firms in question have been operating in a region that has displayed some evidence of recovery and indeed has generated an economic performance more robust than anticipated by most (Noland, 1999, 1). Marcus Noland was somewhat skeptical of a sustained recovery (3). Supporting his skepticism is the theory that the crisis actually uncovered the weaknesses of financial systems in the crisis countries, in particular their vulnerability to large outflows of foreign capital (Cambodian Centre for Conflict Resolution, 2000, 4). Although foreign capital offers various benefits to jurisdictions receiving it, it was seen as volatile and pro-cyclical in nature, and indeed influenced by economic conditions in the home countries of foreign investors (5). Thus foreign capital, although useful and perhaps even necessary, marries jurisdictions receiving it to the international economy and more specifically its sources.

Certainly these circumstances lend themselves to potentially significant contributions on the part of major international accounting firms and other providers of facilitative business services. If the firms through their facilitative service offerings are able to contribute to financial and economic stability in the jurisdictions concerned, they may also contribute to a lasting recovery. If they are able to encourage stability vis-à-vis financial capital or assist in its procurement, they have a major part to play. Certainly by facilitating international transactions and inserting a degree of understanding (confidence?) in financial markets through sound business procedures, they can contribute to recovery and beyond it to growth.

Some have blamed the Asian crises on developments in the global financial system (see Khor, 2000a, 1). More specifically blame was attributed to financial deregulation and liberalization in a global sense, and the growing interconnection of markets, coupled with the speed of transactions through computer technology, and the rise of large institutional financial players, including speculative hedge funds, the investment banks and very large mutual and pension funds (1). Martin Khor points to the size and volatility of financial flows and how market leaders can stimulate herd instincts (2). Demonstration effects can trigger domestic outflows (2–3), which of course speak to the linkages between local and foreign financial markets. Uncertainties revolving around these matters can be mitigated to some extent by the good offices of major international accounting firms in servicing their clients.

Khor in analyzing the Asian crisis has suggested a need for regulating the global financial system (2000b, 1). Throughout the current volume, country and firm specific examples of various services offered by the major international accounting firms that may assist in facilitating international business and economic dealings have been documented. Of course, those services should assist in issues facing the global financial system. Khor sees the crises as having demonstrated dangers inherent in volatile large short-term capital flows to economic stability in emerging nations and calls for greater transparency in regard to international participants and global markets, together with both domestic and international reforms geared to regulating speculative flows. Hopefully the present volume points to ways in which the major accounting firms can assist in these matters.

As recognized in the case of expanding economies, two aspects of accounting reporting require consideration (McKee and Garner, 1996b, 156). One concern revolves around who controls the authority to set accounting and reporting standards, while the other relates to the impacts of varying economic conditions and diverse business arrangements on the "hows and whys of accounting and reporting procedures" (156). Once again, a significant role for major international accounting firms appears to be indicated.

Khor stressed the importance for emerging nations to effectively manage the interface between international developments and national policies, especially in relation to planning a nation's financial system and policy (2000b, 4). He pointed to the need for policy makers to understand what is occurring and thus have a feel for policy instruments to deal with it including as mentioned earlier in this volume (Chapter 1): "Adequate regulatory policy and legal frameworks and the enforcement capability" (Khor, 2000b, 5). He suggested the need for private-sector participants including banks and other financial institutions and private corporations to understand and control processes like fund inflows from loans and portfolio investment, and their appropriate recycling (5). Beyond that he cited the need to handle risks of changes in foreign currency rates (5). Again it appears as though the major accounting firms and other purveyors of facilitative business services are well equipped to assist.

Of course Khor's concerns do imply the need for more predictability in the international dealings under discussion. The current authors concur with this. Indeed they see evidence that various jurisdictions highlighted in the present study are moving toward more regulation and control of their environments. "The recent financial crises in the Asian markets would seem to have led the nation states in the affected areas to bolster national regulations and requirements for financial markets, financial reporting, accounting and auditing" (Garner, McKee and AbuAmara, 2001, 50).

It has been suggested that the auditing, accounting and reporting systems of various Pacific Rim jurisdictions would be expected to pursue an evolutionary process in keeping with the laws, cultures and ways of doing business in each jurisdiction (McKee and Garner, 1996b, 37). It is possible that the Asian crises may have had an accelerating effect in Asian jurisdictions' willingness and political resolve to move toward improving accounting standards (Garner, McKee and AbuAmara, 2001, 51). Certainly the refining of regulations can be expected to vary with the degree to which economic expansion has progressed in specific jurisdictions (51). Assuming that jurisdictional controls and regulations are on the upswing, it would seem to be almost tautological to suggest an expanding role for major accounting firms.

As is known, historically accounting standards have generally been the preserve of individual jurisdictions that have established them through governmental agencies or on occasion have commissioned professional accounting associations to act on their behalf (McKee and Garner, 1996b, 156). Efforts to harmonize national accounting standards internationally date from as far back as the 1970s but to date are hardly a global success. Certainly the major international accounting firms have interests in supporting such endeavors. Indeed their very existence and day-to-day operations tend to contribute to some degree of international understanding if not actual uniformity.

The present volume has shown the jurisdictions under discussion to have domestic legal and accounting systems in place. The major accounting firms have not been sidetracked from offering wide ranges of services to clients through locations throughout the region. In many cases such service offerings have been available throughout the crises and have contributed to sustaining or reasserting the international business and economic linkages so necessary for jurisdictions that rely so heavily upon sustaining global interactions.

Such linkages should hardly be taken for granted in the aftermath of a crisis that has been compared in terms of destructive impact to the Great Depression of 1929 (Oxfam International, October 1998, 1). Beginning as a financial crisis, the malaise soon became a full-fledged social and economic crisis with what was seen as devastating consequences for human development (1). Oxfam saw the international response to the crisis as worse than inadequate and indeed as contributing to the severity of the situation (1). They saw the prospects for East Asia as bleak, citing among underlying causes of the crisis domestic mismanagement, corruption and the politicization of loans through a banking system both unaccountable and nontransparent (4).

The macro-economic collapse began as a crisis in confidence occasioned most notably by massive flights of capital beginning in Thailand and following with Indonesia, Malaysia and in a lesser degree the Philippines (Sussangkarn, Flatters and Kittiprapas, 1999, 1). In the most heavily impacted jurisdictions the loss of confidence was traced to a large and fast-rising dependence on short-term capital flows and related current account deficits (1). Nations throughout the region were experiencing a range of regulatory and prudential weaknesses, obscured by rapid growth and the presumed endless appreciation of real estate and stocks (1). Such a convergence of circumstances seem to be obvious candidates for positive inputs from the major accounting firms, most especially through their wide ranging menus of services aimed at facilitating and/or stabilizing international business operations.

The accounting firms in question are of course private profit-seeking organizations, relying for their success upon their ability to provide for the needs of their clients. In many cases those clients are multinational firms or at least foreign business interests doing business in the jurisdictions concerned. Of course the success of such international business ventures benefits the firms themselves, their private sector clients and the nations in which those clients operate. The symbiosis is generated by the accounting firms operating profitably in providing their facilitative services.

On occasion the operations of a specific firm may benefit clients in ways that may well favor one jurisdiction over another. For example, in the preceding chapter an instance was cited where an accounting firm was encouraging clients or potential clients to operate through Vanuatu rather than Indonesia. The implication was that such operations might prove more successful in Vanuatu given the ongoing turmoil in Indonesia. Other examples of firms, through their operations, benefiting one jurisdiction over another were evident in their dealings in the Mediterranean and the Middle East. Due to uncertainties in Lebanon, various jurisdictions eclipsed Beirut as a financial center and the firms were clearly facilitating the operations of their clients in those jurisdictions (see McKee, Garner and AbuAmara McKee, 1999 and 2000).

The previous Chapter summarizes the role of major accounting firms in the three groupings of jurisdictions that have been discussed in this volume. It appears as though the jurisdictions known as the Asian Tigers have been rebuilding their international role in the post-crisis international economy and that the firms are quite active in those jurisdictions. Among the cohort of emerging nations the economic picture is somewhat less clear, especially in Indonesia and to a lesser extent the Philippines. The island nations were less obviously impacted by the crisis, thus the role of the firms has been somewhat less driven by adjustments, the incident involving Vanuatu cited above notwithstanding.

It seems quite clear from the preceding Chapter that the jurisdictions known as the Asian Tigers have resumed their international focus in the post-crisis world. That focus appears to be of major significance if the economies in question are to sustain their recoveries and resume the material progress that signaled their performance in the last half of the twentieth century. The major accounting firms are in a strong position to assist with international economic and business dealings involving clients housed in those jurisdictions or with operations involving them.

As was the case before the recent crisis, international linkages and dealings are very significant inputs to the development potential and material strength of the economies in question. If anything this has increased the significance of the major accounting firms and other purveyors of international facilitative business services. In such a climate various large accounting firms have become active.

The emerging nations that have been discussed in this volume have also cast their lots with the international economy. Among them Indonesia appears to have been most seriously impacted. As was seen in Chapter 11, that nation has been undergoing serious political difficulties in addition to the problems that appear to be more general among the nations under discussion. Thailand appears to be recovering well, although the financial crisis originated in that nation. Malaysia and the Philippines are also experiencing recovery. The accounting firms are quite active in offering their services through the emerging nations in question. They appear to have much to offer in facilitating international dealings.

With respect to the small island nations discussed in this volume it may be that they were impacted less in negative ways than members of the other two groupings of jurisdictions discussed. Of course Papua New Guinea has been suffering from serious problems relating to economic integration within its borders although it now boasts a very serviceable international airport. The crises appear not to have impacted the type of foreign linkages enjoyed by Fiji in major or lasting ways. In general problems associated with those linkages have not been crisis-driven.

In the case of Vanuatu the crises may even have stimulated business in the offshore financial sector. The extent of that sector has been dealt with elsewhere (McKee, Garner and AbuAmara McKee, 2000). The willingness of one international accounting firm to assist in moving the activities of client firms to Vanuatu in the face of difficulties elsewhere has been alluded to in the preceding chapter. Without making major generalizations it seems clear that the major accounting firms and/or other international business facilitators may well be able to expand their use of the offshore financial sector in the wake of the Asian crisis.

In general it seems clear that major international accounting firms have maintained and perhaps expanded their operations in jurisdictions discussed in this volume through the crisis and beyond. One indication of this is the fact that various rather large firms that are not numbered among the Big Five are offering extensive services in the region.

It has been known that various business services, including those available through the accounting firms are quite capable of influencing business climates in jurisdictions of all sizes and levels of development (McKee and Garner, 1996b, 158). Although the impacts of such services are location specific, it seems clear that they have been generally available in the economies discussed in this volume. No one would suggest that the services in question have been the prime movers in bringing their host jurisdictions through the crises. Nonetheless it seems clear that they have been facilitating the activities of their clients in those jurisdictions.

As was suggested elsewhere nations that are heavily reliant upon exports to fuel their economies can be expected to have definite and perhaps rising needs for services that facilitate international business dealings (158). The crises in the region hardly seem to have altered that perception. Indeed the impact of such services and the firms providing them in specific economies may be related to the size and sophistication of the domestic sectors of the economies, the skill and availability of local accountants and the nature and extent of export activities (158).

How the offerings of the accounting firms benefit domestic economic circumstances is destination specific. In the past Hong Kong and Singapore as virtual city-states were seen as benefiting from demonstration effects from the activities of the firms, while domestic impacts from the firms in South Korea, Taiwan and Thailand were somewhat less visible (158). Domestic impacts in Malaysia seemed potentially more widely distributed since the firms were operating in regional centers as well as the capital (158).

Clearly the demonstration effects and domestic impacts cited above have sustained themselves beyond the recent crises. Thus the accounting firms are asserting positive influences in the jurisdictions that have been highlighted in the present volume. Those influences can be seen in both foreign linkages and domestic matters. The services offered by the firms have much to offer in facilitating businesses and economic dealings as the jurisdictions discussed strive for economic recovery. Indeed the needs of recovery appear to have provided more potential avenues of service for the firms. At this writing (April 2001), the global economy is experiencing shocks from financial and economic difficulties emanating from the United States and Japan. Since those nations are major players vis-à-vis many of the jurisdictions featured in this volume, it can only be hoped that the major accounting firms will be able to offer their services to assist clients throughout the Pacific region in ways that will be able to dampen potential difficulties.

Bibliography

AbuAmara, Yosra. (1991). *Selected International Trade in Services and Development in Small Island Economies*. Ph.D. dissertation, Kent State University.

ACPA International. (2000). *Association Member Directory*. (On-line). Available: http://www.acpaintl.org/firm-db/index.htm

Akathaporn, Parporn, Adel M. Novin and Mohammad J. Abdolmohammadi. (1993). "Accounting Education and Practice in Thailand: Perceived Problems and Effectiveness of Enhancement Strategies." *The International Journal of Accounting*, Vol. 28, No. 3, pp. 259–272.

Alam, M. Shahid. (1989). *Governments and Markets in Economic Development Strategies: Lessons from Korea, Taiwan and Japan*. New York: Praeger.

Amara, Yosra A. (1993a). "Externally Traded Services and the Development of Small Economies." In David L. McKee (ed.), *External Linkages and Growth in Small Economies*. Westport, CT: Praeger, pp. 7–14.

Amara, Yosra A. (1993b). "Services and Growth in Small Developing Countries." In David L. McKee (ed.), *External Linkages and Growth in Small Economies*. Westport, CT: Praeger, pp. 17–26.

American Institute of Certified Public Accountants. (1965). *Accounting Research Study No. 7, "Inventory of Generally Accepted Accounting Principles for Business Enterprises."* New York: American Institute of Certified Public Accountants.

American Institute of Certified Public Accountants. (1991). *International Accounting and Auditing Standards*. New York: American Institute of Certified Public Accountants.

Amsden, Alice H. (1989). *Asia's Next Giant: South Korea and Late Industrialization*. New York: Oxford University Press.

APEC. (August 29, 2000). *THAILAND Overall Economic Performance*. (On-line). Available: http://www.apecsec.org.sg/member/thaiec-report.html

Ariff, Mohamed. (1991). *The Malaysian Economy: Pacific Connections*. New York: Oxford University Press.

Ariff, Mohamed and Hal Hill. (1985). *Export-Oriented Industrialisation: The ASEAN Experience*. Boston: Allen and Unwin.

Arthur Andersen. (1999). *Singapore Guide to Business & Taxes*. New York: Arthur Andersen.

Arthur Andersen Malaysia. (1998). *Arthur Andersen, Malaysia*. (On-line). Available: http://www.arthurandersen.com/MALAYSIA/malaysl2.asp

Arthur Andersen Thailand. (2000a). *About Us (1)*. (On-line). Available: http://www.aathai.com/about/profile.html

Arthur Andersen Thailand. (2000b). *About Us (2)*. (On-line). Available: http://www.aathai.com/about/service.html

Arthur Andersen Thailand. (2000c). *Corporate Finance*. (On-line). Available: http://www.aathai.com/corporate/alter.html

Balassa, Bela and John Williamson. (1990). *Adjusting to Success: Balance of Payments Policy in the East Asian NIC's*. 2nd ed. Washington, DC: Institute for International Economics.

Bank of Ireland Group Treasury. (1997). *Taiwan*. (On-line). Available: http://www.treasury.boi.ie/country/taiwan.htm

Bavishi, Vinod. (1991). *International Accounting and Auditing Trends*. 2nd ed. Princeton, NJ: Center for International Analysis and Research.

BDO International. (1999). *BDO International*. (On-line). Available: http://www.vanuatu.net.vu/bdo.html

Bello, Walden F. (1982). *Development Debacle, the World Bank in the Philippines*. San Francisco: Institute for Food and Development Policy.

Beresford, Dennis. (2001). "Congress Looks at Accounting for Business Combinations." *Accounting Horizons*, Vol. 15, No. 1, pp. 73–86.

Bertram, I. G. and R. F. Watters. (1985). "The MIRAB Economy In South Pacific Microstates." *Pacific Viewpoint*, Vol. 26, No. 3, pp. 497–519.

Bertram, I. G. and R. F. Watters. (1986). "The MIRAB Process: Some Earlier Analysis in Context." *Pacific Viewpoint*, Vol. 27, No. 1, pp. 47–59.

Birenbaum, D. E. and S. Rosenblatt. (1985). "Trade Trends and Trade Issues in the Pacific Basin." *Philippine Economic Journal*, Vol. 24, No. 4, pp. 288–301.

Bodeen, Christopher. (November 24, 1998). *Asian Crisis Trickles into Taiwan*. Copyright Nando Media and Associated Press. (On-line). Available: http://www2.nando.net/newsroom/ntn/world/112498/world28-23009-noframes.html

Bosworth, S. W. (1992). "The United States and Asia." *Foreign Affairs*, Vol. 71, No. 1, pp. 113–129.

Boyce, J. K. (1992). "The Revolving Door? External Debts and Capital Flight: A Philippine Case Study." *World Development*, Vol. 20, No. 3, pp. 335–349.

Bradford, Colin I., Jr. and William H. Branson. (1987). *Trade and Structural Change in Pacific Asia*. National Bureau of Economic Research Conference Report Series. Chicago and London: University of Chicago Press.

British Club. (January 1999). *Economy & Currency*. (On-line). Available: http://www.expatsingapore.com/general/economy.htm

Browne, Christopher with Douglas A. Scott. (1989). *Economic Development in Seven Pacific Island Countries*. Washington, DC: International Monetary Fund.

Buckley, Peter J. and Jeremy Clegg (eds.). (1991). *Multinational Enterprises in Less Developed Countries*. New York: St. Martin's Press.

Byrne & Co. (1988). *The Accounting Profession in Hong Kong*. New York: American Institute of Certified Public Accountants.

Cambodian Centre for Conflict Resolution. (2000). (On-line). Available: http://www.phnompenhdaily.com/16-07-98t1.htm

Castle, Leslie and Christopher Findlay (eds.). (1988). *Pacific Trade in Services*. Sydney: Allen & Unwin.

Chan, P.K.L. and J.H.Y. Wong. (1985). "The Effect of Exchange Rate Variability on Hong Kong's Exports." *Hong Kong Economic Papers*, Vol. 16, pp. 27–39.

Chang, Chin-ru. (1996). *Taiwan Economy*. (On-line). Available: http://web.indstate.edu/cimt/classes/websites/elsie/Economy.html

Chen, E.K.Y. (1984). "Exports of Technology by Newly Industrialized Countries: Hong Kong." *World Development*, Vol. 12, Nos. 5–6, pp. 481–490.

Cheng, C. Y. (1985). "Economic Development on Both Sides of the Taiwan Straits: New Trends for Convergence." *Hong Kong Economic Papers*, Vol. 16, pp. 54–73.

Chew, Soon Beng. (1988). *Small Firms in Singapore*. New York: Oxford University Press for the National University of Singapore, Faculty of Arts and Social Sciences, Center for Advanced Studies.

Cho, George. (1990). *The Malaysian Economy: Spatial Perspectives*. London: Routledge.

Chow, P.C.Y. (1990). "Output Effect, Technology Change and Labor Absorption in Taiwan, 1952–1986." *Economic Development and Cultural Change*, Vol. 39, No. 1, pp. 77–88.

Chowdhury, A. and C. H. Kirkpatrick. (1990). "Human Resources, Factor Intensity and Comparative Advantage of ASEAN." *Journal of Economic Studies*, Vol. 17, pp. 14–26.

Chun, Charles In-Chang and John C. Beck. (January 1999). *Why the Rules are Changing in Asia*. (On-line). Available: http://www.accenture.com/xd/xd.asp?it=enWeb&xd=ideas\outlook\1.99\over_currente6.xml

CIA. (2000a). *The World Factbook 2000: Fiji*. (On-line). Available: http://www.odci.gov.cia/publications/factbook/geos/fj.html

CIA. (2000b). *The World Factbook 2000: Malaysia*. (On-line). Available: http://www.odci.gov/cia/publications/factbook/geos/my.html

CIA. (2000c). *The World Factbook 2000: Singapore*. (On-line). Available: http://www.odci.gov/cia/publications/factbook/geos/sn.html

CIA. (2000d). *The World Factbook 2000: Taiwan*. (On-line). Available: http://www.odci.gov/cia/publications/factbook/geos/tw.html

CIA. (2000e). *The World Factbook 2000: Thailand*. (On-line). Available: http://www.odci.gov/cia/publications/factbook/geos/th.html

CIA. (2001a). *The World Factbook 2000: Indonesia*. (On-line). Available: http://www.odci.gov/cia/publications/factbook/geos.id.html

CIA. (2001b). *The World Factbook 2000: Philippines*. (On-line). Available: http://www.odci.gov/cia/publications/factbook/geos.rp.html

CIA. (2001c). *The World Factbook 2000: Vanuatu*. (On-line). Available: http://www.odci.gov/cia/publications/factbook/geos/nh.html

Coats, Warren. (1999). "The Asian Meltdown of 1997: The Role of the Financial

Sector and of Bank Exit Policies." *The Fletcher Forum of World Affairs*, Vol. 23, No. 1, pp. 77–86.

Coffey, William J. and Antoine Bailly. (1991). "Producer Services and Flexible Production: An Exploratory Analysis." *Growth and Change*, Vol. 22, No. 4, pp. 95–117.

Cole, R. V. and T. G. Parry. (1986). *Selected Issues in Pacific Island Development: Papers from the Islands/Australia Project*. Pacific Policy Papers Series, No. 2. Canberra: Australian National University, National Center for Development Studies.

Collins, Stephen H. (March 1989). "The Move to Globalization: An Interview with Ralph E. Walters." *Journal of Accountancy*, Vol. 167, No. 3, pp. 82–85.

Commission of the European Communities. (2000). *EU Financial Reporting Strategy: The Way Forward*. (On-line). Available: http://www.iasb.org.uk/news/cen8-175.htm

Cooper, Richard. (1988). "Survey of Issues and Review." In Leslie Castle and Christopher Findlay (eds.), *Pacific Trade in Services*. Sydney: Allen & Unwin, pp. 247–262.

Coopers & Lybrand. (1991). *International Accounting Summaries*. New York: John Wiley & Sons.

Coopers & Lybrand. (1992). *International Accounting Summaries 1992 Supplement*. New York: John Wiley & Sons.

The CPA Journal. (October 1992). "International Accounting Standards: Are They Coming to America?" Vol. 62, No. 10, pp. 16–18, 21–24.

Cragg, Claudia. (1993). *Hunting with the Tigers: Doing Business with Hong Kong, Indonesia, South Korea, Malaysia, the Philippines, Singapore, Taiwan, Thailand and Vietnam*. San Diego, CA: Pfeiffer & Company.

David Tong & Company. (1993). *The Accounting Profession in Singapore*. New York: American Institute of Certified Public Accountants.

Dean, Gary. (September 1999). *Indonesia's Economic Development in Comparison to South Korea and Taiwan*. (On-line). Available: http://www.okusi.org/garydean/works/IndEcDev.html

Deloitte Touche Tohmatsu. (1999). "Philippine Business Topics: C. L. Manabat & Co." *The Philippine Accountancy Profession and Globalization* (by Dr. C. L. Manbabat). (On-line). Available: http://www.deloitteap.com/pubs99/papg.html

Deloitte Touche Tohmatsu. (2000a). *Our Practice in the Philippines*. (On-line). Available: http://www.deloitteap.com/practices/prac-phil.html

Deloitte Touche Tohmatsu. (2000b). *Philippine Business Topics*. (On-line). Available: http://www.deloitteap.com/pubs99/papg.html

Deloitte Touche Tohmatsu. (2000c). *Deloitte Touche Tohmatsu Jaiyos*. (On-line). Available: http://www.deloitteap.com/practices/prac-thai.html

Deloitte Touche Tohmatsu. (2001a). *IAS PLUS, Country Updates: Indonesia*. (On-line). Available: http://www.iasplus.com/country/indonesi.htm

Deloitte Touche Tohmatsu. (2001b). *IAS PLUS, Country Updates: Korea*. (On-line). Available: http://www.iasplus.com/country/korea.htm

Deloitte Touche Tohmatsu. (2001c). *IAS PLUS, Country Updates: Malaysia*. (On-line). Available: http://www.iasplus.com/country/malaysia/htm

Deloitte Touche Tohmatsu. (2001d). *IAS PLUS, Country Updates: Philippines*. (On-line). Available: http://www.iasplus.com/country/philippi.htm

Deloitte Touche Tohmatsu. (2001e). *IAS PLUS, Country Updates: Taiwan*. (On-line). Available: http://www.iasplus.com/country/taiwan.htm

Deloitte Touche Tohmatsu. (2001f). *IAS PLUS, Country Updates: Thailand*. (On-line). Available: http://www.iasplus.com/country/thailand.htm

Deloitte Touche Tohmatsu. (2001g). *International Forum for Accountancy Development*. (On-line). Available: http://www.iasplus.com/resource/ifad.htm

Deloitte Touche Tohmatsu. (2001h). *IAS PLUS. The IASC Structure*. (On-line). Available: http://www.iasplus.com/restruct/restruct.htm

DFK International. (2000a). *What Is DFK International?* (On-line). Available: http://www.dfkintl.com/whatis.html

DFK International. (2000b). *History*. (On-line). Available: http://www.dfkintl.com/history.html

DFK International. (2000c). *Objectives*. (On-line). Available: http://www.dfkintl.com/object.html

DFK International. (2000d). *Services and Clients*. (On-line). Available: http://www.dfkintl.com/clients.html

Diamond, Walter H. and Dorothy B. Diamond. (1998). *Tax Havens of the World*. 3 vols. New York: Matthew Bender.

Diamond, Walter H. and Dorothy B. Diamond. (2000). *Tax Havens of the World* (rev. ed.). 3 vols. New York: Matthew Bender.

Disclosure and Accounting Standards Committee. (2001). *Consultative Paper, Compliance with Accounting Standards*. (On-line). Available: http://www.mof.gov.sg/cor/dasc_cpaper.html

The Economist. (June 1989). "A Survey of Hong Kong: Weighing the Odds." In *The Economist* Supplement (1991). "A Survey of Asia's Emerging Economies: Where Tigers Breed," November 16.

The Economist. (1993). "A Survey of Indonesia: Wealth in Its Grasp." April 17, p. 3.

Eichengreen, Barry. (1999). "Bailing in the Private Sector: Burden Sharing in International Financial Crisis Management." *The Fletcher Forum of World Affairs*, Vol. 23, No. 1, pp. 57–75.

Elegant, Robert. (1990). *Pacific Destiny: Inside Asia Today*. New York: Crown Publishers.

Encarta. (2001). *Encyclopedia, Taiwan*. (On-line). Available: http://encarta.msn.com/find/print.asp/&pg-8&ti-06631000&sc-9&pt-1&pn-2

Enderwick, Peter. (1991). "Service Sector Multinationals and Developing Countries." In Peter J. Buckley and Jeremy Clegg (eds.), *Multinational Enterprises in Less Developed Countries*. New York: St. Martin's Press, pp. 292–309.

Enderwick, Peter (ed.). (1989). *Multinational Service Firms*. New York: Routledge.

Ernst & Young. (1990). *Doing Business in Thailand*. New York: Ernst & Young International, Ltd.

Ernst & Young. (1998a). *Ernst & Young in Indonesia*. (On-line). Available: http://www.doingbusinessin.com/cgi_bin/...nfo&record={5dd}&softpage=Document-pass

Ernst & Young. (1998b). *Ernst & Young in Malaysia*. (On-line). Avail-

able: http://www.doingbusinessin.com/cgi_bin/...nfo&record={60A}
&softpage=Document-pass

Ernst & Young. (1998c). *Ernst & Young in Taiwan*. (On-line). Available:
http://www.doingbusinessin.com/cgi_bin...nfo&record={4F9}&softpage=
Document-pass

Ernst & Young. (2001a). *Korean Tax Bulletin*. (On-line). Available: http://www.
youngwha.co.dr/tb/tax9812-4.htm

Ernst & Young. (2001b). *Korean Tax Bulletin: Proposed Revisions for Corporate Restructuring*.   (On-line).   Available: http://www.youngwha.co.kr/tb/
tax200002-8.htm

Ernst & Young. (2001c). *Korea Tax Bulletin: Summary of Differences Between Korean
GAAP and US GAAP*. (On-line). Available: http://www.youngwha.co.
kr/tb/tax9908-9.htm

Ernst & Young. (2001d). *Worldwide Corporate Tax Guide*. (On-line). Available: http:
//www.ey.com/GLOBAL/gcr.nsf/EYPassport/Welcome-Worldwide-
Corporate-Tax-Guide-EYPassport

Ernst & Young International. (1999). *Doing Business in the Philippines*. (On-line).
Available: http://www.ey.com/global/gcr.nsf/EYPassport/Philippines-
EYPassport#1

Estanislao, J. P. (1984). "A Perspective on Our Economic Crisis." *Philippine Economic Journal*, Vol. 23, no. 1, pp. 12–22.

Euh, Yoon-Dae and James C. Baker. (1990). *The Korean Banking System and Foreign
Influence*. London and New York: Routledge.

European Accountants Co., Ltd. (1999–2000a). *Company Profile of European
Accountants*, Bangkok. (On-line). Available: http://www.european
accountants.co.th/profile.htm

European Accountants Co., Ltd. (1999–2000b). *Description of Services*. (On-line).
Available: http://www.europeanaccountants.co.th/services.htm

Fairbairn, T'eo. (1985). "Economic Prospects for the Pacific Islands." In Robert C.
Kiste and Richard A. Herr (eds.), *The Pacific Islands in the Year 2000*. Working Paper Series, Pacific Islands Study Program. Manoa: Center for Asian
and Pacific Studies, University of Hawaii, in collaboration with the Pacific
Islands Development Program, East-West Center, Honolulu, pp. 44–69.

Fairbairn, T'eo I. J. and Thomas T. G. Parry. (1986). *Multinational Enterprises in
the Developing South Pacific Region*. Honolulu: East-West Center. In Feke-
tekuty, Geza. (1988). *International Trade in Services*. Cambridge: Ballinger
Publishing Company.

FASB. (2000). *Response to SEC Concept Release, International Accounting Standards*.
(On-line).   Available: http://accounting.rutgers.edu/raw/fasb/IASC/
index.html

Fiji Trade and Investment Board. (1999a). *About Fiji Islands*. (On-line). Available:
http://www.ftib.org.fj/aboutfiji.htm

Fiji Trade and Investment Board. (1999b). *Role of the FTIB*. (On-line). Available:
http://www.ftib.org.fj/ftibiunfio.htm

Fischer, Stanley. (June 19, 1998). *The Asian Crisis and Implications for Other Economies*. International Monetary Fund. (On-line). Available: http://www.
imf.org/external/np/speeches/1998/061998.htm

FND. (1997–1998). *Vanuatu*. (On-line). Available: http://www.fnd.cz/vanuatu2. htm

Gardner, Paul F. (1989). *New Enterprise in the South Pacific: The Indonesian and Melanesian Experience*. Washington, DC: National Defense University Press.

Garner, Don E., David L. McKee and Yosra AbuAmara. (2001). "The Asian Financial Crises and Financial Reporting Standards." *Proceedings of the American Society of Business and Behavioral Sciences Addendum 2001*.

Government of Singapore. (2001). *WebPages, eCitizen Set Up a Business*. (On-line). Available: http://www.gov.sg.reb/information/busquest.html

Grabowski, Richard. (2000). "Economic Reform and South Asian Development: Review of Lessons Learned from the Experience of East and Southeast Asia." *International Journal of Commerce and Management*, Vol. 10, No. 2, pp. 1–19.

Grant Thornton Thailand. (April 1998). *Grant Thornton Thailand*. (On-line). Available: wysiwyg://21/http://www.gt-thai.com/

Grant Thornton Thailand. (2000). *Services*. (On-line). Available: http://www.gt-thai.com/services.html

Grone, Donald K. (1983). *The ASEAN States: Coping with Dependence*. New York: Praeger.

Gullick, J. M. (1981). *Malaysia: An Economic Expansion and National Unity*. Boulder, CO: Westview Press.

Hakchung, C. (1989). "The Asian Newly Industrializing Economies (NIES): Are Economic Miracles Equally Miraculous?" *Singapore Economic Review*, Vol. 34, No. 1, pp. 2–12.

Hamilton, Clive and Richard Tanter. (1987). "The Antinomies of Success in South Korea." *Journal of International Affairs*, Vol. 41, No. 1, pp. 63–90.

Heely, James A. and Roy L. Nersesian. (1993). *Global Management Accounting: A Guide for Executives of International Corporations*. Westport, CT: Quorum Books.

Heng, T. M. and L. Lon. (December 1990). "An Asian NIC's View on Service Trade Liberalization: Singapore's Case." *Journal of Economic Development*, pp. 57–82.

Hoenig, Thomas M. (1998). "The International Community's Response to the Asian Financial Crisis." *Economic Review: Federal Reserve Bank of Kansas City*, Vol. 83, No. 2, pp. 5–7.

Holmes, Sir Frank (ed.). (1987). *Economic Adjustment: Policies and Problems*. Washington, DC: International Monetary Fund.

Hong Kong Trade Development Council. (June 1999). *Why Is Hong Kong's Economic Recovery Slower than Other Economies in the Region*? (On-line). Available: http://www.tdctrade.com/econforum/sc/chartersc13.htm

Igbal, B. A. and S. U. Faroogi. (1985). "Taiwan's Trade: Problem of Plenty." *Journal of World Trade Law*, Vol. 19, No. 6, pp. 673–674.

IMF. (May 1998). "Financial Crises, Causes and Indicators." *World Economic Outlook*, p. 3.

Independent Accountants International. (1998). *IA Accounting: A Global Approach*. (On-line). Available: http://www.iai.org/consulting/BODY.cfm

Indonesian Business Magazine Ltd. (May 2000). *Indonesian Business*. (On-line). Available: http://www.indonesianbusiness.com/issues/200005/ceo.htm

The Institute of Certified Accountants and Auditors of Thailand. (2001a). *The Institute of Certified Accountants and Auditors of Thailand*. Bangkok, Thailand: The Institute of Certified Accountants and Auditors.

The Institute of Certified Accountants and Auditors of Thailand. (2001b). *Current Status and Agenda, March 2001*. Bangkok, Thailand: The Institute of Certified Accountants and Auditors of Thailand.

Institute of Certified Public Accountants of Singapore. (2001). *Web Page*. (On-line). Available: http://www.accountants.org.sp/institute.html

International Accounting Standards Board. (2001a). *IASB, National Standard-Setter Chairs to Meet to Discuss Common Agenda, IASB Press Release*. (On-line). Available: http://www.iasb.org.uk

International Accounting Standards Board. (2001b). *IASC Trustees Announce New Standard-Setting Board*. (On-line). Available: http://www.cfodirect.com/

International Accounting Standards Committee (IASC). (1990). *International Accounting Standards*. Reprinted in American Institute of Certified Public Accountants (1991). *International Accounting and Auditing Standards*. New York: American Institute of Certified Public Accountants.

International Accounting Standards Committee (IASC). (2001a). *Core Standards*. (On-line). Available: http://www.iasc.org.uk/frame/cen3-5.htm

International Accounting Standards Committee (IASC). (2001b). *Stock Exchanges that Allow IAS Financial Statements*. (On-line). Available: http://www.iasb.org.uk/frame/cen1-10.htm

International Accounting and Auditing Standards. Chicago: Commerce Clearing House.

International Federation of Accountants. (2001). *Twenty-three International Accountancy Firms Launch Effort to Create a Global Quality Standard for Auditing*. (On-line). Available: http://www.ifad.net/content/ie/ie-f-whatsnew-ifad.htm

International Forum on Accountancy Development (IFAD). (2001). *Forces for Change*. (On-line). Available: http://www.ifad.net/content/ie/ie-f-iff-forcesfor.htm

An Introduction to the Fiji Islands. (1999). (On-line). Available: http://www.multimania.com/remisat/fiji2.htm

Islam, I. and C. Kirkpatrick. (June 1986). "Export-Led Development, Labour-Market Conditions and the Distribution of Income: The Case of Singapore." *Cambridge Journal of Economics*, Vol. 10, No. 2, pp. 13–127.

Jacque, Laurent. (1999). "The Asian Financial Crisis: Lessons from Thailand." *The Fletcher Forum of World Affairs*, Vol. 23, No. 1, pp. 87–107.

Jansen, Karel. (1990). *Finance, Growth and Stability: Financing Economic Development in Thailand, 1960–1986*. Sydney: Gower, Avebury.

Jomo, Kwame Sumdaram. (1990). *Growth and Structural Change in the Malaysian Economy*. New York: St. Martin's Press.

Journal of Accountancy. (March 1989). "IASC Study Confirms Use of International Standards." Vol. 167, No. 3, p. 85.

Journal of Accountancy. (January 1994). "IASC Completes Comparability Project, Receives IOSCO Endorsement." Vol. 177, No. 1, p. 23.

Karacadag, Cem and Barbara Samuels II. (1999). "In Search of the Market Failure in the Asian Crisis." *The Fletcher Forum of World Affairs*, Vol. 23, No. 1, pp. 131–143.

Kelly, Brian and Mark London. (1989). *The Four Little Dragons*. New York: Simon & Schuster.

Khor, Martin. (2000a). *The Economic Crisis in East Asia: Causes, Effects, Lessons*. Third World Network. (On-line). Available: http://www.ifg.org/khor.html

Khor, Martin. (2000b). *The Economic Crisis in East Asia: Causes, Effects, Lessons*, Part 2. Third World Network. (On-line). Available: http://www.ifg.org/khor2.html

Kim, Chungsoo and Kihong Kim. (1990). "Asian NIE's and Liberalization of Trade in Services." In H. E. English (ed.), *Pacific Initiatives in Global Trade*. Vancouver: The Institute for Research on Public Policy, pp. 181–198.

Kim, Kihwan. (January 1988). "Korea in the 1990s: Making the Transition to a Developed Economy." *World Development*, Vol. 16, No. 1, pp. 7–18.

Kim, W. C. and A. E. Tschoegl. (January 1986). "The Regional Balance of Industrialization: An Empirical Investigation of the Asian Pacific Area." *Journal of Developing Areas*, Vol. 20, No. 2, pp. 173–183.

Koesoetjahjo, Irene. (May 2000). *Indonesian Business*. Profile. (On-line). Available: http://www.indonesianbusiness.com/issues/200005/ceo.htm

Korean Institute of Certified Public Accountants. (2001). *Homepage in English*. (On-line). Available: http://www.kicpa.or.kr/english/about.htm

KPMG. (1998). *KPMG Malaysia*. (On-line). Available: http://www.aspac.kpmg.com/malay/mal-kpmg.htm

KPMG. (February 1998). *Global Supply Chain Management Benchmarking Study, 1998*. (On-line). Available: http://www.aspac.kpmg.com/reg-consulting/defauly.htm

KPMG. (April 1998). *KPMG Services: Regional Reach—Understanding Business in Asia Pacific*. (On-line). Available: http://www.aspac.kpmg.com/aspac/regional-reach.html

KPMG. (November 1998a). *Regional Consulting*. (On-line). Available: http://www.aspac.kpmg.com/reg_consulting/default.htm

KPMG. (November 1998b). *Hong Kong—Office Information*. (On-line). Available: http://www.aspac.kpmg.com/hk/hk-kpmg.htm

KPMG. (November 1998c). *KPMG International*. (On-line). Available: http://www.kpmg.net/library/97/june/hongkong.asp

KPMG. (March 2000a). *KPMG Services: Regional Reach—Understanding Business in Asia Pacific*. (On-line). Available: http://www.aspac.kpmg.com/aspac/regional-reach.html

KPMG. (March 2000b). *Linking Businesses in Asia Pacific*. (On-line). Available: http://www.aspac.kpmg.com/aspac/linking-business.html

KPMG. (March 2000c). *Industry Expertise*. (On-line). Available: http://www.aspac.kpmg.com/aspac/expertise.html

KPMG. (2001). *Hong Kong Reporting Requirements*. (On-line). Available: http://www.kpmg.com.hk/HongKong/hkgeneral-facts-revised.htm

KPMG Indonesia. (2000). *KPMG Indonesia*. (On-line). Available: http://www.aspac.kpmg.com/country/indonesia.htm

KPMG San Tong & Co. (2000). *The Accounting Profession in South Korea*. New York: American Institute of Certified Public Accountants.

KPMG Singapore. (2000a). *About KPMG*. (On-line). Available: http://www.kpmg.com.sg/about-us/spore.htm

KPMG Singapore. (2000b). *KPMG Consulting*. (On-line). Available: http://www.kpmg.com.sg/consulting/

KPMG Singapore. (2000c). *Banking & Finance Consulting*. (On-line). Available: http://www.kpmg.com.sg/consulting/banking

KPMG Singapore. (2000d). *Business Advisory Services*. (On-line). Available: http://www.kpmg.com.sg/consulting/bas/

KPMG International. (2001a). *Country Information—Fiji*. (On-line). Available: http://www.aspac.kpmg.com/about/fiji-country-info.html

KPMG International. (2001b). *Country Information—Vanuatu* (On-line). Available: http://www.kpmg.com.vu/country-profile.htm

Kraus, Willy and Wilfried Lutkenhorst. (1986). *The Economic Development of the Pacific Basin: Growth Dynamics, Trade Relations and Emerging Cooperation*. New York: St. Martin's Press; London: Hurst.

Krause, L. B. (1988). "Hong Kong and Singapore: Twins or Kissing Cousins?" *Economic Development and Cultural Change*, Supplement, Vol. 36, No. 3, pp. 45–66.

Kreston International. (1999a). *Who Are We*. (On-line). Available: http://www.kreston.com/WHO.html

Kreston International. (1999b). *List of Services*. (On-line). Available: http://www.kreston.com/service.html

Kulessa, Manfred. (1990). *The Newly Industrializing Economies of Asia: Prospects of Co-operation* Europe-Asia-Pacific Studies in Economy and Technology. New York: Springer, pp. 211, 360.

Larson, James K. (1998). *Taiwan Country Report*. MIT Advanced Study Program. (On-line). Available: http://curricula.mit.edu/~market/Docs/14/JimlarsonCountryReport.html

Lav, Lawrence J. (1986). *Models of Development: A Comparative Study of Economic Growth in South Korea and Taiwan*. San Francisco: Institute of Contemporary Studies Press.

Lee, C. H. (1992). "The Government, Financial System and Large Private Enterprises in the Economic Development of South Korea." *World Development*, Vol. 20, No. 2, pp. 187–197.

Lee, Chung H. and Ippei Yamazawa. (1990). *The Economic Development of Japan and Korea: A Parallel with Lessons*. New York: Praeger.

Levinson, Jerome. (1999). "The International Financial System: A Flawed Architecture." *The Fletcher Forum of World Affairs*, Vol. 23, No. 1, pp. 1–56.

Levitt, Arthur. (2001). "The World According to GAPP." *Fianancial Times*. (On-line). Available: http://news.ft.com/ft/gx.cgi/ftc?pagename=View&c=Article&cid=FT3ZGQWZ7MC&live=tru&useoverridetemplate=IXL3/05/01

Li, Kuo-Ting. (1988). *The Evolution of Policy Behind Taiwan's Development Success*. New Haven, CT: Yale University Press.

Lim, Chong Yah et al. (1989). *Policy Options For the Singapore Economy*. New York: McGraw-Hill.

Lim, David. (1985). *Asian-Australia Trade in Manufacturers*. Melbourne: Longman Cheshire.

Lim, Patricia. (1984). *ASEAN: A Bibliography*. Singapore: Institute of Southeast Asian Studies.

Linder, S. B. (1985). "Pacific Protagonist-Implications of the Rising Role of the Pacific." *American Economic Review*, Vol. 75, No. 2, pp. 279–284.

Linder, Staffan Burenstam. (1986). *The Pacific Century: Economic and Political Consequences of Asian-Pacific Dynamism*. Stanford, CA: Stanford University Press.

Livingstone, John M. (August 1990). "Accounting Standards and Practices." *Management Accounting*, Vol. 72, No. 2, p. 33. Reprinted from Livingstone, John M. (1989). *The Internationalization of Business*. New York: St. Martin's Press.

Martin, Linda G. (1987). *The ASEAN Success Story: Social, Economic, and Political Dimensions*. Honolulu: East-West Center, University of Hawaii.

McKee, David L. (1988). *Growth, Development and the Service Economy in the Third World*. New York: Praeger.

McKee, David L. (1991). *Schumpeter and the Political Economy of Change*. New York: Praeger.

McKee, David L. (ed.). (1993). *External Linkages and Growth in Small Economies*. Westport, CT: Praeger.

McKee, David L., Yosra A. Amara and Don E. Garner. (1995). "International Services as Facilitators." *Foreign Trade Review*, Vol. 29, No. 4, pp. 254–264.

McKee, David L., Yosra A. Amara and Don E. Garner. (1997). "The Positive Functions of Offshore Financial Centers." *Journal of Global Competitiveness*, Vol. 5, No. 1, pp. 406–413.

McKee, David L., Yosra A. Amara and Don E. Garner. (1999). "Offshore Financial Centers, Accounting Services and the Facilitation of Global Business: Some New World Perspectives." *Journal of Global Business*, Vol. 7, No. 1, pp. 383–392.

McKee, David L. and Don E. Garner. (1992). *Accounting Services, the International Economy and Third World Development*. Westport, CT: Praeger.

McKee, David L. and Don E. Garner. (1996a). *Accounting Services, Growth and Change in the Pacific Basin*. Westport, CT: Quorum Books.

McKee, David L. and Don E. Garner. (1996b). "The Major Accounting Firms and Development Prospects for Small Pacific Island Nations." *METU—Studies in Development*. Vol. 22, No. 1, pp. 56–66.

McKee, David L., Don E. Garner and Yosra AbuAmara McKee. (1998). *Accounting Services and Growth in Small Economies*. Westport, CT: Quorum Books.

McKee, David L., Don E. Garner and Yosra AbuAmara McKee. (1999). *Accounting Services, the Islamic Middle East and the Global Economy*. Westport, CT: Quorum Books.

McKee, David L., Don E. Garner and Yosra AbuAmara McKee. (2000). *Offshore Financial Centers, Accounting Services and the Global Economy*. Westport, CT: Quorum Books.

McKee, David L., Xiannuan Lin and Haiyang Chen. (1991). "Hong Kong's Investment in China and the Hong Kong Economy." *Philippine Economic Journal*. Vol. 30, Nos. 3–4, pp. 224–236.

McKee, David L. and Clem Tisdell. (1990). *Developmental Issues in Small Island Economies*. New York: Praeger.

McKee, Robert. (2000a). *Taiwan: The Lone Survivor*. (On-line). Available: wysiwyg://15/http://www.megastories.com/seasia/taiwan/taiwan.htm

McKee, Robert. (2000b). *Indonesia: No Growth, No Investment*. (On-line). Available: wysiwyg://www.megastories.com/seasia/indonesi/mckee/indonesia.htm

McKee, Robert. (2000c). *Philippines: Could Be Worse*. (On-line). Available: wysiwyg://21/http://www.megastories.com/seasia/philippi/philippi2.htm

McKee, Robert. (2000d). *Malaysia: Conflict in the Government*. (On-line). Available: wysiwyg://27/http://www.megastories.com/seasia/malaysia/malaysia2.htm

McLellan, S. (1985). "Malaysia's New Economic Policy: The Role of the Transnational Corporations." *Canadian Journal of Development Studies*, Vol. 6, No. 1, pp. 65–75.

Meller, Norman. (1987). "The Pacific Island Microstates." *Journal of International Affairs*, Vol. 41, No. 1, pp. 109–134.

Metraux, Daniel Alfred. (1991). *Taiwan's Political and Economic Growth in the Late 20th Century*. Lewiston, NY: E. Mellen Press.

Midsnell Group International. (2000a). *International Representation*. (On-line). Available: http://www.bargallo.com.mx/midsnell.htm

Midsnell Group International. (2000b). *Midsnell Group International*. (On-line). Available: http://www.ztke.com/midsnell.html

Mody, A. (1990). "Institutions and Dynamic Comparative Advantage: The Electronics Industry in South Korea and Taiwan." *Cambridge Journal of Economics*, Vol. 14, No. 3, pp. 291–314.

Moores Rowland. (September 30, 1997). *Vanuatu: The South Pacific's Premiere Tax Haven*. (On-line). Available: http://www.mooresrowland.com/vanuatu.html

Moores Rowland. (1998a). *Welcome to Moores Rowland—Vanuatu*. (On-line). Available: http://www.mooresrowland.com/welcome.html

Moores Rowland. (1998b). *Services Offered by Moores Rowland*. (On-line). Available: http://www.mooresrowland.com/services.html

Moores Rowland. (1998c). *Offshore News & Links*. (On-line). Available: http://www.mooresrowland.com/news.html

Moores Rowland. (2001). *Business and Tax Guide—Vanuatu* (On-line). Available: http://www.mooresrowland.com/vanuatu.html

Moores Rowland International. (June 1998). *Welcome to Moores Rowland International*. (On-line). Available: http://www.mri-world.com/Pages/welcome.html

Moore Stephens, P. C. (2000a). *Firm Profile*. (On-line). Available: wysiwyg://Home.85/http://www.moorestephensnyc.com/firmprofile.html

Moore Stephens, P. C. (2000b). *Services*. (On-line). Available: wysiwyg://Home85/http://www.moorestephensnyc.com/services.html

Morison, Charles Edward. (1985). *Japan, the United States, and a Changing Southeast Asia*. Lanham, MD: University Press of America.

Morison International Asia Pacific. (1999a). *Products & Services*. (On-line). Available: http://www.miap.com/60.htm

Morison International Asia Pacific. (1999b). *Our Professionals*. (On-line). Available: http://www.miap.com/5.htm

Morison International Asia Pacific. (1999c). *Regional Outlook*. (On-line). Available: http://www.miap.com/7.htm

Most, Kenneth S. (1988). *Advances in International Accounting*, Vol. 2, *A Research Annual*. Greenwich, CT: JAI Press.

Mueller, Gerhard G., Helen Gernon and Gary Meek. (1991). *Accounting—An International Perspective*. 2nd ed. Homewood, IL: Richard D. Irwin.

NAI'A Cruises Fiji. (1998). *Historical Overview of the Fiji Islands*. (On-line). Available: http://www.naia.com.fj/fiji/history.html

Naughton, Barry. (1997). "The Emergence of the China Circle." In Barry Naughton (ed.), *The China Circle*. Washington, DC: Brookings Institution Press, pp. 3–37.

New Zealand Trade Development Board. (January 1998). *Indonesia*. (On-line). Available: http://www.tradenz.govt.nz/intelligence/profiles/indonesia.html

New Zealand Trade Development Board. (March 1998). *Fiji*. (On-line). Available: http://www.tradenz.govt.nz/intelligence/profiles/fiji.html

New Zealand Trade Development Board. (April 1998). *Singapore*. (On-line). Available: http://www.tradenz.govt.nz/intelligence/profiles/singapore.html

New Zealand Trade Development Board. (July 1998). *Thailand*. (On-line). Available: http://www.tradenz/intelligence/profiles/thailand.html

New Zealand Trade Development Board. (December 1998). *Taiwan*. (On-line). Available: http://www.tradenz.govt.nz/intelligence/profiles/taiwan.html

New Zealand Trade Development Board. (April 1999). *Hong Kong Special Administrative Region*. (On-line). Available: http://www.tradenz.govt.nz/intelligence...kong-special-administrative-region.html

New Zealand Trade Development Board. (June 1999a). *Republic of South Korea*. (On-line). Available: http://www.tradenz/intelligence/profiles/republic-of-south-korea.html

New Zealand Trade Development Board. (June 1999b). *Papua New Guinea*. (On-line). Available: http://www.tradenz/intelligence/profiles/papua-new-guinea.html

New Zealand Trade Development Board. (July 1999). *Malaysia*. (On-line). Available: http://www.tradenz.govt.nz/intelligence/profiles/malaysia.html

New Zealand Trade Development Board. (February 2000a). *Philippines*. (On-line). Available: http://www.tradenz/intelligence/profiles/philippines.html

New Zealand Trade Development Board. (February 2000b). *Asia Watch: Indonesia Update*. (On-line). Available: http://www.tradenz.govt.nz/intelligence.../asiawatch/south/indonesia20000217.html

New Zealand Trade Development Board. (February 2000c). *Thailand Economic Update*. (On-line). Available: http://www.tradenz.govt.nz/intelligence/news/asiawatch/south/thailand20000216.html

New Zealand Trade Development Board. (March 2000). *Asia Watch: South East Asia*

Update by Market. (On-line). Available: http://www.tradenz.gov.nz/ intelligence/news/asiawatch/south/asean200003.html

New Zealand Trade Development Board. (June 2000). *Asia Watch: Regional Update—South East Asia*. (On-line). Available: http://www.tradenz/ intelligence/news/asiawatch/south/asean20000201.html

Nobes, Christopher W. (ed.). (2000). *GAAP 2000: A Survey of National Accounting Rules in 53 Countries*. (On-line). Available: http://www/cfodirect.com/ cfopublic.nsf/vContent/MSRA-4TP5VJ

Nobes, Christopher and Robert Parker (eds.). (1991). *Comparative International Accounting*. 3rd ed. New York: Prentice-Hall.

Noland, Marcus. (1990). *Pacific Basin Developing Countries*. Washington, DC: Institute for International Economies.

Noland, Marcus. (1999). *Asian Economic Recovery*. Institute for International Economics. (On-line). Available: http://www.iie.com/TESTMONY/mansf. htm

Noyelle, Thierry J. and Anna B. Dutka. (1988). *International Trade in Business Services*. Cambridge: Ballinger Publishing Company.

Nurkse, Ragnar. (1967). *Problems of Capital Formation in Underdeveloped Countries and Patterns of Trade and Development*. New York: Oxford University Press.

O'Malley, Shaun F. (March/April 1992). "Accounting Across Borders." *Financial Executive*, Vol. 8, No. 2, pp. 28–31.

Orsini, Larry L. and Lawrence R. Hudack. (October 1992). "EEC Financial Reporting: Another Source of Harmonization of Accounting Principles." *The CPA Journal*, Vol. 62, No. 10, p. 20.

Oxfam International. (October 1998). *East Asian "Recovery" Leaves the Poor Sinking*. (On-line). Available: http://www.oxfam.org.uk/policy/papers/eabrief/ eabrief2.htm

Paauw, D. S. (1984). "Economic Growth, Employment, and Productivity: Prospects for Indonesia." *Singapore Economic Review*, Vol. 29, No. 2, pp. 111–125.

Pacific Basin Economic Council. (June 24, 1998). *Destination ASEAN: Malaysia: Hitting Heavy in High-Tech*. (On-line). Available: http://www.pbecus.org/ damalay.htm

Palmer, Ronald D. and Thomas J. Reckford. (1987). *Building ASEAN: 20 Years of Southeast Asian Cooperation*. New York: Praeger.

Park, Y. C. (August 1986). "Foreign Debt, Balance of Payments, and Growth Prospects: The Case of the Republic of Korea, 1965–1988." *World Development*, Vol. 14, No. 8, pp. 1019–1058.

Parry, T. G. (1988). "Foreign Investment and Industry in the Pacific Islands." *Journal of Developing Areas*, Vol. 22, No. 3, pp. 381–399.

Parry, Thomas G. (1973). "The International Firm and National Economic Policy." *Economic Journal*, Vol. 84, No. 332, pp. 84–88.

Peavey, Dennis E. and Stuart K. Webster. (August 1990). "Is GAAP the Gap to International Markets?" *Management Accounting*, Vol. 72, No. 2, pp. 31–35.

Peebles, Gavin. (1988). *Hong Kong's Economy: An Introductory Macro Economic Analysis*. New York: Oxford University Press.

Perroux, François. (1950). "Economic Space: Theory and Applications." *Quarterly Journal of Economics*, Vol. 64, No. 1, pp. 90–97.

Perroux, François. (1970). "Note on Concept of Growth Poles." In David L. McKee, Robert D. Dean and William H. Leahy (eds.), *Regional Economics*. New York: Free Press, pp. 93–104.

Philippines Institute of Certified Public Accountants. (2001). *Home Page*. (On-line). Available: http://www.picpa.com/ph/aboutus.html

PKF International Association. (1995–1997). *Pannell Kerr International Association*. (On-line). Available: http://www.pkf.com/

PKF International Association. (2000a). *About Us*. (On-line). Available: http://www.pkf.com/about.html

PKF International Association. (2000b). *Services*. (On-line). Available: http://www.pkf.com/services.html

Posen, Adam. (1999). "Financial Fracility and the Risks of Crisis: The Case of Japan." *The Fletcher Forum of World Affairs*, Vol. 23, No. 1, pp. 109–130.

Price Waterhouse. (1989a). *Doing Business in Fiji*. New York: Price Waterhouse World Firm Limited.

Price Waterhouse. (1989b). *Doing Business in Indonesia*. New York: Price Waterhouse World Firm Limited.

Price Waterhouse. (1989c). *Doing Business in the Philippines*. New York: Price Waterhouse World Firm Limited.

Price Waterhouse. (1990a). *Doing Business in Malaysia*. New York: Price Waterhouse World Firm Limited.

Price Waterhouse. (1990b). *Doing Business in Papua New Guinea*. New York: Price Waterhouse World Firm Limited.

Price Waterhouse. (1990c). *Doing Business in Singapore*. New York: Price Waterhouse World Firm Limited.

Price Waterhouse. (1991a). *Doing Business in Taiwan*. New York: Price Waterhouse World Firm Limited.

Price Waterhouse. (1991b). *Doing Business in Western Samoa*. New York: Price Waterhouse World Firm Limited.

Price Waterhouse. (1992a). *Doing Business in Hong Kong*. New York: Price Waterhouse World Firm Limited.

Price Waterhouse. (1992b). *Doing Business in Korea*. New York: Price Waterhouse World Firm Limited.

Price Waterhouse. (1992c). *Doing Business in Malaysia: Supplement*. New York: Price Waterhouse World Firm Limited.

Price Waterhouse. (1992d). *Doing Business in Vanuatu*. New York: Price Waterhouse World Firm Limited.

Price Waterhouse. (1993a). *Doing Business in Indonesia*. New York: Price Waterhouse World Firm Limited.

Price Waterhouse. (1993b). *Doing Business in the Philippines*. New York: Price Waterhouse World Firm Limited.

Price Waterhouse. (1993c). *Doing Business in Singapore*. New York: Price Waterhouse World Firm Limited.

Price Waterhouse. (1994a). *Doing Business in Fiji*. New York: Price Waterhouse World Firm Limited.

Price Waterhouse. (1994b). *Doing Business in Malaysia*. New York: Price Waterhouse World Firm Limited.

Price Waterhouse Coopers. (November 1998). *Welcome to Price Waterhouse Coopers in Hong Kong*. (On-line). Available: http://www.pwcglobal.com/hk/eng/main/home/index.html

Price Waterhouse Coopers. (1999a). *Industries*. (On-line). Available: http://www.pwcglobal.com/hk/eng/about/ind/index.html

Price Waterhouse Coopers. (1999b). *Services*. (On-line). Available: http://www.pwcglobal.com/hk/eng/about/svcs/index.html

Price Waterhouse Coopers. (2000). *Doing Business and Investment Series 2000 Edition (CD-ROM)*. New York: Price Waterhouse Coopers.

Putnam Retail Management, Inc. (1998). *The Asia Crisis: Causes and Consequences*. (On-line). Available: http://www.putnaminv.com/frames/f14.htm

Rabushka, Alvin. (1987). *The New China: Comparative Economic Development in Mainland China, Taiwan, and Hong Kong*. Boulder, CO: Westview Press.

Rahmon, M. Z. and J. E Finnerty. (1986). "International Accounting Standards and Transnational Corporations." *Revista Internationale di Scienze Economiche e Commercial*, Vol. 33, Nos. 6–7, pp. 697–714.

Rana, P. B. and J. M. Dowling, Jr. (1988). "The Impact of Foreign Capital on Growth: Evidence from Asian Developing Countries." *Developing Economies*, Vol. 26, No. 1, pp. 3–11.

Rhee, Yung Whee, Bruce Ross-Larson and Garry Pursell. (1984). *Korea's Competitive Edge: Managing the Entry into World Markets*. Baltimore, MD: Johns Hopkins University Press.

Riahi-Belkaoui, Ahmed. (1994). *Accounting in the Developing Countries*. Westport, CT: Quorum Books.

Sassen, Saskia. (1991). *The Global City: New York, London, Tokyo*. Princeton, NJ: Princeton University Press.

Schive, C. and B. A. Majumdar. (1990). "Direct Foreign Investment and Linkage Effects: The Experience of Taiwan." *Canadian Journal of Development Studies*, Vol. 11, No. 2, pp. 325–342.

Schlosstein, Steven. (1991). *Asia's New Little Dragons*. Chicago: Contemporary Books.

Securities and Futures Commission. (1999). *Annual Report, Regulation of Accountants*. (On-line). Available: http://www.sfc.gov.tw/e-sfc/e-database/e-annual/1999/e-div6.htm

Securities and Futures Commission. (2000). *Annual Report, Regulation of Accountants*. (On-line). Available: http://www.sfc.gov.tw/e-syc/e-database/e-annual/2000/e-div6.htm

Segal-Horn, Susan. (1993). "The Internationalization of Services Firms." *Advances in Strategic Management*, Vol. 9, pp. 31–55.

SGV & Co. and Arthur Andersen & Co. (1989). *The Accounting Profession in the Philippines*. New York: American Institute of Certified Public Accountants.

Siamwalla, A. (1990). "The Thai Rural Credit System: Public Subsidies, Private Information, and Segmented Markets." *World Bank Economic Review*, Vol. 4, No. 3, pp. 271–295.

Skully, Michael T. (1985). *ASEAN Financial Co-operation: Developments in Banking, Finance, and Insurance*. New York: St. Martin's Press.

Skully, Michael T. and George J. Viksnins. (1987). *Financing East Asia's Success: Comparative Financial Development in Eight Asian Countries*. New York: St. Martin's Press.

Smith, Bruce J. (1987). "Some Aspects of Economic Adjustment in Small Island Economies." In Sir Frank Holmes (ed.), *Economic Adjustment: Policies and Problems*. Washington, DC: International Monetary Fund.

Soesastro, Hadi. (July 10, 2000a). *The Economic Crisis in Indonesia: Lessons and Challenges for Governance and Sustainable Development (1)*. Pacific Link. (On-line). Available: http://www.pacific.net.id/pakar/hadisusastro/economic.html

Soesastro, Hadi. (July 10, 2000b). *The Economic Crisis in Indonesia: Lessons and Challenges for Governance and Sustainable Development (2)*. Pacific Link. (On-line). Available: http://www.pacific.net.id/pakar/hadisusastro/economic-2.html

Soesastro, Hadi. (July 10, 2000c). *Implications of Indonesia's Crisis for the Asia Pacific Region: A Literature Survey*. Pacific Link. (On-line). Available: http://www.pacific.net.id/pakar/hadisusastro/000508.html

Soesastro, Hadi. (July 10, 2000d). *The Indonesian Economy Under Wahid*. Pacific Link. (On-line). Available: http://www.pacific.net.id/pakar/hadisusastro/indonesianeconomy.html

Soong, T. N. & Co. (1992). *The Accounting Profession in Taiwan, Republic of China*. New York: American Institute of Certified Public Accountants.

State of Hawaii. (1999). *Country Profile: Singapore*. (On-line). Available: http://www.hawaii.gov/dbedt/ert/co/singa.html

State of Hawaii. (August 29, 2000). *Thailand Demand Assessment*. (On-line). Available: wysiwyg://58/http://www.hawaii.gov/dbedt/ert/cp/thail.html

Stiglitz, Joseph E. (1999). "Beggar-Thyself versus Beggar-Thy-Neighbor Policies: The Dangers of Intellectual Incoherence in Addressing the Global Financial Crisis." *Southern Economic Journal*, Vol. 66, No. 1, pp. 1–38.

Streeten, Paul. (1988). *Beyond Adjustment: The Asian Experience*. Washington, DC: International Monetary Fund.

Suarez-Villa, L. and P. H. Han. (1990). "The Rise of Korea's Electronics Industry: Technological Change, Growth, and Territorial Distribution." *Economic Geography*, Vol. 66, No. 3, pp. 273–292.

Sudit, E. F. (1984). "The Role of Comparative Productivity Accounting in Export Decisions." *Journal of International Business Studies*, Vol. 15, No. 1, pp. 105–118.

Summers, Lawrence H. (January 20, 2000). *Indonesia and the Challenge of Lasting Recovery*. U.S. Embassy, Jakarta. (On-line). Available: http://www.usembassyjakarta.org/Summers2000.html

Sundrum, R. M. (December 1986). "Indonesia's Rapid Economic Growth, 1968–1981." *Bulletin of Indonesian Economic Studies*, Vol. 22, No. 3, pp. 40–69.

Sung, Yun Wing. (1988). "A Theoretical and Empirical Analysis of Entropot Trade: Hong Kong and Singapore and Their Roles in China's Trade." In Leslie Castle and Christopher Findlay (eds.), *Pacific Trade in Services*. Sydney: Allen & Unwin, pp. 173–208.

Sussangkarn, Chalongphob. (August 30, 2000). *Economic Crisis and Recovery in Thailand: The Role of the IMF*. (On-line). Available: http://www.tdri.or.th/thai-imf.htm

Sussangkarn, Chalongphob, Frank Flatters and Sauwalak Kittiprapas. (1999). "Comparative Social Impacts of the Asian Economic Crisis in Thailand,

Indonesia, Malaysia and the Philippines: A Preliminary Report." *TDRI Quarterly Review*, Vol. 14, No. 4, pp. 3–9. (On-line). Available: http://www.info.tdri.or.th/econwatch/qr/text/m99-1.htm

Sutherland, W. M. (1986). "Microstates and Unequal Trade in the South Pacific: The Sparteca Agreement of 1980." *Journal of World Trade Law*, Vol. 20, No. 3, pp. 313–328.

Technical Committee of the International Organization of Securities Commissions (IOSC). (2000). *IOSC Standards: Report of the Technical Committee of the International Organization of Securities Commissions*. New York: International Organization of Securities Commissions.

Thoburn, John T. (1977). *Primary Commodity Exports and Economic Development: Theory, Evidence and a Study of Malaysia*. London and New York: Wiley.

Tisdell, Clem. (1993). *"Small Island Economies in a World of Economic Change."* The University of Queensland (mimeographed).

Todaro, Michael P. (1994). *Economic Development*. 5th ed. New York: Longman.

Trade Partners Limited. (2000a). *About Us*. (On-line). Available: http://www.thailand-accounting.com/about.html

Trade Partners Limited. (2000b). *Legal & Professional Services*. (On-line). Available: http://www.thailand-accounting.com/services.html

Tucker, Ken and Mark Sundberg. (1988). *International Trade in Services*. London: Routledge.

Turner, Lynn. (2001). "Classified Recruitment: The 'Best of Breed' Standards." *Financial Times*. (On-Line). Available: http://globalarchive.ft.com/globalarchive/article.htm?id=010308001563&query=IASB

United Nations. (1987). *Foreign Direct Investment, the Service Sector and International Banking*. New York: United Nations Center on Transnational Corporations.

Valentine, Charles F., Ginger Lew and Roger M. Poor. (1991). *The Ernst & Young Resource Guide to Global Markets*. New York: Wiley.

Vogel, Ezra F. (1991). *The Four Little Dragons: The Spread of Industrialization in East Asia*. Cambridge, MA: Harvard University Press.

Wallace, R., S. Olusegun, John M. Samuels and Richard J. Briston. (1990). *Research in Third World Accounting*, Vol. 1. London: JAI Press.

Walter, Ingo. (1990). *The Secret Money Market*. New York: Harper & Row Publishers, Ballinger Division.

Wawn, Brian. (1982). *The Economies of the ASEAN Countries: Indonesia, Malaysia, Philippines, Singapore, and Thailand*. New York: St. Martin's Press.

Westphal, L. E. (1990). "Industrial Policy in an Export-Propelled Economy: Lessons from South Korea's Experience." *Journal of Economic Perspectives*, Vol. 4, No. 3, pp. 41–59.

Westphal, L. E. et al. (May/June 1984). "Exports of Technology by Newly Industrializing Countries: Republic of Korea." *World Development*, Vol. 12, Nos. 5–6, pp. 505–533.

Wie, T. K. (1991). "The Surge of Asian NIC Investment into Indonesia." *Bulletin of Indonesian Economic Studies*, Vol. 27, No. 3, pp. 55–88.

World Bank. (1992). *World Development Report*. New York: Oxford University Press.

World Bank. (1993). *The East Asian Miracle: Economic Growth and Public Policy.* New York: Oxford University Press.

Wright, Ian. (2001). "Towards Global Accounting Standards: A European Perspective." *CFOdirectNetwork.* (On-Line). Available: http://www.cfodirect. com/cfopublic.nsf/0/8A56A99E428514E885256A4200641432

Wyatt, Arthur R. (September 1992). "Seeking Credibility in a Global Economy." *New Accountant,* Vol. 8, No. 1, pp. 4–6, 51, 52.

Yamazawa, Il, T. Nohera and H. Osada. (1986). "Economic Interdependence in Pacific Asia: An International Input-Output Analysis." *Development Economics,* Vol. 24, No. 2, pp. 95–108.

Young Wha. (2000a). *Ernst & Young International.* (On-line). Available: http:// www.youngwha.co.kr/GCF-introduction01.htm

Young Wha. (2000b). *Services-u.* (On-line). Available: http://www.youngwha. co.kr/services-u.htm

Young Wha. (2000c). *Services2-u.* (On-line). Available: http://www.youngwha. co.kr/services2-u.htm

Young Wha. (2000d). *Services3-u.* (On-line). Available: http://www.youngwha. co.kr/services3-u.htm

Young Wha. (2000e). *Services4-u.* (On-line). Available: http://www.youngwha. co.kr/GCF-Finance04.htm

Young Wha Consulting. (2000). *Major Services.* (On-line). Available: http:// www.youngwha.co.kr/eymc-u.htm

Index

About the Authors

DAVID L. McKEE is Professor of Economics in the Graduate School of Management at Kent State University, where he specializes in development economics and economic change. His most recent books, co-authored with Don E. Garner and Yosra AbuAmara McKee, are *Offshore Financial Centers, Accounting Services and the Global Economy* (2000), *Accounting Services, the Islamic Middle East and the Global Economy* (1999) and *Accounting Services and Growth in Small Economies* (1998), all published by Quorum Books.

DON E. GARNER is Professor and former Chair of the Department of Accounting at California State University, Stanislaus. He is a certified public accountant and a certified internal auditor, as well as a specialist in auditing and accounting.

YOSRA ABUAMARA McKEE is an adjunct faculty member in economics at Kent State University. Her work on international trade and services, economic integration and regional development has been aired in various professional publications and presentations.